The Court of the Empress Josephine

Lepagerie Buonaperte

THE COURT

OF

THE EMPRESS JOSEPHINE

BY

IMBERT DE SAINT-AMAND

TRANSLATED BY

THOMAS SERGEANT PERRY

ILLUSTRATED

WILDSIDE PRESS

THE CAXTON PRESS, NEW YORK

CONTENTS.

THE COURT

OF

THE EMPRESS JOSEPHINE

THE

COURT OF THE EMPRESS JOSEPHINE.

I.

THE BEGINNING OF THE EMPIRE.

"TWO-THIRDS of my life is passed, why should I so distress myself about what remains? The most brilliant fortune does not deserve all the trouble I take, the pettiness I detect in myself, or the humiliations and shame I endure ; thirty years will destroy those giants of power which can be seen only by raising the head; we shall disappear, I who am so petty, and those whom I regard so eagerly, from whom I expected all my greatness. The most desirable of all blessings is repose, seclusion, a little spot we can call our own." When La Bruyère expressed himself so bitterly, when he spoke of the court "which satisfies no one," but "prevents one from being satisfied anywhere else," of the court, "·that country where the joys are visible but false, and the sorrows hidden, but real," he had before him the brilliant Palace of Versailles, the unrivalled glory of the Sun King, a monarchy which thought itself immovable and eternal. What would he say in this

1

century when dynasties fall like autumn leaves, and
it takes much less than thirty years to destroy the
giants of power; when the exile of to-day repeats to
the exile of the morrow the motto of the churchyard:
Hodie mihi, cras tibi? What would this Christian
philosopher say at a time when royal and imperial
palaces have been like caravansaries through which
sovereigns have passed like travellers, and when
their brief resting-places have been consumed by the
blaze of petroleum and are now but a heap of ashes?

The study of any court is sure to teach wisdom
and indifference to human glories. In our France of
the nineteenth century, fickle as it has been, incon-
stant, fertile in revolutions, recantations, and changes
of every sort, this lesson is more impressive than it
has been at any period of our history. Never has
Providence shown more clearly the nothingness of
this world's grandeur and magnificence. Never has
the saying of Ecclesiastes been more exactly verified:
" Vanity of vanities ; all is vanity ! " We have
before us the task of describing one of the most
sumptuous courts that has ever existed, and of reviewing splendors all the more brilliant for their
brevity. To this court of Napoleon and Josephine,
to this majestic court, resplendent with glory, wealth,
and fame, may well be applied Corneille's lines : —

> " All your happiness
> Subject to instability
> In a moment falls to the ground,
> And as it has the brilliancy of glass
> It also has its fragility."

We shall evoke the memory of the dead to revive this vanished court, and we shall consult, one after another, the persons who were eye-witnesses of these short-lived wonders. A prefect of the palace, M. de Bausset, wrote: "When I recall the memorable times of which I have just given a faint idea, I feel, after so many years, as if I had been taking part in the gorgeous scenes of the *Arabian Tales* or of the *Thousand and One Nights.* The magic picture of all those splendors and glories has disappeared, and with it all the prestige of ambition and power." One of the ladies of the palace of the Empress Josephine, Madame de Rémusat, has expressed the same thought: "I seem to be recalling a dream, but a dream resembling an Oriental tale, when I describe the lavish luxury of that period, the disputes for precedence, the claims of rank, the demands of every one." Yes, in all that there was something dreamlike, and the actors in that fairy spectacle which is called the Empire, that great show piece, with its scenery, now brilliant, now terrible, but ever changing, must have been even more astonished than the spectators. Aix-la-Chapelle and the court of Charlemagne, the castle of Fontainebleau and the Pope, Notre Dame and the coronation, the Champ de Mars and the distribution of eagles, the Cathedral of Milan and the Iron Crown, Genoa the superb and its naval festival, Austerlitz and the three emperors, — what a setting! what accessories! what personages! The peal of organs, the intoning of priests, the applause of the multitude and of the soldiers, the groans of the dying, the trumpet call, the roll of the drum, ball music, military bands, the cannon's roar, were the joyful and mournful harmonies heard while the play went on. What we shall study amid this tumult and agitation is one woman. We have already studied her as the Viscountess of Beauharnais, as Citizeness Bonaparte, and as the wife of the First Consul. We shall now study her in her new part, that of Empress.

Let us go back to May 18, 1804, to the Palace of Saint Cloud. The Emperor had just been proclaimed by the Senate before the *plébiscite* which was to ratify the new state of things. The curtain has risen, the play begins, and no drama is fuller of contrasts, of incidents, of movement. The leading actor, Napoleon, was already as familiar with his part as if he had played it since his childhood. Josephine is also at home in hers. As a woman of the world, she had learned, by practice in the drawing-room, to win even greater victories. For a fashionable beauty there is no great difference between an armchair and a throne. The minor actors are not so accustomed to their new position. Nothing is more amusing than the embarrassment of the courtiers when they have to answer the Emperor's questions. They begin with a blunder; then, in correcting themselves, they fall into still worse confusion; ten times a minute was repeated, Sire, General, Your Majesty, Citizen, First Consul. Constant, the Emperor's valet de chambre, has given

us a description of this 18th of May, 1804, a day
devoted to receptions, presentations, interviews, and
congratulations: "Every one," he says, "was filled
with joy in the Palace of Saint Cloud; every one
imagined that he had risen a step, like General Bonaparte, who, from First Consul, had become a monarch.
Men were embracing and complimenting one another;
confiding their share of hopes and plans for the future;
there was no official so humble that he was not fired
with ambition." In a word, the ante-chamber, barring
the difference of persons, presented an exact imitation
of what was going on in the drawing-room. It seemed
like a first performance which had long been eagerly
expected, arousing the same eager excitement among
the players and the public. The day which had
started bright grew dark; for a long time there were
threatenings of a thunder-storm; but none looked on
this as an evil omen. All were inclined to cheery
views. The courtiers displayed their zeal with all
the ardor, the passion, the *furia francese*, which is a
national characteristic, and appears on the battle-field
as well as in the ante-chamber. The French fight
and flatter with equal enthusiasm.

Amid all these manifestations of devotion and
delight, the members of the Imperial family alone,
who should have been the most satisfied, and certainly the most astonished by their greatness, wore
an anxious, almost a grieved look. They alone appeared discontented with their master. Their pride
knew no bounds; their irritability was extreme.

Nothing seemed good enough for them in the way of
honors and privileges; and when we recall their
father's modest house at Ajaccio, it is hard to keep
from smiling at the vanity of these new Princes of
the blood. Of Napoleon's four brothers, two were absent and on bad terms with him: Lucien, on account
of his marriage with Madame Jouberton; Jerome, on
account of his marriage with Miss Paterson. His
mother, Madame Letitia Bonaparte, an able woman,
who combined great courage with uncommon good
sense, had not lost her head over the wonderful good
fortune of the modern Cæsar. Having a presentiment that all this could not last, she economized
from motives of prudence, not of avarice. While
the courtiers were celebrating the Emperor's new
triumphs, she lingered in Rome with her son Lucien,
whom she had followed in his voluntary exile, having
pronounced in his favor in his quarrel with Napoleon.
As for Joseph and Louis, who, with their wives, had
been raised to the dignity of Grand Elector and Constable, respectively, one might think that they were
overburdened with wealth and honors, and would be
perfectly satisfied. But not at all! They were indignant that they were not personally mentioned in the
plébiscite, by which their posterity was appointed to
succeed to the French crown. This *plébiscite* ran thus:
" The French people desire the inheritance of the Imperial dignity in the direct, natural, or adoptive line
of descent from Napoleon Bonaparte, and in the
direct, natural, legitimate line of descent from Joseph

Bonaparte and from Louis Bonaparte, as is determined by the organic *senatus-consultum* of the twenty-eighth Floréal, year XII." For the Emperor's family, these stipulations were the cause of incessant squabbles and recriminations. Lucien and Jerome regarded their exclusion as an act of injustice. Joseph and Louis asked indignantly why their descendants were mentioned when they themselves were excluded. They were very jealous of Josephine, and of her son, Eugene de Beauharnais, and much annoyed by the Emperor's reservation of the right of adoption, which threatened them and held out hopes for Eugene. Louis Bonaparte, indignant with the slanderous story, according to which his wife, Hortense, had been Napoleon's mistress, treated her ill, and conceived a dislike for his own son, who was reported to be that of the Emperor. As for Elisa Bacciochi, Caroline Murat, and Pauline Borghese, they could not endure the mortification of being placed below the Empress, their sister-in-law, and the thought that they had not yet been given the title of Princesses of the blood, which had been granted to the wife of Joseph and the wife of Louis, filled them with actual despair.

Madame de Rémusat, who was present at the first Imperial dinner at St. Cloud, May 18, 1804, describes this curious repast. General Duroc, Grand Marshal of the Palace, told all the guests in succession of the titles of Prince and Princess to be given to Joseph and Louis, and their wives, but not to the Emperor's sisters, or to their husbands. This fatal news prostrated Elisa, Caroline, and Pauline.   When they sat down at table, Napoleon was good-humored and merry, possibly at heart enjoying the slight constraint that this novel formality enforced upon his guests. Madame Murat, when she heard the Emperor saying frequently *Princess* Louis, could not hide her mortification or her tears.   Every one was embarrassed, while Napoleon smiled maliciously.

The next day the Emperor went to Paris to hold a grand reception at the Tuileries, for he was not a man to postpone the enjoyment of the splendor which his satisfied ambition could draw from his new title.   In this palace, where had ruled the Committee of Public Safety, where the Convention had sat, whence Robespierre had departed in triumph to preside over the festival in honor of the Supreme Being, nothing was heard but the titles of Emperor, Empress, My Lord, Prince, Princess, Imperial Highness, Most Serene Highness   It was asserted that Bonaparte had cut up the red caps to make the ribbons of the Legions of Honor.   The most fanatical Revolutionists had become conservative as soon as they had anything to preserve.   The Empire was but a few hours old, and already the new-born court was alive with the same rivalries, jealousies, and vanities that fill the courts of the oldest monarchies.   It was like Versailles, in the reign of Louis XIV., in the Gallery of Mirrors, or in the drawing-room of the Œil de Bœuf.   It would have taken a Dangeau to record, hour by hour, the minute points of etiquette.

The Emperor walked, spoke, thought, acted, like a monarch of an old line. To nothing does a man so readily adapt himself as to power. One who has been invested with the highest rank is sure to imagine himself eternal; to think that he has always held it and will always keep it. Indeed, how is it possible to escape intoxication by the fumes of perpetual incense? How can a man tell the truth to himself when there is no one about him courageous enough to tell it to him? When the press is muzzled, and public power rests only on general approval, when there is no slave even to remind the triumphant hero, as in the ancient ovations, that he is only a man, how is it possible to avoid being infatuated by one's greatness and not to imagine one's self the absolute master of one's destiny? The new Cæsar met with no resistance. He was to publish scornfully in the *Moniteur* the protest of Louis XVIII. against his accession. He was to be adored both by fierce Revolutionists and by great lords, by regicides and by Royalists and ecclesiastics. It seemed as if with him everything began, or rather started anew. " The old world was submerged," says Chateaubriand; "when the flood of anarchy withdrew, Napoleon appeared at the beginning of a new world, like those giants described by profane and sacred history at the beginning of society, appearing on earth after the Deluge."

The former general of the Revolution enjoyed his situation as absolute sovereign. He studied the laws of etiquette as closely as he studied the condition of his troops. He saw that the men of the old régime were more conversant in the art of flattery, more eager, than the new men. As Madame de Staël says: "Whenever a gentleman of the old court recalled the ancient etiquette, suggested an additional bow, a certain way at knocking at the door of an ante-chamber, a more ceremonious method of presenting a despatch, of folding a letter, of concluding it with this or that formula, he was greeted as if he had helped on the happiness of the human race." Napoleon attached, or pretended to attach, great importance to the thousand nothings which make up the empty life of courts. He established in the palace the same discipline as in the camps. Everything became a matter of rule. Courtiers studied formalities as officers studied the art of war. Regulations were as closely observed in the drawing-rooms as in the tents. At the end of a few months Napoleon was to have the most brilliant, the most rigid court of Europe. At times the whirl of vanities that surrounded him filled with impatience the great central sun, without whom his satellites would have been nothing. At other times, however, his pride was gratified by the thought that it was his will, his fancy, which evoked from nothing all the grandees of the earth. He was not pained at seeing such eagerness in behalf of trifles that he had invented. He liked to fill his courtiers with raptures or with despair, by a smile or a frown. He thought his sisters' ambition childish, but it amused him; and if they had to cry a little at first, he finally granted them what they wanted.

May 19, after the family dinner, Madame Murat was more and more distressed at not being a Princess, when she was a Bonaparte by birth, while Madame Joseph and Madame Louis, one of whom was a Clary, the other a Beauharnais, bore that title, and burst out into complaints and reproaches. "Why," she asked of her all-powerful brother, "why condemn me and my sisters to obscurity, to contempt, while covering strangers with honors and dignities?" At first these words annoyed Napoleon. "In fact," he exclaimed, "judging from your pretensions, one would suppose that we inherited the crown from the late King our father." At the end of the interview, Madame Murat, not satisfied with crying, fainted away. Napoleon softened at once, and a few days later there appeared a notification in the *Moniteur* that henceforth the Emperor's sisters should be called Princesses and Imperial Highnesses.

The Empress's Maid of Honor was Madame de La Rochefoucauld; her Lady of the Bedchamber was Madame de Lavalette. Her Ladies of the Palace, whose number was soon raised to twelve, and later still more augmented, were at first only four: Madame de Talhouët, Madame de Luçay, Madame de Lauriston, and Madame de Rémusat. These ladies, too, aroused the hottest jealousies, and soon they gave rise to a sort of parody of the questions of vanity that agitated the Emperor's family. The women who were admitted to the Empress's intimacy could never console themselves for the privileges accorded to the Ladies of the Palace.

In essentials all courts are alike. On a greater or smaller scale they are rank with the same pettinesses, the same chattering gossip, the same trivial squabbles as the porter's lodge, ante-chambers, and servants' quarters. If we examine these things from the standpoint of a philosopher, we shall find but little difference between a steward and a chamberlain, between a chambermaid and a lady of the palace. We may go further and say that as soon as they have places and money at their disposal, republicans have courtesies, as much as monarchs, and everywhere and always there are to be found people ready to bow low if there is anything on the ground that they can pick up. Revolutions alter the forms of government, but not the human heart; afterwards, as before, there exist the same pretensions, the same prejudices, the same flatteries. The incense may be burned before a tribune, a dictator, or a Cæsar, there are always the same flattering genuflections, the same cringing.

The new Empire began most brilliantly, but there was no lack of morose criticism. The Faubourg Saint Germain was for the most part hostile and scornful. It looked upon the high dignitaries of the Empire and on the Emperor himself as upstarts, and all the men of the old régime who went over to him they branded as renegades. The title of " Citizen " was suppressed and that of "Monsieur" restored, after having been abandoned in conversation and writing for twelve years. Miot de Mélito tells us in his Memoirs that at first public opinion was opposed to this change; even those who at the beginning had shown the greatest repugnance to being addressed as Citizen, disliked conferring the title of Monsieur upon Revolutionists and the rabble, and they pretended to address as Citizen those whom they saw fit to include in this class. Many turned the new state of affairs to ridicule. The Parisians, always of a malicious humor, made perpetual puns and epigrams in abundance.

The Faubourg Saint Germain, in spite of a few adhesions from personal motives, preserved an ironical attitude. General de Ségur, then a captain under the orders of the Grand Marshal of the Palace, observed that in 1804, with the exception of several obscure nobles, either poor or ruined, and others already attached to Napoleon's civil and military fortune, many negotiations and various temptations were required to persuade well-known persons to appear at the court as it was at first constituted. He goes on: " As a spectator and confidant of the means employed, I witnessed in those early days many refusals, and some I had to announce myself. I even heard many bitter complaints on this subject. I remember that in reply I mentioned to the Empress my own case, and told her what it had cost me to enlist under the tricolor, and then to enter the First

Consul's military household. The Empress understood me so well that she made to me a similar confidence, confessing her own struggles, her almost invincible repugnance, at the end of 1795, in spite of her feeling for Bonaparte, before she could make up her mind to marry the man whom at that time she herself used to call General Vendémiaire."

Although Josephine had become Empress, she remained a Legitimist, and saw clearly the weak points in the Empire. At the Tuileries, in the chamber of Marie Antoinette, she felt out of place; she was surprised to have for Lady of Honor a duchess of an old family, and her sole ambition was to be pardoned by the Royalists for her elevation to the highest rank. Napoleon, too, was much concerned about the Bourbons, in whom he foresaw his successors. "One of his keenest regrets," wrote Prince Metternich, "was his inability to invoke legitimacy as the foundation of his power. Few men have felt more deeply than he the precariousness and fragility of power when it lacks this foundation, its susceptibility to attack."

After recalling the Emperor's attempt to induce Louis XVIII. to abandon his claims to the throne, Prince Metternich goes on: "In speaking to me of this matter, Napoleon said: 'His reply was noble, full of noble traditions. In those Legitimists there is something outside of mere intellectual force.'" The Emperor, who, at the beginning of his career, displayed such intense Republican enthusiasm, was by nature essentially a lover of authority and of the monarchy. He would have liked to be a sovereign of the old stamp. His pleasure in surrounding himself with members of the old aristocracy attests the aristocratic instincts of the so-called crowned apostle of democracy. The few Republicans who remained faithful to the principles were indignant with these tendencies ; it was with grief that they saw the reappearance of the throne ; and thus, from different motives the unreconciled Jacobins and the men of Coblentz who had not joined the court, showed the same feeling of bitterness and of hostility to the Empire.

The trial of General Moreau made clear the germs of opposition which existed in a latent condition. It is difficult to form an idea of the enormous throng that blocked all the approaches to the Palace of Justice the day the trial opened, and continued to crowd them during the twelve days that the trial lasted, which was as interesting to Royalists as to Republicans. The most fashionable people of Paris made a point of being present. Sentence was pronounced June 10. Georges Cadoudal and nineteen of the accused, among whom were M. Armand de Polignac, and M. de Rivière, were condemned to death.

To the Emperor's great surprise, Moreau was sentenced to only two years of prison. This penalty was remitted, and he was allowed to betake himself to the United States. To facilitate his establishing himself there, the Emperor bought his house in the rue d'Anjou Saint Honoré, paying for it eight hundred thousand francs, much more than it was worth, and then he gave it to Bernadotte, who did not scruple to accept it. The sum was paid to Moreau out of the secret fund of the police before he left for Cadiz. Josephine's urgent solicitations saved the life of the Duke Armand de Polignac, whose death-sentence was commuted to four years' imprisonment before being transported. Madame Murat secured a modification of the sentence of the Marquis de Rivière; and these two acts of leniency, to which great publicity was given, were of great service in diminishing the irritation of the Royalists. After Moreau's trial, the opposition, having become discouraged, and conscious of its weakness, laid down its arms, at least for a time. Napoleon was everywhere master.

The Republic was forgotten. Its name still appeared on the coins: "French Republic, Napoleon, Emperor"; but it survived as a mere ghost. Nevertheless, the Emperor was anxious to celebrate in 1804 the Republican festival of July 14; but the object of this festival was so modified that it would have been hard to see in it the anniversary of the taking of the Bastille and of the first federation. In the celebration, not a single word was said about these two events. The official eulogy of the Revolution was replaced by a formal distribution of crosses of the Legion of Honor.

This was the first time that the Emperor and Empress appeared in public in full pomp. It was also the first time that they availed themselves of the privilege of driving through the broad road of the garden of the Tuileries. Accompanied by a magnificent procession, they went in great splendor to the Invalides, which the Revolution had turned into a Temple of Mars, and the Empire had turned again to a Catholic Church. At the door they were received by the Governor and M. de Ségur, Grand Master of Ceremonies, and at the entrance to the church by the Cardinal du Belloy at the head of numerous priests. Napoleon and Josephine listened attentively to the mass; then, after a speech was uttered by the Grand Chancellor of the Legion of Honor, M. de Lacépède, the Emperor recited the form of the oath; at the end of which all the members of the Legion shouted "I swear." This sight aroused the enthusiasm of the crowd, and the applause was loud. In the middle of the ceremony, Napoleon called up to him Cardinal Caprara, who had taken a very important part in the negotiations concerning the Concordat, and was soon to help to persuade the Pope to come to Paris for the coronation. The Emperor took from his own neck the ribbon of the Legion of Honor, and gave it to the worthy and aged prelate. Then the knights of the new order passed in line before the Imperial throne, while a man of the people, wearing a blouse, took his station on the steps of the throne. This excited some surprise, and he was asked what he wanted; he took out his appointment to the Legion. The Emperor at once called him up, and gave him the cross with the usual kiss.

The Empress's beauty made a great impression, as we learn from Madame de Rémusat, who was generally prejudiced against her, but on this occasion was forced to recognize that Josephine, by her tasteful and careful dressing, succeeded in appearing young and charming amid the many young and pretty women by whom she was for the first time surrounded. "She stood there," Madame de Rémusat goes on, "in the full light of the setting sun, wearing a dress of pink tulle, adorned with silver stars, cut very low after the fashion of the time, and crowned by a great many diamond clusters; and this fresh and brilliant dress, her graceful bearing, her delightful smile, her gentle expression produced such an effect that I heard a number of persons who had been present at the ceremony say that she effaced all her suite." Three days later the Emperor started for the camp at Boulogne.

In spite of the enthusiasm of the people and the army, one thing became clear to every thoughtful observer, and that was that the new régime, lacking strength to resist misfortunes, must have perpetual success in order to live. Napoleon was condemned, by the form of his government, not merely to succeed, but to dazzle, to astonish, to subjugate. His Empire required extraordinary magnificence, prodigious effects, Babylonian festivities, gigantic adventures, colossal victories. His Imperial escutcheon, to escape contempt, needed rich coats of gilding, and demanded glory to make up for the lack of antiquity. In order to make himself acceptable to the European monarchs, his new brothers, and to remove the memory of the venerable titles of the Bourbons, this former officer of the armies of Louis XVI., the former second-lieutenant of artillery, who had suddenly become a Cæsar, a Charlemagne, could make this sudden and strange transformation comprehensible only through unprecedented fame and splendor. He desired to have a feudal, majestic court, surrounded by all the pomp and ceremony of the Middle Ages. He saw how hard was the part he had to play, and he knew very well how much a nation needs glory to make it forget liberty. Hence a perpetual effort to make every day outshine the one before, and first to equal, then to surpass, the splendors of the oldest and most famous dynasties. This insatiable thirst for action and for renown was to be the source of Napoleon's strength and also of his weakness. But only a few clear-sighted men made these reflections when the Empire began. The masses, with their easy optimism, looked upon the new Emperor as an infallibly impeccable being, and thought that since he had not yet been beaten, he was invincible. Josephine indulged in no such illusions; she knew the defects in her husband's character, and dreaded the future for him as well as for herself. Singularly enough for one so surrounded by flatteries, in her whole life her head was never for a moment turned by pride or infatuation.

II.

BEFORE having himself crowned by the Pope, after the example of Charlemagne, Napoleon was anxious to go to meditate at the tomb of the great Carlovingian Emperor, of whom he regarded himself as the worthy successor. A journey on the banks of the Rhine, a triumphal tour in the famous German cities which the France of the Revolution had been so proud to conquer, seemed to the new sovereign a fitting prologue to the pomp of the coronation. Napoleon was desirous of impressing the imaginations of people in his new Empire and in the old Empire of Germany. He wished the trumpets of fame to sound in his honor on both banks of the famous and disputed river.

The Empress, who had gone to Aix-la-Chapelle to take the waters, arrived there a few days before her husband. Napoleon wrote to her, August 6, 1804 : —

"MY DEAR: I have been here at Calais since midnight; I am thinking of leaving this evening for Dunkirk. I am satisfied with what I see, and I am tolerably well. I hope that you will get as much

20

good from the waters as I get from going about and from seeing the camps and the sea. Eugene has left for Blois. Hortense is well. Louis is at Plombières. I am very anxious to see you. You are always essential to my happiness. A thousand kind messages."

The Emperor wrote again from Ostend, August 14, 1804: —

" MY DEAR: I have not heard from you for several days, though I should have been glad to hear that the waters have done you good and how you pass your time. I have been here a week. Day after to-morrow I shall be at Boulogne for a tolerably brilliant festival. Send me word by the messenger what you mean to do, and when you shall have finished your baths. I am much satisfied with the army and the fleet. Eugene is still at Blois. I hear no more about Hortense than if she were at the Congo. I am writing to scold her. Many kind wishes for all."

Napoleon reached Aix-la-Chapelle September 3. The Emperor Francis had, on the 10th of August, assumed the Imperial title accorded to his house, of Emperor-elect of Germany, Hereditary Emperor of Austria, King of Bohemia and Hungary. He had then given orders to M. de Cobentzel to go to Aix-la-Chapelle to present his credentials to Napoleon. Napoleon received the Austrian diplomatist very kindly, and was soon surrounded by a multitude of foreign ambassadors who came to pay their respects. He re-established the annual honors long before paid to the memory of Charlemagne, went down into the vault, and gave the priests of the Cathedral convincing proofs of his munificence. The Empress was shown a piece of the true cross which the Carlovingian Emperor had long worn on his breast as a talisman. She was offered a holy relic, almost the whole arm of that hero, but she declined it, saying that she did not wish to deprive Aix-la-Chapelle of so precious a memorial, especially when she had the arm of a man as great as Charlemagne to support her.

From Aix-la-Chapelle, Napoleon and Josephine went to Cologne, then to Coblentz, then to Mayence, travelling separately. The Emperor left Cologne September 16 at four in the afternoon, and reached Bonn a little before nightfall, to start again the next morning. The town pleased her very much, and she was sorry she could not remain there longer. She stayed at a fine house with a garden opening on a terrace that looked out over the Rhine. After supper she walked on the terrace. The delight of the people assembled below, the peacefulness of the night, and the beauty of the river in the moonlight, made the evening most enjoyable. At four the next morning the Empress started off again in her travelling carriage, and at ten she entered Coblentz. The Emperor did not get there until six in the evening, having left Cologne the same day. At Bonn he got on horseback to examine for himself everything that demanded close inspection. From Coblentz, where a

ball was given them, Napoleon and Josephine went
to Mayence, each by a different route. The Emperor
followed the highway on the edge of the Rhine; the
Empress ascended the river in a yacht which the
Prince of Nassau Weilburg had placed at her disposal. It was a picturesque voyage.

The morning mist soon cleared away. Josephine,
who had breakfast served on deck, admired the many
charming scenes between Boppard and Bacharach,
the fertile fields, the towns perched on the steep
banks; in the distance, the mountains covered with
forests; then the narrowing river, the bounded view,
the cliffs crowded together, where nothing can be
seen but the river, the sky, and the crags crowned by
the mirrored towns of mediæval castles. The light
boat, as it glided smoothly over the stream, with its
gilded Neptune at the bow, recalled Cleopatra's barge.
At times the silence was profound, then the church-
bells would be heard, as well as the cheers of the peasants on the river-banks. The pettiest villages had
sent guards of honor, had hoisted flags, and raised
triumphal arches. Curiously enough, the right bank,
which did not belong to France, seemed to display
quite as much zeal and enthusiasm as the left bank,
the French one; on both sides were the same shouts
of welcome, the same demonstrations, the same salutes. When she reached Saint Goar, on the left
bank, the Empress saw the authorities of the town
coming out to meet her, with military music, in boats
decorated with branches of trees; and on the other

side of the river, on the terrace of the castle of Hesse Rheinfels, the Hessian garrison was presenting arms, and their salutes joined with those of the inhabitants of Saint Goar. Further on, they shouted through a speaking-trumpet to hear the famous echo of the Lorelei, with its wonderfully distinct and frequent repetitions. Then they passed the fantastic castle of the Palatinate, built in the middle of the stream, and in old times the refuge of the Countesses Palatine, where their children were born and kept in security during their babyhood. The Empress landed at Bingen, where she spent the night, starting again the next morning. Towards three in the afternoon she reached Mayence, where twelve young girls belonging to the best families of the city were awaiting her. Almost simultaneously, the cannon at the other gate announced the Emperor's arrival.

On his way, Napoleon had noticed on an island in the Rhine, at the very extremity of the French Empire, the convent of Rolandswerth. He was told that the nuns who lived there had refused to leave it during the last war, and that very often the cannon-balls of the contending armies had often fallen on the island without damaging the convent where those holy women were praying. The Emperor became interested in their fate, and made over to them the forty or fifty acres of which the little island consisted.

On their arrival at Mayence, September 21, Napoleon and Josephine were most warmly greeted. In the evening all the streets and public buildings were illuminated. The Prince Archchancellor of the Germanic Empire, who owed to the French sovereign the preservation of his wealth and of his title, desired to pay his respects. The Emperor was surrounded by a real court of German Princes. The Princess of the House of Hesse, the Duke and Duchess of Bavaria, the Elector of Baden, who was more than seventy-five years old, and had come with his son and grandson, appeared as if vassals of the new Charlemagne, the second Théâtre Français had been summoned from Paris, and played before this public of Highnesses. Every one was struck by the celerity with which this crowned soldier had acquired the appearance of a sovereign belonging to an old line, while he still preserved the language and appearance of a soldier. One day he asked the hereditary Prince of Baden: "What did you do yesterday?" The young Prince replied with some embarrassment that he had strolled about the streets. "You did very wrong," said Napoleon. "What you ought to have done was to visit the fortifications and inspect them carefully. How can you tell? Perhaps some day you will have to besiege Mayence. Who would have told me when I was a simple artillery officer walking about Toulon that I should be destined to take that city?" It was at Mayence that the treasures unjustly extorted from the German Princes were restored to them. It was at Mayence that Gutenberg's name for the first time received formal homage.

General de Ségur, in his Memoirs, narrates an anecdote about Napoleon's stay in this old German city. The Emperor had gone incognito and without escort to an island in the Rhine, not far from the town. As he was walking in this almost deserted island, he noticed a wretched hut in which a poor woman was lamenting that her son had been drafted. "Console yourself," said Napoleon, without letting her know who he was, and giving her an assumed name: "Come to Mayence to-morrow and ask for me; I have some influence with the ministers and I will try to help you." The poor woman appeared punctually. With delight and surprise she saw that the stranger was the Emperor of the French. Napoleon was delighted to tell her that her house which had been destroyed by the war should be rebuilt, that he would give her a little herd and several acres of land, and that her son should be restored to her.

A letter in the *Moniteur* thus described the departure of Napoleon and Josephine: "Mayence, 11 Vendémiaire (October 3). The Empress left yesterday for Paris, by way of Saverne and Nancy. The Emperor is just leaving; he means to visit Frankenthal, Kaiserslanten, and Kreutznach; then he will take the road to Treves. The stay of Their Majesties has been for us a source of lasting pleasure and advantage. The most important interests of our department have been favorably regulated. We have nothing now to wish for except an opportunity to show our gratitude, our devotion, and our fidelity, and the sincerity of the good wishes our citizens expressed by their unanimous cheers. The Electors, the Princes, and the many distinguished strangers who have given our city the appearance of a great capital, are now taking their departure."

This journey on the banks of the Rhine made a deep impression in France and throughout Europe. It must be confessed that no one has ever equalled the Emperor in the art of keeping himself picturesquely before the public. Napoleon in the crypt at Aix-la-Chapelle, face to face with the shade of Charlemagne is a subject to inspire a painter or a poet! At Brussels, in the church of Saint Gudule, Napoleon evoked the memory of Charles V.; at Aix-la-Chapelle in the Cathedral vault he questioned the shade of Charlemagne. And as he meditated on the tomb of the Carlovingian hero, so now do monarchs on their way through Paris meditate in their turn over his tomb beneath the gilded dome of the Invalides. They go down into the crypt, look at the porch upheld by twelve great statues of white marble, each one commemorating a victory, at the mosaic pavement representing a huge crown with fillets, the sarcophagus of red granite from Finland, placed on a foundation of green granite from the Vosges. Then they enter the subterranean chamber, the black marble sanctuary, which contains, among numerous relics, the sword that Napoleon carried at Austerlitz, the decorations he wore on his uniform, the gold crown voted him by the city of Cherbourg, and finally sixty flags won in his victories. The church of the Invalides inspires the same thoughts as the Cathedral of Aix-la-Chapelle. In the two temples kings and great men may make the same reflection about glory, about death, about the handful of dust which is all that is left of heroes.

III.

THE time for the coronation was drawing near. Napoleon, who had already received the official recognition of foreign powers, was anxious to have his Imperial title consecrated by a great religious ceremony, the fame of which should resound throughout the whole Catholic world. The first date proposed for the solemnity was the 26th Messidor, Year XII. (July 14, 1804), then that of the 18th Brumaire, Year XIII. (Nov. 9, 1804). But the choice in each case was unfortunate. It was hard to combine the memory of the taking of the Bastille with the coronation of a sovereign, and the 18th Brumaire would have recalled the regrets of Republicans and the services of Lucien Bonaparte, who, after being the main aid of his brother's fortune, was living at Rome, in disgrace and exile. On the other hand, the Pope's hesitation, for it was with the greatest difficulty that he could make up his mind to go to Paris, had further postponed the date, which was at last fixed for the beginning of December.

Josephine awaited with impatience and fear an

event on which, she felt, her future fate depended.
The Pope, that mysterious and holy person, had
started. Was he to prove her saviour? Was she to
be a repudiated wife or a crowned Empress? The
clergy were untiring in their laudations of Napoleon's
glory. Bishops, in their charges, spoke of him as
God's elect. One prelate, speaking of the Empire,
had said: "One God and one monarch! As the
God of the Christians is the only one deserving to be
adored and obeyed, you, Napoleon, are the only man
worthy to rule the French!" Another had said:
"Napoleon, whom God called from the deserts of
Egypt, like another Moses, will bring peace between
the wise Empire of France and the divine Empire of
Christ. The finger of God is here. Let us pray the
Most High to protect with his powerful hand the
man he has chosen. May the new Augustus live
and rule forever! Submission is his due because he
is ordered by Providence!" Yet in spite of these
extravagant outbursts which came from every pulpit
in the whole French Empire, this restorer of the
altars, this saviour of religion was married only by
civil right! From the ecclesiastic point of view, he
was living in concubinage. He had had his brother
Louis's marriage with Hortense de Beauharnais, and
his sister Caroline's with Murat blessed by Cardinal
Caprara, but in spite of Josephine's entreaties, he had
denied her this pious satisfaction. It was on the
Pope that the Empress put all her hope; she thought
that he would take pity on her, and by bringing her

into conformity with the rules of the church, would put an end to a condition of things humiliating to her as a sovereign, and painful to her as a Catholic.

At the same time Josephine was anxiously wondering whether she was to be crowned. Her brothers-in-law became more venomous in their intrigues against her, and desired not only that she be excluded from any part in the coronation, but also that she should be condemned to divorce on the pretext of barrenness. Joseph Bonaparte was never tired of saying that Napoleon ought to marry some foreign Princess, or at least some daughter of an old French family, and he skilfully laid stress on his own unselfishness in urging a plan which would necessarily remove himself and his descendants from the line of inheritance. The Emperor's sisters showed the same hostility towards Josephine, whom they hated, although she well deserved their love. Since Napoleon maintained an absolute silence about his intentions concerning the coronation, the Bonapartes already imagined that she was going to be divorced, and hence exhibited an untimely delight which displeased the Emperor and brought him closer to his wife. At last, tired with family bickerings, he suddenly put an end to them and filled Josephine with joy by telling her that she was to be crowned at Notre Dame.

The reader should turn to the curious account in Miot de Mélito's Memoirs of the council held at Saint Cloud, November 17, 1804, to arrange the formalities of the coronation. Of Napoleon's four brothers, two were in disgrace, Lucien and Jerome, and they were not to be present at the ceremony. As for Joseph and Louis, it was decided that they should appear, not as Princes of the blood, but only as high dignitaries of the Empire. Joseph, it will be remembered, was Grand Elector, and Louis was Constable.

This decision once taken, Joseph said in the council of November 17: "Since it has been recognized that, with the exception of the Head of the State, no one else, whatever his rank, can be regarded as partaking the honors of sovereignty, and that we especially are not treated as Princes, but only as high dignitaries, it would not be right that our wives, who henceforth are only wives of high dignitaries, should as Princesses carry the train of the Empress's robe, which consequently must be carried by Ladies of Honor or of the Palace." This remark displeased the Emperor, and many members of the council cited many examples to refute it, notably that of Maria de' Medici. Joseph, who had foreseen their arguments, displayed unexpected erudition: "Maria de' Medici," he said, "was accompanied only by Queen Margaret, the first wife of Henri IV., and by Madame (Catherine of Bourbon), the King's sister. The train was carried by a very distant relative. Queen Margaret had, indeed, offered a fine example of generosity by being present at the coronation of the woman who took her place and who, more fortunate than herself, had borne heirs to Henri IV. But she was not asked to carry the train of Maria de' Medici, and yet Maria de' Medici had a right to every honor, because she was a mother." This very transparent allusion to Josephine's barrenness so exasperated Napoleon that he arose suddenly from his chair and addressed his brother with the intensest bitterness and violence. After the meeting Joseph proposed to his brother retiring to Germany. Napoleon relented and, November 27, he said to his brother: "I have given a great deal of thought to the difference that has arisen between you and me, and I will confess that during the six days that this quarrel has lasted, I have not had a moment's peace. I have even lost my sleep over it, and you are the only person who has this power over me; I know nothing that disturbs me to this degree. This influence comes from my old affection for you and from my recollection of what you did for me in my boyhood, and I am much more dependent than you think on feelings of that sort. . . . Take your position in an hereditary monarchy and be the first of my subjects. That is a fine enough position, to be the second man in France, perhaps in Europe. . . . Comply with my wishes; follow my ideas; do not flatter the patriots when I drive them away; do not oppose the nobles when I summon them; form your household according to the principles that have guided me. In a word, be a Prince, and do not disturb yourself about the importance of the title."

Joseph at last yielded, and promised that his wife

should conform without a murmur to the ceremonies established for the coronation. Only this concession was made to their susceptibilities : that in the rules the phrase, *bear the cloak* was substituted for *carry the train*, " for," as Miot de Mélito says, " Vanity will clutch at a straw."

As for Madame Bonaparte, Napoleon's mother, she persisted in remaining at Rome with Lucien. In spite of frequent messages from Paris, she was not to get there until some days after the coronation, a fact which did not prevent her appearing in the great picture commemorating the event, painted by David, who was successively Jacobin and Imperialist, and beginning with the apotheosis of Marat, celebrated that of Napoleon.

Pope Pius VII., then sixty-two years old, had left Rome November 2, after praying for a long time at the altar of Saint Peter's. The populace had followed his carriage for a long distance, weeping with terror at his undertaking a journey to revolutionary France. At Florence he had been received by the Queen of Etruria, then a widow and her son's Regent. At Lyons he became less anxious ; a number of the inhabitants crowded about him, and fell on their knees, asking for the blessing of the Vicar of Christ. Meanwhile, Napoleon was putting the last touches to the repairs he had commenced at the Palace of Fontainebleau, to put it in a suitable condition to receive the Sovereign Pontiff. In less than twenty days the furnishing of the palace had been completed, and the castle had, as if by magic, resumed its old-time splendor.

Every one wondered how the first meeting between the Pope and the Emperor would take place. Many points of etiquette arose which Napoleon managed to elude. Pius VII. was to arrive through the forest of Fontainebleau, and the Emperor was to go to meet him through the forest of Nemours. To prevent all formality, Napoleon made an excuse of a hunting party. All the huntsmen, with their carriages, met in the forest. Napoleon was on horseback, in hunting dress. When he knew that the Pope and his suite were due at the cross of Saint Hérene — at noon, Sunday, November 25, 1804 — he turned his horse in that direction, and as soon as he reached the half-moon at the top of the hill, he saw the Pope's carriage arriving.

According to the account given in the Memoirs of the Duke of Rovigo, the carriage of Pius VII. stopped, and the pontiff in his white robes got out by the left-hand door. The road was muddy, and he was averse to stepping into it with his white silk slippers ; but there was nothing to be done. Napoleon got off his horse to receive him, and sprang cordially into his arms. These two famous men, who, although they were entire strangers, had already thought so often of each other, and were to exercise such great influence over each other's destiny, now met with deep emotion. As they were embracing, one of the Emperor's carriages, which had been ordered to drive up, pushed on a few steps as if by an oversight of the coachman ; the footmen held both doors open ; the Emperor took

that on the right; a court official pointed to that on
the left for the Pope, so that the two sovereigns
entered the same carriage simultaneously by the two
doors.   The Emperor sat down naturally on the right-
hand side, and this first step established the etiquette
for the whole time of the Pope's stay, without discussion.

At the entrance of the Palace of Fontainebleau,
the Empress, the high dignitaries of the Empire, the
generals, were formed in a circle to receive and
salute Pius VII.   He was welcomed with the utmost
reverence.   His fine, noble face, his air of angelic
kindness, his soft, yet sonorous voice, produced a
deep impression.   Josephine was especially moved by
the presence of the Vicar of Christ.   After resting a
few moments in his private apartment, to which he
had been conducted by M. de Talleyrand, High Chamberlain, by General Duroc, Grand Marshal of the
Palace, and by M. de Ségur, Grand Master of Ceremonies, the Pope paid a visit to Napoleon, who, after
an interview of about half an hour, conducted him
back to the hall that was at that time called that
of the High Officers.   The two sovereigns dined
together, and the Pope went early to bed, to rest
himself after the fatigues of his long journey.   The
next evening some singers had been summoned to
the Empress's apartment, but Pius VII. withdrew
just as the concert was about to begin.

In the course of the day Josephine had had a private interview with the Pope, and had confided to

him the secret which so distressed her. She who was reigning over the greatest of Catholic nations, the consort of the successor of the very Christian Kings, the wife of a ruler about to be crowned by the Pope, was married only by civil rite! She entreated Pius VII. to use all his influence with Napoleon to put an end to a situation which was a continual torture and reproach to her as a wife and as a Christian. The Pope appeared touched by the confidence of his dear daughter, as he always called the Empress, and promised to demand, and, if necessary, to insist, upon the celebration of the Emperor's religious marriage, as a condition of the coronation, and this promise filled Josephine with joy.

The presence of the Pope and the Emperor, the throng of prelates, generals, courtiers, and beautiful women, the combination of religious and Imperial pomp gave to the Castle of the Valois, a few days before dilapidated and abandoned, new splendor and magnificence. Never in the most brilliant days of the reign of Francis I., or Henri II., or of Louis XIV., had this sumptuous residence appeared in greater state. This wonderful palace is renowned for its superb and picturesque architecture, its majestic façades, its five courts: that of the White Horse, of the Fountain, of the Dungeon, of the Princes, of Henri IV. The Festival Hall is very beautiful, with its rich and abundant ornamentation, its walnut floor, divided into octagonal panels richly outlined with inlaid gold and silver, its monumental mantel-

piece, with its figures, emblems, and fantastic fres-
coes, the brilliant masterpieces of Primaticcio, and of
Nicolo d'Abati.

Alas! this splendid Fontainebleau, the gorgeous
palace where Pope and Emperor were then living in
triumph, was later to be to both an accursed spot.
The Pope was to return to it a prisoner, maltreated
though old, though a priest, though the Vicar of
Christ, and there the Emperor was to drink the cup
of humiliation, of despair, to the dregs.   It was there
that, conquered, broken, betrayed by fortune, he was
to sign his abdication.   It was there that he was to
utter those heart-rending words: "It is right; I
receive what I have deserved.   I wanted no statues,
for I knew that there was no safety in receiving
them at any other hands than those of posterity.
A man to keep them while he lives, needs constant
good fortune.   I think of France, which it is terrible
to leave in this state, without frontiers when it had
such wide ones!—that is the bitterest of the humiliations that overwhelm me.   To leave France so small
when I wished to make it so great!"   It was there
that, overcome by immeasurable grief, the conqueror
of so many battles wished to seek in suicide a refuge
from the tortures of thought, and that he was to
fail to find death, he who on the battle-field had
squandered so many lives.   O mortals, ignorant of
your own fates, how happy you are not to have
foreknowledge of them!

IV.

THE Empress left Fontainebleau, Thursday, November 29, 1804, in company with Madame de La Rochefoucauld, Maid of Honor, and Madame d'Arberg, Lady of the Palace, and reached Paris the same day, a few hours before the Emperor and the Pope, who left Fontainebleau in the same carriage and entered the Tuileries at eight in the evening. A platoon of Mamelukes escorted the Imperial carriage, and it was a singular sight to see the Mussulman escorting the Vicar of Christ. The Pope was installed at the Tuileries in the Pavilion of Flora. There were attached to his person M. de Viry, the Emperor's Chamberlain; M. de Luçay, Prefect of the Palace, and Colonel Durosnel, Equerry.

All Paris was excited by the approach of the great event. The hotels were crowded; the population of the capital was nearly doubled, so vast was the throng of provincials and foreigners. Tradesmen were working night and day to prepare the dresses and uniforms. In every workshop there was unparalleled activity. Leroy, who previously had been

39

only a milliner, had decided for this occasion to undertake dressmaking, and had made Madame Raimbault, a celebrated dressmaker of the time, his partner. From their shop came the magnificent robes to be worn by the Empress on Coronation Day. Her jewels, consisting of a crown, a diadem, and a girdle, were the work of the jeweller Margueritte. The crown was formed of eight branches meeting under a gold globe surmounted by a cross. The branches were set with diamonds, four in the shape of a palm leaf, four in the shape of a myrtle leaf. Around the curve was a ribbon inlaid with eight enormous emeralds. The frontlet was bright with amethysts. The diadem was formed of four rows of pearls interlaced with diamond leaves, with many large brilliants, one alone weighing one hundred and forty-nine grains. The girdle was a gold band, enriched with thirty-nine pink gems. The Emperor's sceptre had been made by Odiot; it was of solid silver, enlaced by a gold serpent, and surmounted by a globe on which was a miniature figure of Charlemagne seated. The hand of justice, the crown, and the sword came from the workshops of Biennais. The dress of the courtiers was to be very magnificent; it consisted of a French coat of different colors according to the duties of the wearer under the Grand Marshal, the High Chamberlain, and the Grand Equerry, with silver embroidery for all; a cloak worn over one shoulder, of velvet, lined with satin; a scarf, a lace band, and the hat caught up in front, and adorned with a feather. The women were to appear in ball dress, with a train, with a collar of blond-lace, called a *chérusque*, which was fastened on both shoulders and rose high behind the head, recalling the fashions of the time of Catherine de' Medici.

There were rehearsals of the coronation as if it were a spectacular play. Every one, from the principal actors to the most insignificant assistants, studied his part most conscientiously; the Masters of Ceremonies were to act as prompters to those who might forget. The Imperial carriages and those of the Princes and Princesses one morning were all driven empty to the neighborhood of Notre Dame, that coachman, postilions, and grooms might know the route they were to take, and when they were to draw up. The carriages were superb, the horses magnificent, the liveries sumptuous. Never in the most extravagant days of the monarchy had such luxury been seen.

M. de Bausset says that a week before the coronation the Emperor commanded of the artist Isabey seven drawings representing the seven principal ceremonies to take place at Notre Dame, which, however, could not be rehearsed in the Cathedral on account of the number of workmen busy day and night in decorating it. To ask at once for seven drawings each containing more than a hundred persons in action, was asking for the impossible. Isabey skilfully eluded the difficulty. He bought at the toy shops all the little dolls he could find, dressed them

up as Pope, Emperor, Empress, Princes, high dignitaries, Chamberlains, Equerries, Ladies of Honor,
Ladies of the Palace. These dolls thus arrayed he
arranged on a plan in relief of the interior of Notre
Dame, and carrying it to the Emperor, said: "Sire,
I bring Your Majesty something better than the
drawings." Napoleon thought the idea ingenious,
and used the dolls and the plan to make every official
understand his place and his duty.

The *Moniteur* of the 9th Frimaire, Year XIII.
(November 30, 1804), published in advance all the
details of the ceremony, which the Emperor had fixed
with as much care as if it had been the plan of a
battle. A difficulty arose on this occasion. The
Pope had wished Napoleon to receive the holy communion in public on the day of the coronation, and
Napoleon had given the matter thought. The Grand
Master of Ceremonies, M. de Ségur, brought up
against the proposition the necessity of a preliminary
confession and the possibility that absolution might
be denied him. "That's not the difficulty," said the
Emperor, "the Holy Father knows how to distin-
guish between the sins of Cæsar and those of the
man." Then he added: "I know that I ought to
give an example of respect for religion and its
ministers; so you see that I treat the priests well,
go regularly to mass, and listen to it with all due
seriousness and solemnity. But every one knows me,
and how would it be for me, and for others, if I should
go too far? Would not that be setting an example

of hypocrisy, and committing a sacrilege?" The Pope did not insist upon it. This dread of committing sacrilege Napoleon referred to again at Saint Helena, in 1816: "Everything was done," he said then, "to persuade me to go in great pomp to communion at Notre Dame, after the fashion of our kings; I absolutely refused; I did not believe enough, I said, to get any good from it, and yet I believed too much to consent to be guilty of sacrilege."

Another difficulty which gave the Pope much anxiety, and was not settled in the formalities of the coronation, was whether the Emperor should receive the crown from the hands of the Sovereign Pontiff. Pius VII. had brought up the question before leaving Rome, and Cardinal Consalvi had written on this matter, to which the Vatican attached great importance, as follows: "All the French Emperors, all those of Germany, who have been crowned by the Popes, have accepted the crown from them. The Holy Father, before undertaking this journey, requires to receive from Paris the assurance that there will be no innovation made in the present case, in the way of a diminution of the honor and dignity of the Sovereign Pontiff." At Rome only vague and dilatory answers had been received. In Paris the Emperor, leaving the matter to be decided on the spur of the moment, had only said: "I will arrange that myself."

The preparations at Notre Dame had come to an end. They had been very considerable. Several houses that hid the north façade had been destroyed. Before the great entrance, still scarred by the ravages of the Revolutionists, there had been set up a decoration of painted wood, representing a vast Gothic porch with three arches upholding the statues of the thirty-six good cities, the mayors of which were to be present at the coronation. To the right and the left stood images of Clovis and Charlemagne, sceptre in hand. Above, between two golden eagles, appeared the Imperial coat-of-arms. This was intended for the sole entrance of the Pope and the Emperor. It was connected with the Archbishop's palace by large, covered, wooden galleries, adorned within by gobelin tapestry. This palace, to which Pius VII. and Napoleon were to go before they entered the Cathedral, no longer exists; it was destroyed, February 14, 1831, in an insurrection. It used to stand just by the side of the church. It was built in 1161 by Maurice de Sully, rebuilt in 1697 by the Cardinal of Noailles, embellished in 1750 by the Archbishop de Beaumont, and was the meeting-place of the Constituent Assembly from October 19 to November 9, 1789. There the Pope and the Emperor were to alight on their way from the Tuileries and put on their grand coronation robes before entering the Cathedral.

The whole church of Notre Dame had been hung with crimson stuffs adorned with gold fringe, with the arms of the Empire embroidered on the corners. On each side of the nave and around the choir had been built three rows of galleries, decorated alike with silk and velvet stuffs fringed with gold, and flags had been arranged like a trophy about each pillar. Above the trophies were winged and gilded victories, holding candelabra with a vast number of candles. There were, besides, twenty-four chandeliers hanging from the roof. The galleries kept out the light, especially at the season when the days were short; consequently it had been decided that the Cathedral should be artificially lit during the ceremony, thus augmenting the pomp and beauty of the spectacle. The choir, shut off by a railing, was reserved for the clergy. To the right of the high altar, on a platform with eleven steps, had been raised the pontifical throne, above which was a golden dome adorned with the arms of the Catholic, Apostolic, and Roman Church. In front and on each side of the pontifical throne were benches with backs for the cardinals and prelates. For the Emperor and the Empress had been prepared what was called the great and the little throne. The little throne was formed of two armchairs, one for Napoleon, the other for Josephine. These two chairs stood on a platform with four steps, opposite the high altar. The Emperor and Empress were to occupy them during the first part of the ceremony. The grand throne was at the other end of the church, with its back against the great door, which was thus closed. This great throne stood on a large semicircular platform, and was reached by twenty-four steps. It stood under a canopy in the shape of a triumphal arch, upheld by eight

columns, and it overlooked the whole church. The
Emperor and the Empress were not to ascend this
throne till after the coronation.

For the coronation Napoleon had given to the
Cathedral a number of holy vessels in silver-gilt,
enriched with diamonds, and very valuable lace albs,
a processional cross, chandeliers, and incense-burners.
At the same time he restored to the Cathedral a great
number of relics with which the piety of Saint Louis
had endowed the Sainte Chapelle. In 1791 they had
been deposited in the treasury of Saint Denis, by
order of Louis XVI., thence in 1793 they had been
transferred to the cabinet of curiosities in the National Library, and had been exposed under the
Directory, in the Hall of Antiquities. The Emperor
restored them to the worship of the faithful.

The preparations were completed, and the ceremony promised to be magnificent. Madame Junot,
afterwards the Duchess of Abrantès, breakfasted
with the Empress at the Tuileries, December 1, 1804,
the day before the coronation. Josephine was much
excited and radiantly happy. At breakfast she told
how amiably the Emperor had talked with her that
morning and how he had tried on her head the crown
which she was to put on the next day at Notre
Dame. As she said that she shed tears of gratitude.
She spoke then of her pain when Napoleon had
refused her request for Lucien's return. "I wanted
to plead this great day," she said, "but Bonaparte
spoke so harshly that I had to keep silent. I wanted

to show Lucien that I could return good for evil; if you have a chance, let him know it."

In the evening the Senate came to the Tuileries to announce to the Emperor the result of the *plébiscite* which approved of the Empire and the matter of inheritance; 3,521,660 citizens having voted for, and 2,579 against. Napoleon replied to the President of the Senate with the infatuation that springs from success and the consciousness of strength: " I ascend the throne to which I have been called by the unanimous voices of the Senate, the people, and the army, with my heart full of feeling of the great destinies of this people whom, from the midst of camps, I first saluted with the name of great. Since my youth all my thoughts have been devoted to it, and I must say here, my pleasures and my pains now are nothing but the pleasures and the pains of my people. My descendants will long fill this throne. They will never forget that contempt of laws and the overthrow of the social order are only the results of the weakness and indecision of rulers."

The hour of disaster was approaching, but it had not yet struck; the morrow was to be radiant. Salvos of artillery were fixed every hour from six in the evening till midnight; at each salvo, the towers, spires, and public buildings were illuminated for a few minutes by Bengal lights. Imperial insignia, among others the sword of Charlemagne, were already in the Church of Notre Dame. General de Ségur, then a captain under the command of the Grand Marshal of the Palace, was charged to watch that precious relic during the night. He records one thing about it which clearly shows the bellicose spirit of the men of the time. One of the officers guarding the Imperial sword conceived the mad idea of using it against one of his comrades, who defended himself with his own sabre, and consoled himself for his defeat and for a slight wound with the thought that he was beaten by so glorious a weapon.

That same night, the one before the coronation, Josephine's wishes were granted. Her union with Napoleon was blessed by the church. An altar was mysteriously raised in the Tuileries, and there, in the presence of M. de Talleyrand and the Marshal Berthier, who were the only witnesses, Cardinal Fesch celebrated, in the profoundest secrecy, the religious marriage of the Emperor and Empress. The scruples of Pius VII. were thus allayed. Josephine could be crowned the next day.

V.

THE CORONATION.

IT was December 2, 1804. Since early morning all Paris had been alive. It was very cold; the sky was covered, but no one thought of the unpleasant weather. All the streets through which the procession was to pass had been carefully swept and sprinkled with sand. The inhabitants had decorated the fronts of their houses according to their tastes and means, with draperies, tapestry, artificial flowers, and branches of evergreens. Two lines of infantry were drawn up for a space of about half a league. Long before the hour of the departure of the Pope and the Emperor from the Tuileries, a vast throng had gathered in the streets, was crowding every window, and assembling on every roof. Marshal Murat, Governor of Paris, offered at an early hour a sumptuous breakfast to the Princes of Germany who had come to Paris for the coronation — the Elector Archchancellor of the German Empire, the Princes of Nassau, of Hesse, and of Baden. After the breakfast they drove to Notre Dame in four superb carriages, drawn by six horses each, with an escort under the

49

command of one of his aides-de-camp, and he himself
mounted his horse to take his place at the head of
the twenty squadrons of cavalry which were to go in
front of the Emperor's carriage.

At the Tuileries Napoleon put on what was called
the undress attire; this he was to wear on his way
from the palace to the Archbishop's. He was not to
put on full dress, that is to say, the Imperial robes
and cloak, until he was to enter the church. The
undress is thus described by Constant, the Emperor's
valet: silk stockings embroidered with gold; low
boots of white velvet, embroidered with gold on the
seams; with diamond buttons and buckles on his
garters; a coat of crimson velvet faced with white
velvet; a short cloak of crimson lined with white
satin, covering the left shoulder and fastened on the
right-hand side by a double clasp of diamonds; a
black velvet cap, surmounted by two aigrets, a diamond loop, and for button, the most celebrated of
the crown jewels, the Regent.

The Empress's costume was no less magnificent.
She wore a dress, with a train, of silver brocade
covered with gold bees; her shoulders were bare,
but on her arms were tight sleeves embroidered with
gold, the upper part adorned with diamonds, and
fastened to them was a lace ruff worked with gold
which rose behind half up her head. The tight-
fitting dress had no waist, after the fashion of the
time, but she wore a gold ribbon as a girdle, set with
thirty-nine pink gems. Her bracelets, ear-rings,

and necklace were formed of precious stones and antique cameos. Her diadem consisted of four rows of pearls interlaced with clusters of diamonds. The Empress, whose hair was curled, after the fashion of the reign of Louis XIV., although forty-one years old, looked, according to Madame de Rémusat, no more than twenty-five. The Emperor was much struck by Josephine's beauty in this sumptuous attire; all this luxury impressed him. He recalled the days of his childhood, and turning to his favorite brother, he said: " Joseph, if father could see us ! "

Nine o'clock sounded, the hour set for the departure of the Pope, who was to reach Notre Dame before the Emperor. The Sovereign Pontiff, clad in white, went down the staircase of the Pavilion of Flora and entered his carriage, which was drawn by eight horses; above it was a large tiara. At Rome it was the custom that when the Pope went forth to officiate at one of the great churches, — for instance, to Saint John Lateran, — for one of his chamberlains to start a moment before him, mounted on a mule, and carrying a great processional cross. Pius VII. asked that the same thing might be done at Paris; consequently the pontifical procession was headed by a chamberlain whose mule did not fail to amuse the vast crowd that lined the quays; yet when the Pope passed, all knelt down and received his blessing with due respect. With cavalry in front and behind, the Pope's carriage and the eight carriages in which were the cardinals, Italian prelates and officers who had come from

Rome with him, drove slowly along the quays to the
Archbishop's Palace.   There were awaiting him all
the French cardinals, archbishops, and bishops, and
he was received by the Cardinal du Belloy, the Archbishop of Paris, as he entered to put on his pontifical robes.   The pontifical procession entered Notre
Dame in the following order: a priest, carrying the
apostolic cross; seven acolytes, carrying the seven
golden candlesticks; more than a hundred bishops,
archbishops or cardinals, in cope and mitre, marching two by two; and last of all the Holy Father, his
tiara on his head, under a canopy between two cardinals who held up the ends of his golden cope.   The
clergy intoned the hymn *Tu es Petrus*, which was
very impressive, and the Sovereign Pontiff, after
kneeling for a few moments before the high altar,
took his seat in the middle of the choir on the pontifical throne, above which was a dome adorned with
the coat-of-arms of the church.

The Emperor and the Empress, who were to leave
the Tuileries at ten, did not start till half past ten.
They got into the magnificent coronation carriage
which excited the hearty admiration of the crowd,
always fond of show.   It was drawn by eight superb
horses, splendidly harnessed; upon it was a golden
crown upheld by four eagles with outstretched wings.
The four sides of the coach were of glass, set in
slender carved uprights, so that there was an unob-
structed view of Napoleon and Josephine on the
back seat, with Joseph and Louis Bonaparte opposite

them. Salvos of artillery announced the Emperor's
departure from the Tuileries. Twenty squadrons of
cavalry, with Marshal Murat at their head, led the
procession. Eighteen carriages, with six horses each,
followed, conveying the high dignitaries and the
courtiers. Bands played triumphal marches, and all
along the way a vast crowd saluted this sovereign.
The procession starting from the Tuileries by the
Carrousel went along the rue Saint Honoré as far as
the rue de Lombards, crossed the Pont au Change,
and then along the quay to the rue du Parvis Notre
Dame and the Archbishop's Palace. Just as the
Emperor and the Empress were entering the palace
courtyard, the mist, which had been thick all the
morning, cleared away, and the sun came out glisten-
ing on the gilded decorations of the Imperial coach.
The *Moniteur*, with its official enthusiasm, spoke of
"the orb of day escaping, against every expectation,
from the rigid rule of a stormy season to light up the
festal day."

At the Archbishop's Palace, Napoleon changed his
dress, putting on his coronation robes. This differed
entirely from the costume he had worn from the
Tuileries to the palace, and consisted of a tight-fit-
ting gown of white satin, embroidered with gold on
every seam, and of an Imperial mantle of crimson
velvet, all over which were golden bees; it was
bordered by worked branches of olive-tree, laurels,
and oak, in circles enclosing the letter N, with a
crown above each one; the lining, the border, and

the cape were of ermine. This cloak, fastened on the right shoulder, while leaving the arm free, reached to just above the knee, and weighed no less than eighty pounds, and though it was held by four persons, Prince Joseph, Prince Louis, the Archchancellor Cambacérès, the Archtreasurer Lebrun, was for the Emperor, who was a short man, a sumptuous, but heavy load. He carried it, however, with fitting majesty. On his head he had put a crown of golden laurel, the laurel of Cæsar; around his neck he wore the diamond necklace of the Legion of Honor; on his left side he carried a sword with a large handle — the scabbard was of blue enamel adorned with gold eagles and bees. At the same time Josephine completed her dressing, putting on a long red velvet cloak, sprinkled with gold bees, and lined with ermine; its skirts were upheld by Princesses Joseph, Louis, Elisa, Pauline, and Charlotte.

The Imperial procession proceeded from the Arch-bishop's Palace to Notre Dame through the wooden gallery, and entered the church, not through the mid-dle entrance, which was blocked by the great throne, but through one of the side-doors. They advanced in the following order, with an interval of ten paces between each group: the ushers, four abreast, the heralds at arms, two abreast; the Chief Herald at Arms; the pages, four abreast; the aides of the masters of ceremonies; the masters of ceremonies; the Grand Master of Ceremonies, M. de Ségur; Mar-shal Sérurier, carrying on a cushion the Empress's

ring; Marshal Moncey, carrying the basket which
was to receive her cloak; Marshal Murat, carrying
her crown on a cushion; the Empress, with her First
Equerry on her right, and her First Chamberlain on
her left; she wore the Imperial cloak, which was
supported by the five Princesses, the cloak of each
one of these being supported by an officer of her
household; Madame de La Rochefoucauld, Maid of
Honor, and Madame de Lavalette, the Empress's
Lady of the Bedchamber; Marshal Kellermann, carrying the crown of Charlemagne, a diadem with six
branches adorned with valuable cameos; Marshal
Perignon, carrying Charlemagne's sceptre, at the end
of which was a ball representing the world, with a
small figure of the great Carlovingian Emperor; Marshal Lefebvre, carrying Charlemagne's sword; Marshal
Bernadotte, carrying Napoleon's necklace; Colonel
General Eugene de Beauharnais, the Emperor's ring;
Marshal Berthier, the Imperial globe; M. de Talleyrand, the basket destined to receive the Emperor's
cloak. Then came the Emperor, the crown of golden
laurel on his head, holding in one hand his silver
sceptre, topped by an eagle, and encircled by a golden
serpent, and in the other his hand of justice. His
cloak was supported by his two brothers, Joseph,
Grand Elector, and Louis, Constable, as well as
by the Archchancellor Cambacérès and the Archtreasurer Lebrun. Then followed the Grand Equerry,
the Colonel General of the Guard, and the Grand
Marshal of the Palace, the three abreast, the min-

isters, four abreast, and the high officers of the
army.

As Napoleon entered the church, the twenty thousand spectators shouted, " Long live the Emperor !"
A cardinal gave holy water to Josephine ; the Cardinal, the Archbishop of Paris, presented it to Napoleon ; and the two prelates, after complimenting the
Emperor and the Empress, conducted them in a procession, under a canopy held by canons, to the smaller
throne in the middle of the choir.   There they were
to sit during the first part of the ceremony, near the
high altar, on a platform with four steps.   As the
Emperor and the Empress entered the choir, the
Pope came down from the pontifical chair, and intoned the *Veni Creator*.   The Emperor handed to the
Archchancellor his hand of justice ; to the Archtreasurer, his sceptre ; to Prince Joseph, his crown ; to
Prince Louis, his sword ; to the Grand Chamberlain,
his Imperial cloak ; to Colonel General Eugene de
Beauharnais, his ring.   The six objects formed what
were called " the Emperor's ornaments."   They were
placed on the altar by the representative dignitaries,
and were to be handed again to the Emperor by the
Pope in the course of the ceremony.   The same was
true of the " Empress's ornaments," her ring, cloak,
and crown, which were placed on the altar ; the ring,
by Marshal Sérurier ; the cloak, by Marshal Moncey ;
the crown, by Marshal Murat.   Charlemagne's insignia, his crown, sceptre, and sword, remained during
the whole ceremony in the hands of Marshals Keller-

mann, Perignon, and Lefebvre, who stood at the right
of the small throne in the choir.

As soon as the ornaments of the Emperor and
Empress had been placed on the altar, the Pope
asked the Emperor in Latin if he promised to use
every effort to have law, justice, and peace rule
in the church and among his people; Napoleon
touched the gospels with both hands, as it was held
out to him by the Grand Almoner, and answered
Profiteor. Then the Pope, the bishops, archbishops,
and cardinals knelt before the altar and began the
litany. When they reached the three verses used only
at coronations, the Emperor and Empress also knelt.

After the litany, the Grand Almoner, another cardinal, and two bishops advanced towards the small
throne, and bowed low before Napoleon and Josephine, and conducted them to the foot of the altar to
receive sacred unction. The Emperor and Empress
knelt on blue velvet cushions placed on the first step
of the altar. The Pope anointed Napoleon on the
head and his two hands, uttering the prayer of consecration: "Mighty and Eternal God, who didst appoint Hazael to be king over Syria, and Jehu to be
king over Israel, making known thy wishes through
the prophet Elijah; and who didst pour holy oil of
kings upon the head of Saul and of David, through
the prophet Samuel, send down through my hands,
the treasures of thy grace and of thy blessings upon
thy servant Napoleon, whom, in spite of our unworthi-
ness, we consecrate to-day as Emperor, in thy name."

Then the Pope anointed the Empress in the same way, reciting this prayer: " May the Father of eternal glory be thy aid; and may the Omnipotent bless thee; may he hear thy prayers, and give thee a long life, ever confirming this blessing and maintaining it forever with all thy people; may he confound thy enemies; may the sanctification of Christ and the anointing of this oil ever aid thee, so that he who on earth has given thee his blessing may give thee in heaven the happiness of the angels, and that thou mayst be blessed and guarded for eternal life by Jesus Christ, our Saviour, who lives and reigns forever and ever."

The Emperor and Empress were then conducted to the small throne, that is to say, to their two chairs; before each one was a praying-stand. Then high mass began; it was said by the Pope; the music had been composed by Paesiello, the Abbé Rose, and Lesueur. There were three hundred performers, singers, and musicians; among the soloists were the great singer Laïs, and two famous violinists, Kreutzer and Baillot. At the *Gradual* the mass was interrupted for the blessing of the ornaments which the Emperor and Empress then put on.

Napoleon, followed by the Archchancellor, the Archtreasurer, the Grand Chamberlain, the Grand Equerry, and two chamberlains, and Josephine, accompanied by her Lady of Honor, her Lady of the Bedchamber, her First Chamberlain, and her First Equerry, advanced towards the altar, and

ascended the steps at the same time; the Sovereign
Pontiff, with his back to the altar, was sitting on a
sort of folding-chair. He blessed the Imperial ornaments, reciting a special prayer for each one. His
Holiness then handed them to the Emperor in the
following order: first the ring, which Napoleon
placed on his finger; then the sword, which he put
in its scabbard; the cloak, which his chamberlains
fastened on his shoulders, then the hand of justice
and the sceptre which he handed to the Archchancellor and the Archtreasurer.

The only ornament left to be given to the Emperor .
was the crown. It will be remembered that there
had been a long negotiation at Rome to ascertain
whether the Emperor would be crowned by the Pope
or would crown himself. The question was left
uncertain, and Napoleon had said that he would
settle it himself at Notre Dame when the time came.
Still Pius VII. was convinced that he was going to
place the crown on the sovereign's head. He had
just handed him the ring, the sword, the cloak, the
hand of justice, and the sceptre, and was preparing
to do the same thing with the crown. But the
Emperor, who had ascended the last step of the altar,
and was following every motion of the Pope, grasped
from his hands the sign of sovereign power and
proudly placed it on his own head. Pius VII., out-
witted and surprised, made no attempt at resistance.

After thus crowning himself, Napoleon proceeded
to crown the Empress. This was the most solemn

moment in Josephine's life; the moment which dispelled all her incessant dread of divorce, the brilliant
verification of her fondest hopes, the completion of
her triumph. Napoleon advanced with emotion to
this companion of his happiest days, to the woman
who had brought him happiness; she was kneeling
before him, shedding tears of joy and gratitude, with
her hands clasped and trembling. He recalled all
that he owed her: his happiness, for, thanks to her,
he had been blessed with a requited love; his glory,
for it was she who, in 1796, had secured for him the
command of the Army of Italy, the origin of all his
triumphs. He must have been glad at this moment
that he had not followed his brother's malicious
suggestions and had not separated from his dear
Josephine! The affection of the young General
Bonaparte revived in the heart of the sovereign.
He thought Josephine more gracious, more touching,
more lovable than ever, and it was with an outburst
of happiness that he placed the Imperial diadem on
her charming and cherished head.

The Emperor and Empress, once crowned, proceeded to the great throne, at the entrance of the
church, by the great door, being solemnly led there
by the Pope and the Cardinals. The Imperial procession then formed again in the order in which it
had come to Notre Dame, the Empress going before
the Emperor. At this moment the Princesses seemed
to hesitate about carrying the skirt of the Empress's
cloak; Napoleon noticed this, and said a few severe,

firm words to his sisters, and all was smoothed.
The procession reached the foot of the great throne;
the Emperor ascended the twenty-four steps and sat
down in full majesty, wearing his crown and Imperial
cloak, holding the hand of justice and the sceptre.
At his right, on a seat like his, but one step lower,
the Empress placed herself. Another step lower, sat
the Princesses on simple seats. At the Emperor's
left, two steps below him, were the Princes and high
dignitaries. On each side of the platform the marshals, high officers, and ladies of the court took their
places. The sight was most impressive. The Pope
in his turn ascended the twenty-four steps, and thus
commanding the whole Cathedral, extended his hands
over the Emperor and the Empress, and uttered these
Latin words, the formula used for taking the throne:
"*In hoc solio confirmare vos Deus, et in regno æterno
secum regnare faciat Christus!*" — "May God establish you on your throne, and may Christ cause you
to reign with him in his eternal kingdom!" Then
he kissed the Emperor on the cheek, and turning
towards the assembled multitude, said: "*Vivat Imperator in æternum!*" — "May the Emperor live forever!" This was what had been said ten centuries
before at Saint Peter's in Rome when the ruler of the
same people, Charlemagne, had been proclaimed Emperor of the West.

Applause broke forth and three hundred musicians
intoned the *Vivat Imperator*, a hymn composed by
the Abbé Rose. The pontifical procession and the

Imperial procession returned to the choir; the Emperor and Empress resumed their places on the chairs, and the Pope began the *Te Deum*. After this, which was sung by four choirs and two orchestras, the mass, which had been interrupted by the ceremony with the ornaments and the taking possession of the throne, went on. At the offertory, Napoleon and Josephine, followed by the two Princes and the five Princesses, went to lay their offerings before the Pope; these consisted of a silver-gilt vase, a lump of gold, a lump of silver, and a candle about which were inlaid thirteen pieces of money. At the elevation Prince Joseph removed the Emperor's crown, and Madame de La Rochefoucauld, Maid of Honor, that of the Empress. Napoleon and Josephine knelt before the Host, and when they rose, put their crowns on again.

When mass was over, the Emperor took the political oath prescribed by the constitution, which had aroused much opposition in Rome. The presidents of the great bodies of the state brought him the formula, and with one hand held over the gospels, the Emperor swore to maintain the principles of the Revolution, to preserve the integrity of the territory, and to rule with an eye to the interest, happiness, and glory of the French people. The First Herald-at-Arms then called forth in a loud voice: "The most glorious and most august Emperor Napoleon, Emperor of the French, is crowned and enthroned: Long live the Emperor!" That was the end of the ceremony. Salvos of artillery mingled with the applause.

The solemnity had been most successful, and Napoleon could say with truth to his brother Joseph: "For me it is a battle won; by my art and the measures I took, I have succeeded beyond my expectations." Had he not prophesied accurately when he said to his secretary at the signing of the Concordat: "Bourrienne, you will see what use I shall make of the priests!" The golden chasubles had made a brilliant spectacle by the side of the uniforms; the crosses and the tiara by the side of the swords and the sceptre. Napoleon, always a master of theatrical effect, had known how to lend antiquity to his newborn glory by borrowing from the past all its majesty and pomp, and by skilfully decking himself with what was most brilliant in the chronicles of remote centuries. From Charlemagne he took his insignia; from Cæsar his golden laurel. The head of a nation that had grown great by the cross and the sword, he desired to make his coronation the festival of the church and of the army.

The Imperial and the pontifical processions returned to the Archbishop's Palace, and half an hour later proceeded to the Tuileries, through the New Market, the Place du Châtelet, the rue Saint Denis, the boulevards, the rue and the Place de la Concorde, the Pont Tournant, and the grand roadway of the castle. Night had fallen; the houses were illuminated. Five hundred torches cast their light on the two processions, and by their imposing and strange brilliancy, the crowd gazed with interest on the new Charlemagne and the Vicar of Christ.

Napoleon and Josephine re-entered the Tuileries at half past six; the Pope at about seven. The Emperor, who was somewhat tired by all this ceremony, gladly resumed his modest uniform of Colonel of the Chasseurs of the Guard. He dined alone with Josephine, asking her to keep on her head the becoming diadem which she wore so gracefully. That evening he chatted pleasantly with the ladies-in-waiting, and praised the rich dresses they had worn in such splendor at Notre Dame; he said to them, laughing: "It's I who deserve the credit for your charming appearance." Then they looked out of the windows on the illuminated garden, the large flower-garden surrounded with porches covered with lights, the long alley adorned with shining colonnades, on the terraces of orange-trees all aglow, with a number of glasses of various colors on every tree, and finally on the Place de la Concorde, one blazing star. It was like a sea of flame.

It was the painter who had been a member of the Convention, the *montagnard*, the regicide who had insulted Louis XVI., who had painted the apotheosis of Marat, and with a malicious hand had drawn the features of Marie Antoinette on her way to the scaffold; it was this artist, this fierce demagogue, the ardent Revolutionist, who was commissioned with painting the official representation of the coronation. He carried his gallantry so far as to choose for his subject, not the moment when Napoleon crowned himself, but that of the coronation of the Empress;

and when a critic accused him of making Josephine
too young, he said: "Go and say that to her!"
When the picture was finished, the Emperor and the
court went to see it in the artist's studio. Napoleon
walked up and down for half an hour, bareheaded,
before the canvas, which is about twenty feet high,
about thirty long, and contains one hundred portraits.
(It is now at Versailles in the Hall of the Guards, at
the top of the marble staircase.) The Emperor examined it with the closest attention, while David and
all who were present maintained a respectful silence.
This long waiting made the artist very anxious. At
last Napoleon turned towards him and said: "It's
good, David, very good. You have divined all my
thought; you have made me a French knight. I
thank you for transmitting to ages to come the proof
of affection I wanted to give to her who shares with
me the pains of government." Then taking two steps
towards the artist, he raised his hat and said, in a
loud voice: "David, I salute you."

Sometimes at Notre Dame in Holy Week, at evening service, when the Cathedral is lit up as at the
coronation, I recall the various ceremonies of this
church: the royal baptisms and marriages there celebrated; the banners hung from its roof; the *Te Deums*
and *De Profundis* so often sung there; Bossuet uttering the funeral oration of the Prince of Condé; the
shameless goddess of Reason profaning the sanctuary.
I close my eyes in meditation, and seem to be present
at the coronation, to see Pius VII. on his pontifical

throne, and, before the altar, Napoleon crowning Josephine with his own hands. I hear the echo of distant litanies, of the trumpets, of the organ, and of the applause. Then I think of the nothingness of all human glory and grandeur. Of all the illustrious persons who have knelt in this old basilica, what is left? Scarcely a few handfuls of dust. I open my eyes. The days are silent; the crowd has quietly withdrawn. The lights are out, and at the end of the church, in the shadow, like a timid star in a cloudy day, burns a solitary lamp.

VI.

THE coronation was the signal for a succession of festivities. Napoleon was anxious that all classes of society should take part in the rejoicings; that commerce should be benefited; that luxury should do wonders; and that Paris should take the position of the first city in the world, the capital of capitals. The day after the coronation was to be the popular holiday, and the day when the flags were distributed was to be the festival of the army. Monday, December 3, booths were open on every side for the entertainment of the crowd. Adulation assumed every guise, even the humblest; and every form of language, even that of the markets, was employed to flatter the new sovereign. There was sung, " The joyous round on the lottery of thirteen thousand fowls, with an accompaniment of fountains of wine." It was a description of the food distributed to the poor people of Paris. This song was sung in every street and place, as the *Ça ira* was sung in '93.

The compliment of the marketmen and of their ladies ran thus: "I have reasoned it out with my wife that a house a thousand times as large as Notre Dame would not be able to hold all those who have reason to bless you." In the way of incense, nothing was too gross for the sovereign. One district said of Napoleon : —

> " He received for us when God formed him,
> The arm of Romulus, the mind of Numa."

The Empress too was praised : —

> " Spouse of the hero whom the universe regards,
> The Graces accompany you to the temple,
> Every one sees in your face the bounty
> Of which you distribute the gifts."

In allusion to her love of flowers this quatrain was composed : —

> " Josephiniana ! this is the new flower
> Whose beauty catches my eye.
> To join the laurels of Cæsar
> Nothing less is needed than an immortal flower."

The Emperor was sung, too, in mythological language, for his flatterers tried to exhaust all sorts of adulation. On Coronation Day the Prefect of Police had distributed a poem entitled *The Crown of Napoleon brought from Olympus by command of Jupiter :* —

> " Mounting one of the coursers of the proud Bellona,
> Mercury brings a crown from Olympus;
> The king of the gods sends it to the hero of the French
> As the reward of his success.
> Ye whom he guided a hundred times in the fields of glory,
> Phalanx of warriors, children of victory,
> Braving the impotent fury of the English,
> Sing Napoleon, sing your Emperor."

December 3 the public rejoicings organized by the government extended from the Place de la Concorde to the Arsenal. Heralds-at-arms walked through the city, distributing medals struck to commemorate the coronation. These medals bore on one side the head of the Emperor, his brow wearing the crown of the Cæsars; on the other, the image of a magistrate, and of an ancient warrior, supporting on a buckler a crowned hero, wearing an Imperial mantle. Beneath was the inscription: "The Senate and the People."

As soon as the heralds-at-arms had passed by, the merry-making began, continuing till late in the night. There was a distribution of food, as well as sports of all kinds, reminding one of the times of the Roman Emperors: *panem et circenses.* On the Place de la Concorde had been built four large wooden halls for public balls. The cold was severe; there was a hard frost, but this did not check the universal enjoyment. On the boulevards there were at every step puppet shows, wandering singers, rope dancers, greased poles, bands of music. From the Place de la Concorde to the end of the boulevard Saint Antoine sparkled a double row of colored lights arrayed like garlands. The Garde Meuble and the Palace of the Legislative Body were ablaze with lights. The arches of Saint Denis and of Saint Martin were all covered with lights; the crowd was enraptured with the fireworks, which had never been so fine.

The people of Paris had been invited to illuminate the fronts of their houses, and moved either by enthusiasm or self-interest, they had spent large sums for this purpose. Among the notable illuminations was that of the engineer Chevalier, on the Pont Neuf. There was a transparency in which, amid encircling laurels and myrtles, was to be seen an optician turning his glass up to the sky towards a bright star, around which was this inscription: " *In hoc signo salus !* " — " In this sign is safety ! "

December 3 was the first day of the coronation festivities. The third day was devoted to what the *Moniteur* called, " arms, valor, fidelity." This was the day when Napoleon formally presented to the army and to the National Guard of the Empire the eagles, " which they were always to find on the field of honor." This ceremony took place on the Champ de Mars. To quote once more from the *Moniteur:* " This vast field, crowded with deputations representing France and the army, bore the aspect of a brave family assembled under the eyes of its chief." The main front of the Military School had been decorated with a huge gallery, with several tents as high as the apartments on the first floor. The middle one, resting on four columns which supported winged victories, covered the thrones of the Emperor and the Empress. The Princes, the high dignitaries, the ministers, the marshals of the Empire, the high officers of the crown, the civil officers, the ladies of the court, were to take their places at the right of the throne. The gallery, in the middle of which was the Imperial tent, was in front of the Military School, and was divided into sixteen parts, eight on each side, representing the sixteen cohorts of the Legion of Honor. A broad staircase led from this gallery to the Champ de Mars; the first step was for the presidents of cantons, the prefects, sub-prefects, and the members of the municipal councils. On the other steps, there stationed themselves colonels of regiments and presidents of the electoral colleges of the departments, holding flags surmounted with eagles. On each side of the staircase were colossal figures of France, one at war, the other at peace. Twenty-five thousand soldiers, in faultless trim, had been under arms since six in the morning.

Unfortunately, the weather was terrible; a thaw had begun and it was raining in torrents. The Champ de Mars was a sea of mud. The courtiers who, on the 2d of December, had so belauded the sun, representing it as a sharer in the festival, a docile slave of the Emperor, were obliged to acknowledge that it was raining. Madame de Rémusat made a very true remark about this; she said with truth that one of the commonest, though one of the absurdest, flatteries of every time, was that of pretending that a sovereign's need of fine weather was sure to bring it. "At the Tuileries," she said, "I noticed the opinion that the Emperor needed only to appoint a review or a hunt for a certain day, and that day would be pleasant. Whenever that happened, a great deal was said about it, while silence was kept about rainy or foggy weather. This is exactly what

used to happen under Louis XIV. For the honor of
sovereigns I should prefer that they accepted this
childish flattery with indifference or disgust, and
that no one would think of offering it. It was
impossible to deny that it rained during the distribution of the eagles at the Champ de Mars; but how
many people I met the next day, who assured me
that the rain had not wet them!"

In spite of the bad weather, an enormous crowd
lined the road through which the Imperial procession
was to pass. The terraces of the Tuileries, the Place
de la Concorde, the *quais* were thronged. Numberless spectators covered the slopes of the Champ de
Mars. The ever obsequious *Moniteur*, in its official
account of the ceremony, said: "If the spectators
were uncomfortable, there was not one who was not
consoled by the feeling that held him there, and by
the expression of his wishes which the applause made
very clear."

At noon the Emperor and the Empress, followed
by their suite, left the Tuileries in the order observed at the coronation, passed down the broad
road, over the Pont Tournant, through the Place
de la Concorde, to the Champ de Mars. Before
their carriage rode the Chasseurs of the Guard and
a squadron of Mamelukes; behind it came the
mounted grenadiers and the chosen Legion. On
reaching the Military School, Napoleon and Josephine received the compliments of the Diplomatic
Body; then they put on their coronation robes, and

took their place in the gallery in front of the building. As soon as the Emperor had seated himself on the throne, cannon were fired, drums beat, bands played. The deputations from the army, who were assembled in the Champ de Mars, formed in close columns and came forward. Then Napoleon arose and said in a loud voice: "Soldiers! These are your flags; these eagles will always be your rallying point; they will be wherever your Emperor may think necessary for the defence of his throne and of his people. You will swear to offer your life in their defence, and by your courage to keep them always on the path to victory. You swear it?" Officers and men replied: "We swear it!"

Alas! these flags were to be always on the path of honor, but not always on the path of victory, for victory is a female goddess and a fickle one. Against how many enemies these flags were to be defended, beneath scorching suns, under avalanches of ice and snow! What heroism, what miracles of bravery, were to be witnessed by these standards on many a battle-field! What fatigue, what suffering, what sacrifices, dangers, wounds, how many glorious deaths, what seas of blood, to come at last to the most lamentable disasters! Had the future been seen, those drums would have been draped in black. But the army imagined itself invincible. The thought of defeat would have called forth a smile of pity. Proud of itself, of its commander, it shouted with joy and pride as it passed before the throne.

A single incident disturbed this martial ceremony. Suddenly an unknown young man approached the Imperial gallery, and shouted: "Down with the Emperor! Liberty or death!" This ardent Republican was at once arrested. His voice had been lost in the music and clatter of arms.

The rain continued, and soon soaked through the canvas and stuffs sheltering the throne. The Empress. was obliged to leave, with her daughter, who had recently given birth to a child. The other Princesses followed this example, with the exception of Madame Murat, who, although lightly clad, remained exposed to the showers. She said that she was learning how to endure the inevitable discomforts of the highest rank.

At five o'clock Napoleon and Josephine were once more at the Tuileries where a state dinner was given in the Gallery of Diana. In the middle of this gallery the table of the Emperor and the Empress was placed beneath a magnificent canopy, on a platform. The Empress sat there with the Emperor on the right and the Pope on her left. The high officers of the crown, as well as a colonel-general of the Guard and a prefect of the palace, remained standing near the Imperial table.

Pages waited on the tables. The Archchancellor of the German Empire took his place at that of the Emperor. In the same gallery were set other tables for the French Princes and for the hereditary Prince of Baden, for the ministers, for the ladies and officers of the Imperial household. After the dinner was a concert, at which the Pope consented to be present. When that was over Pius VII. withdrew, and the evening ended with a ballet danced by the dancers of the opera in the great hall called since the Empire the Hall of the Marshals.

VII.

THE winter of 1804–5 was very brilliant. Napoleon was anxious to give the beginning of his reign an air of splendor. He allowed his officials generous salaries, but he insisted on their spending all they received in sumptuous living, in entertaining freely, and receiving distinguished foreigners. Luxury became compulsory, and trade flourished beyond all expectations. Paris had never, even in the grandest days of the old monarchy, known greater social animation. This martial generation, accustomed to desire a short but merry life, aware that the festivities of one day would be interrupted by the battles of the next, were as eager in the ball-room as on the battle-field. They hastened to enjoy their present prosperity as if they foresaw the disasters to come. French gallantry, which had been forgotten during the Revolution, resumed its sway. The women were like the fair mistresses of castles in the Middle Ages who gave their hearts to the bravest knights. Love and glory both became the fashion. The former Lady of the Bedchamber to Marie Antoinette, Madame

Campan, who taught most of the young women of the court in her school at Saint Germain, had formed a group of beauties, trained in aristocratic manners, at the head of whom was her ablest, most intelligent pupil, Hortense de Beauharnais, who had been married to Prince Louis Bonaparte. The Grand Chamberlain, M. de Talleyrand, a poor bishop but an excellent specimen of a grand lord, and the Grand Master of Ceremonies, M. de Ségur, whose success as ambassador of Louis XVI. at the court of Catherine was very great, set the tone in the households of the Emperor and the Empress.

Napoleon set an example of luxury and elegance. Grand dinners, concerts, official entertainments succeeded one another with startling rapidity. Josephine, who was wildly fond of dress, was glad of an excuse to indulge her extravagant tastes. The Emperor's three sisters lived like real princesses, rivalling one another in magnificence. Princes Joseph and Louis displayed the pomp of future kings.

Almost all the women of the court were young and pretty. It would have been hard to confer on any one, to the exclusion of the rest, the palm of beauty. There were three who were especially distinguished: Madame Maret (later the Duchess of Bassano); Madame Savary (later the Duchess of Rovigo); and Madame de Canisy (later the Duchess of Vicenza). The last named had married M. de Canisy, the Emperor's equerry. Later, she got a divorce and married M. de Caulaincourt, Duke of Vicenza and Grand Equerry.

At Saint Helena Napoleon thus recounted the origin of this famous beauty: "Madame de Loménie, the Cardinal's niece, before being put to death in the Revolution, entrusted to Father Patrault her two young daughters. When the terror was over, Madame de Brienne, their aunt, who had weathered the storm and still possessed a large fortune, demanded them of Father Patrault, who refused to give them up for a long time, on the ground that their mother had urged him to bring them up as peasants." And Napoleon went on: "I was then General of the Army of the Interior; and was able to secure the return of the two children, though with some difficulty, for Patrault resisted in every way in his power. They were the women whom you afterwards knew as Madame de Marnésia and as the beautiful Madame de Canisy."

The Duchess of Abrantès, in recalling the brilliant winter of 1804–5, says, in her Memoirs: "One especially impressive beauty, particularly in the ball-room, was Madame de Canisy. I have often compared her to a muse. It would be impossible for a single face to present a fuller combination of charms than hers: she possessed regular features, a delightful expression, an attractive smile; her hair was silky and glossy. Seldom have I seen anything more charming than Madames de Canisy, Maret, and Savary in entering a ball-room together."

There was no lack of entertainments at which these beauties shone. The one given at the Hotel de

Ville, December 16, 1804, to the Emperor and the Empress, was so costly that it kept the city of Paris for many years in debt. Napoleon, Josephine, Princes Joseph and Louis drove to it in the coronation coach. Batteries of artillery, stationed on the Pont Neuf, announced the moment of their arrival, while tables covered with poultry, and fountains of wine, attracted an enormous crowd to the place; almost every one had a share in this distribution of food, thanks to the precautions taken by the authorities of delivering it only to those who presented a ticket. The front of the Hotel de Ville was illuminated with colored lanterns. When the Empress entered the apartments reserved for her, she found there a complete and magnificent gold toilet-service: it was a present from the City Council. The President of the Council thus addressed her: "Madame: How could the Parisians, who are so capable of distinguishing what is good, delicate, and noble, let slip this opportunity of paying their homage to the profound tenderness, the touching grace, the true dignity that characterize Your Majesty? The happy influence of these rare qualities already makes itself felt in all classes of society, and while your august spouse elevates France in glory, you inspire it to resume the first rank among the races most renowned for urbanity." The hall in which the Imperial banquet was to be given was called the Hall of Victories. On the door was the inscription *Fasti Napoleoni*, and at intervals, separated by military trophies and standards, were Latin inscriptions in honor of Napoleon. Before dinner he was presented with a table-service of silver-gilt by the city of Paris. Then he took his seat, with the Empress, on a platform beneath a canopy, and the meal began. During dinner, a band, hidden behind green foliage, played a symphony of Haydn's, and then was sung a cantata full of flattery for the Emperor and the Empress.

After the dinner there were magnificent fireworks. As the first rockets rose, a second cantata was sung. One of the pieces of fireworks represented a man-of-war with eighty guns; its decks, masts, sails, and rigging were represented by glowing lights. Another, which the Emperor himself set off, represented Mount Saint Bernard sending forth a volcanic eruption from snow-covered rocks. In the centre appeared the image of Napoleon at the head of his army, riding up the steep slope of the mountain.

This entertainment, which closed with a ball at which seven hundred persons were present, was a real apotheosis. Madame de Rémusat, speaking of the extravagant adulation devised for this occasion, says: "A great deal has been said about the fulsome flatteries of Louis XIV. during his reign; I am sure that altogether they would not amount to a tenth part of those that Bonaparte received. I remember that at another festivity given by the city to the Emperor a few years later, since all inscription had been exhausted, there were placed above the throne on which he was to sit, these words from Scripture, in gold letters: *Ego sum qui sum,*—and no one was shocked."

The Senate and the Legislative Body also gave grand entertainments in honor of the coronation. That of the Legislative Body was particularly brilliant. This assembly, which rivalled the Senate in obsequiousness, had decided that a marble statue should be raised to the Emperor in the room where it sat, in honor of the drawing up of the civil code. The day when this statue was to be inaugurated was chosen for the festivity. The Empress, followed by a magnificent suite, reached the Palace of the Legislative Body at about seven in the evening. As she entered, musicians intoned Glück's famous chorus, which used to be sung on formal occasions in the reign of Louis XVI., in honor of Marie Antoinette:—

"What charms! What majesty!"

Unanimous applause emphasized the allusions. Then on the President's invitation, Marshals Murat and Masséna raised the veils that covered the statue, and all eyes beheld the figure of Napoleon, wearing on his brow a laurel wreath, in which were mingled oak and olive leaves. Later, at the time of his abdication at Fontainebleau, Napoleon expressed a regret that he had permitted his statue to be made during his lifetime.

Then M. de Vaublanc ascended the tribune, and made a speech full of extravagant praise; it ended thus: "You live, all of you, threatened by the perils

of the times; you live, and you owe your life to him
whose statue you behold.   You return unfortunate
exiles; you breathe once more the delicious air of
your own country; you embrace your fathers, your
children, your wives, your friends; all this you owe
to him whose statue you behold. There is no longer
any question of his glory; I say nothing about it; I
invoke humanity on one side, gratitude on the other;
I ask you to whom you are indebted for this great,
extraordinary, unexpected good fortune. You all
answer with me, It is to the great man whose statue
you behold." Throughout the whole speech, a perfect
masterpiece of official composition, adulation came in
like a chorus. The President in his turn uttered a
similar eulogy: " Very few at the time," says Constant, who describes this occasion, " found this praise
extravagant; possibly their opinions have changed
since then."

After the speeches, dinner was served to three hundred guests, followed by a magnificent ball.   Though
in the middle of the winter, there was a great show
of shrubs and flowers.   The Halls of Lucretia and of
the Reunion, in which there was dancing, were like
one large bed of roses, laurels, lilacs, jonquils, lilies,
and jasmine.

Perhaps the finest of all the entertainments was
that given to the Emperor and Empress by the marshals of the Empire in the Opera House.   It cost each
marshal ten thousand francs.   The Opera House at
that time was in the rue de Richelieu, where it had

been since 1794. (It was the one torn down during the Restoration, on account of the murder of the Duke of Berry, who was killed on the threshold.) By means of a floor placed level with the stage over the orchestra and the pit, there was made a magnificent ball-room. Twenty-four chandeliers hung from the ceiling, and candelabra were set on each side of every box. The decorations consisted of silver gauze, and wreaths of flowers. The uniforms of the men and the dresses of the women were almost equally magnificent. The eyes of the spectators were dazzled by dresses trimmed with precious stones. Never had there been seen such profusion of light, flowers, perfumes, and diamonds. In this magical setting, fashionable beauties, with their dresses worked with silver and gold foil, their turbans of Eastern stuffs, their jewels and ancient cameos, appeared like sultanas. It was a most sumptuous and fairy-like show.

The marshals arrived at eight in the evening, the Empress at ten, the Emperor at eleven ; as he entered the ball-room, the applause was so violent that it was feared that the candles would be put out. A military march was played, and then there was a concert, closing with the Abbé Rose's *Vivat Imperator*, which had made such an impression on the Coronation Day. After the concert, Prince Louis Bonaparte, Marshal Murat, Eugene de Beauharnais, and Marshal Berthier opened the ball with the Princesses. The Emperor walked twice around the hall, as if he were reviewing troops. Then he sat down by the side of the Empress on a raised platform, and withdrew before the end of the ball.

Besides all these entertainments there were the grand levees and concerts at the Tuileries. The Hall of the Marshals was an impressive sight on those evenings, filled, as it was, with young and pretty women, in gorgeous dresses, and with men resplendent with stars, epaulettes, feathered hats, and sword-belts set with diamonds. After the concert the company would go to the Gallery of Diana, where the supper-tables were set: that of the Empress, those of the Princesses, of the Lady of Honor, of the Lady of the Bedchamber, of the Ladies of the Palace. "All these tables," says the Duchess of Abrantès, "were occupied by women with roses on their heads, and smiles on their lips, and often with tears in their eyes; for vanity, everywhere triumphant, holds its court especially at court. There, favor is everything, disgrace is everything. A chance word or glance of the Emperor or Empress is a blow and a serious one. What, then, must be the result of an invitation sent or withheld?"

During the concert the Empress made up the supper-table; that is to say, chose the women who were to sit at her table, commissioning her chamberlain to notify those she had selected. The Princesses did the same, and the officers of their households likewise informed the women whom they had chosen. There were but twelve places at the Empress's table; eight or ten at those of the Princesses. When the chamberlains came to bring these most welcome invitations, there fluttered through the eight hundred or thousand women present at the concerts and grand levees an anxious emotion which amused observers. The aspect of the Gallery of Diana was most impressive. On the Empress's table shone a golden service amid glass and Sèvres ware. During the supper the men strolled up and down the gallery, but as soon as the Emperor appeared, awe and fear appeared on every face. It seemed as if the times of Louis XIV. had returned, of which La Bruyère said: "Nothing so disfigures certain courtiers as the presence of their Prince; I can sometimes scarcely recognize them, so altered are their features, so degraded their faces. The proud and haughty ones are the most disturbed, for they change the most; and the upright and modest man comes out best; he has nothing to change." The Duchess of Abrantès, recalling the intimidation caused by Napoleon's approach, wrote: "Even those who nowadays talk about the Corsican with a great show of scorn, those very ones (I have seen them, and I am not the only one,) were the most timid before the very shadow of his hat." The women trembled even more. They dreaded the questions the Emperor might put to them, and, according to Madame de Rémusat, there was not one who would not gladly have been anywhere else. During the First Empire, everything, even the festivities, wore a military air. The sovereign always had the air of a commanding general. Discipline prevailed at a ball as well as in a camp, and the young men took part in those pleasures only to return with renewed zeal and courage to the battle-field.

VIII.

BY the beginning of 1805 the court was definitely formed. After laborious studies on the part of a special commission, and long discussions in which Napoleon took as interested a part as he did in the preparation of the civil code, all the wheels of etiquette had been arranged, and the machinery worked with perfect regularity. The Emperor attached great importance to the subject, from both a political and a social point of view. In his eyes, etiquette had the great advantage of drawing between him and those who had recently been his superiors, a distinct line of separation. He looked upon it as a useful tool of government, as an accompaniment of glory absolutely essential for a sovereign, especially for one of recent origin. He was very proud of his court, of the wealth it displayed, and of the vast results he obtained at a comparatively small expense, and at Saint Helena he liked to recall its agreeable memory.

"The Emperor's court," we read in the *Memorial*, "was in every respect much more magnificent than

87

anything that had been seen up to that time, and cost infinitely less. The suppression of abuses, order and regularity in the accounts, made the great difference. His hunting, with the exception of a few useless or absurd particulars, such as the use of falcons, was as splendid and as crowded as that of Louis XIV., and it cost only four hundred thousand francs a year, while the King's cost seven millions. It was the same way with the table; Duroc's order and severity wrought wonders. Under the kings, the palaces were not permanently furnished; the same furniture was transported from one palace to another; there were no accommodations for the people of the court; every one had to provide for himself. Under him, however, there was no one in attendance, who, in the room allotted him, was not as comfortable as at home, or even more comfortable, so far as what was essential and proper was concerned."

The court moved as smoothly as a well-drilled regiment. Napoleon would have shown no mercy to the slightest disregard of the rules he had himself drawn up after long meditation. The courtiers were expected to be as familiar with the code of etiquette as were the officers with the manual of arms. The Emperor noticed the minutest details, busied himself with everything, saw everything. There had been much more latitude at court under the old monarchy, and those of the old régime who entered the Emperor's court were soon wearied by the inflexible severity of its discipline. The court, moreover, was very splendid. The Faubourg Saint Germain brought to it its politeness and conversational charm. For his part, Napoleon speedily assumed the manners of a European sovereign, while preserving his martial character. He was at the same time Emperor and commander-in-chief. Yet the military element did not control his court; the civil element was more powerful there than in other European courts, the Russian, for example. Napoleon would never have suffered in his presence the faintest sign of the familiarity of the camp; every one who crossed the threshold of the Tuileries was compelled to preserve the manners, the bearing, the language of a courtier.

The levees and couchees of the sovereign were restored as in the time of the Bourbons; though under the monarchy they were real things, and a mere imitation under the Empire. These moments were not devoted to the petty details of toilette, but rather to receiving, morning and evening, those members of the civil and military household who had to receive his direct orders or enjoyed the right of "paying their court at these privileged hours." At Saint Helena, Napoleon boasted that at the Tuileries he had suppressed in the matter of etiquette "all that was real and commonplace, and had substituted what was merely nominal and decorative." "A king," he said, "is not a natural product; he is a result of civilization. He does not exist nakedly, but only when dressed."

Let us try to retrace the lines of etiquette as they existed in 1805, at the same time indicating the principal members of the Emperor's household and the nature of their duties.   There were many separate duties, each under the control of a high officer of the Crown, with their provinces carefully defined and sedulously distinguished from one another.   There were six high officers of the Crown: the Grand Almoner (Cardinal Fesch); the Grand Marshal of the Palace (General Duroc); the Grand Equerry (General de Caulaincourt); the Grand Chamberlain (M. de Talleyrand); the Grand Master of Ceremonies (M. de Ségur).

The colonels-general were: Marshal Davout, commanding the foot grenadiers; Marshal Soult, commanding the chasseurs-à-pieds; Marshal Bessières, commanding the cavalry; Marshal Mortier, commanding the artillery and sailors.   These colonels-general of the Imperial Guard formed part of the Emperor's household, and enjoyed the same prerogatives as the high officers of the Crown.

The Grand Almoner was the bishop of the court, wherever that might be.   He gave the Emperor and his court a dispensation from fasting.   He accompanied him to church ceremonies and gave him his prayer-book.   At grand dinners he said grace.   He set free the prisoners whom the Emperor pardoned on certain holy days.

The Grand Marshal of the palace had charge of the military command in the Imperial residences; of their maintenance, decoration, and furnishing; of the assignment of rocms, the supply of food, the heating, lights, silver, and livery. He commanded the detachments of the Imperial Guard on duty in the Imperial palaces. He gave orders to beat the reveillé and the tattoo, to open and shut the palace gates. When the Emperor was with the army, or travelling, he had to find him quarters. In 1805 the Grand Marshal's budget amounted to 2,338,167 francs. In 1806 it reached the sum of 2,770,841 francs. There were four tables in the palace, — that of the officers and ladies-in-waiting, that of the officers of the guard and the pages, that of the ladies who read to the Empress and introduced visitors.

The Grand Marshal had under his orders the prefects of the palace: M. de Luçay, M. de Bausset, and M. de Saint Didier. They had charge of the provisions, lighting, heating, the silver, and the liveries. They inspected the kitchens, pantries, cellars, and linen-closet to see that everything was in order. There was always one prefect of the palace on duty for a week at a time. He also carried word to the Emperor and the Empress when a meal was ready, conducted them to the table, and back to their rooms afterwards.

The Grand Marshal had also under his orders the governor of the palaces and the marshals; these last were charged with choosing apartments for the Emperor and the Empress, and quarters for their suite in the Imperial residences and on journeys.

They had for assistants the quartermasters of the palace.

The Master of the Hounds had charge of all the coursing and hunting in the woods and forests belonging to the Crown.

The Grand Equerry looked after the stables, the pages, the couriers, and the Emperor's arms; he also had the supervision of the horses at Saint Cloud. He walked just before the Emperor when he came forth from his rooms to ride, gave him his whip, held his reins and the left stirrup. He was responsible for the good condition of the carriages, the intelligence and skill of the huntsmen, coachman, and the postilions, the safety and the training of the horses. In a procession, or on a journey, he was in the carriage just before the Emperor's. He accompanied the Emperor to the army, and if the sovereign's horse was killed or disabled, it was his duty to pick the Emperor up and to offer him his own horse.

The Grand Equerry had four equerries under his orders: Colonels Durosnel, Defrance, Lefebvre, Vatier, and two equerries in ordinary, M. de Canisy and M. de Villoutrey. An equerry on duty always accompanied the Emperor, whether he was driving or riding. If the Emperor drove, the equerry on duty rode by the right-hand door of the carriage, unless the colonel-general on duty happened to be on horseback, in which case the equerry rode on the other side. The equerry on duty walked before the Emperor when he left or returned to his apartment; he never left the waiting-room during the day, and slept in the palace.

The pages, whose governor was General Gardane, were also under the orders of the Grand Equerry. They were appointed when between fourteen and sixteen, and held the position until they were eighteen. At grand dinners and in the apartments of honor, they waited on the Emperor and Empress, and on the Princes and Princesses. When the Emperor rode out, one followed on horseback ; if he drove, the page got up behind the carriage. When the sovereign went forth in his state-coach, as many pages as possible clambered up behind it and upon the box by the side of the coachman. At receptions, and on days when mass was said, there were eight pages on duty. They stood in a row when the Emperor returned to his apartment, and walked before him when he left it. If the Emperor had not returned to the palace by nightfall, the pages would wait at the entrance-door to walk before him, carrying lights. The pages, too, served as messengers, and when they carried letters of the Emperor, the doors were thrown wide open before them.

The impression produced by the pages, when they were first on duty at the Tuileries in 1804, is thus described by a contemporary: " They have been much noticed, especially in the evening, by the ladies. The fact is, they are all good-looking boys, particularly the oldest ; they have good figures and wear a new and becoming uniform, and since they

are in the service of a severe master, and of a most
kind and indulgent mistress, they have to be very
attentive and considerate. Their full dress differs
from livery only by the lace of their coat which imi-
tates embroidery, by the knot on their left shoulder,
and by the lace frill above their waistcoat. Besides,
in full dress they wear, like footmen, a green coat
with all the seams laced with gold, gold shoe-buckles,
a hat with a white feather, but they have no sword.
Perhaps this is well, for they would be playing with
it. They have all been chosen among the sons of
generals of divisions and of high dignitaries of the
Empire."

At Saint Helena Napoleon said, speaking of the
pages and the Imperial stables: "The Emperor's
stables cost him three million francs; the horses cost
three thousand francs apiece per year. A page, from
six to eight thousand francs; this last was perhaps
the heaviest expense of the palace; but there was
every reason to be satisfied with the education they
received, and with the care taken with them. All
the first families of the Empire sought to get the
places for their sons; and they were right."

The Grand Chamberlain had charge of all the
honors of the palace, the regular audiences, the
oaths taken in the Emperor's study, the admissions,
the levees and couchees, the festivities, receptions,
theatrical performances, the music, the boxes of the
Emperor and Empress at the different theatres, the
Emperor's wardrobe, his library; he also looked after
the ushers and valets de chambre.

The Grand Chamberlain had under his orders (this refers to 1805), a First Chamberlain, M. de Rémusat, and thirteen chamberlains: MM. d'Arberg, A. de Talleyrand, de Laturbie, de Brigode, de Viry, de Thiard, Garnier de Lariboisière, d'Hédouville, de Croy, de Mercy-Argenteau, de Zuidwyck, de Tournon, de Bondy. In the Imperial Almanack of 1805, these men are not named with their titles, even the *de* is in all cases omitted or joined with the name, thus: M. Rémusat, M. Darberg, A. Talleyrand, Laturbie, Tournon, Dethiard, Deviry, Hédouville, etc., etc.

The chamberlain on duty was called the chamberlain of the day. At the palace there were always two chamberlains of the day, one for the grand apartment, the other for the Emperor's apartment of honor. They were relieved every week. The principal duties of the chamberlains were to have charge of introductions to the Emperor, to give orders to the ushers and valets de chambre, to see that the orders about the receptions were carried out, and to attend upon the sovereign's levees and couchees.

Either a chamberlain or one of the Emperor's aides-de-camp served as Master of the Wardrobe. He had charge of the clothes, the linen, the lace, the boots and shoes, and of the ribbons of the Legion of Honor. If he assisted at the Emperor's toilet, he had to hand him his coat, fasten his ribbon or collar, give him his sword, hat, and gloves, in the Grand Chamberlain's absence.

The Grand Master of Ceremonies determined questions of rank and precedence, drew up and enforced the rules for public, formal ceremonies, for the reception of sovereigns and hereditary princes, and foreign ambassadors and ministers.

The colonels-general of the Imperial Guard and the Emperor's aides also made part of the household.

At ceremonies when the Emperor was in his state-coach, there were two colonels-general of the Guard at the left door. When he rode, all four followed close behind. The Grand Equerry, or his substitute, had a place among them.

The colonel-general on duty received directly the Emperor's orders relative to the different requirements of the Imperial Guard, and transmitted them directly to the other colonels-general. He was quartered in the palace, in preference to any other officer of the Crown, and as near as possible to the Emperor's apartment, whether at the residence or when travelling. In the field he slept in the Emperor's tent.

Napoleon had twelve aides-de-camp. The one on duty was called the aide-de-camp of the day. He always had a horse saddled or a carriage harnessed ready in the stable, to carry any messages the Emperor might give. As soon as the Emperor had gone to bed, the aide-de-camp on duty was especially entrusted with guarding him, and he slept in an adjoining room. In the field the Emperor's aides served as chamberlains.

There were two distinct elements in the Emperor's

household: the military, and the aristocratic. Some men owed their position entirely to their merit; others entirely to their birth; these were both patriots of 1792 and émigrés, but it must be confessed the Imperial Almanack shows that the aristocratic element was the more prominent. Napoleon, though certain writers persist in representing him as the crowned champion of democracy and the emperor of the lower classes, had a more aristocratic court than Louis XVIII. He was more impressed by great manners than were the old kings. Even after he had been betrayed, abandoned, denied, insulted by the aristocracy, he had a weakness for it. In 1816 he said: "The democracy may become furious; it has a heart; it can be moved. The aristocracy always remains cold and never pardons." Yet even after this, he blamed himself for not having done enough for the French nobility. "I see clearly," he went on, "that I did either too much or too little for the Faubourg Saint Germain. I did enough to make the opposition dissatisfied, and not enough to win it to my side. I ought to have secured the émigrés when they returned. The aristocracy would have soon adored me; and I needed it; it is the true, the only support of a monarchy, its moderator, its lever, its resisting point; without it, the state is like a ship without a rudder, a balloon in mid-air. Now, the strength, the charm of the aristocracy lies in its antiquity, the only thing I could not create." It must be confessed that from an old Republican general, for the man who had sent Augereau to execute the coup d'état of the 18th Fructidor, and who the 13th Vendémiaire, from the steps of the Church of Saint Roch had crushed the Paris conservatives, this was a very aristocratic way of talking, reminding one of the old régime. In 1816 Napoleon said again: "Old and corrupt nations cannot be governed like the virtuous peoples of antiquity. For one man nowadays who would sacrifice everything for the public welfare, there are thousands who take no thought of anything except their own interests, pleasures, and vanity. Now to pretend to regenerate a people off-hand would be madness. The workman's genius is shown by his knowing how to make use of the materials under his hand, and that is the secret of the restoration of all the forms of the monarchy, of the return of titles, crosses, and ribbons."

The old Republicans of 1796, who used to denounce kings, "drunk with blood and pride," would not have readily recognized their old general under the golden canopies of the Tuileries, where he dined in state. His table stood on a platform, beneath a canopy, and there were two chairs, one for himself, the other for the Empress. As he entered the banquet-hall, he was preceded by a swarm of . pages, masters-of-ceremonies, and prefects of the palace ; he was followed by the colonel-general on duty, the Grand Chamberlain, the Grand Equerry, and the Grand Almoner. The Grand Almoner advanced to the table and blessed the dinner. A general of division, the

Grand Equerry Caulaincourt, offered a chair to Bonaparte. Another general of division, Duroc, the Grand Marshal of the Palace, handed him his napkin and poured out his wine. Not merely high dignitaries, but the Princes of the Empire themselves, deemed it an honor to wait upon him as servants. If a Prince of the Imperial family happened to be in the Emperor's room, any article of dress that he asked for was given by the chamberlain-in-waiting to the Prince, and by the Prince to the Emperor. The time of the Sun King seemed to have returned.

The Imperial apartment at the Tuileries consisted of two distinct parts, the grand state apartments and the Emperor's private apartment. The state apartment contained the following rooms: 1, a concert hall (the Hall of the Marshals); 2, a first drawing-room (under Napoleon III. called the Drawing-room of the First Consul); 3, a second drawing-room (that of Apollo); 4, a throne room; 5, a drawing-room of the Emperor (afterwards called that of Louis XIV.); 6, a gallery (of Diana). The private apartment was itself composed of the apartment of honor, containing a hall of the guards and a first and second drawing-room, and an interior apartment containing a bedroom, a study, an office, and topographic bureau. The ushers had charge of the apartment of honor; the valets de chambre of the other. A rigid etiquette determined the right of entrance into the different rooms composing the state apartment, according to a carefully studied system. The pages were authorized to enter the Hall of the Marshals; members of the household of the Emperor and Empress could enter the first and second drawing-rooms; the Princes and Princesses of the Imperial family, the high officers of the Crown, the presidents of the great bodies of the state, had admission to the throne room. Men and women had to bow to the throne whenever they passed it. The Emperor and the Empress alone had the right of entering the Emperor's drawing-room. No one else could go in except by the Emperor's summons.

An absurd importance was attached to these trivialities, to these empty nothings, to the right of entering this room or that, of walking before this or that person, of handing the Emperor this or that article of dress. "An honest, reasonable man," said Madame de Rémusat, "is often overcome with shame at the pleasures and pains of a courtier's life, and yet it is hard to escape from them. A ribbon, a slight difference of dress, the right of way through a door, the entrance into such and such a drawing-room, are the occasion, contemptible in appearance, of a host of ever new emotions. Vain is the struggle to acquire indifference to them. . . . In vain do the mind and the reason revolt against such an employment of human faculties; however dissatisfied one is with one's self, it is necessary to humiliate one's self before every one and to desert the court, or else to consent to take seriously all the nonsense that fills the air and breathes there."

Vanity of human events! What has become of

these drawing-rooms of the Tuileries, which it was such an honor to enter, which were trod with such respectful awe? Look at the lamentable ruins of this ill-fated palace. There may still be seen, blackened with petroleum and stained by the rain, some of those drawing-rooms, once so brilliant, once thronged with an eager and showy crowd. What an instructive spectacle! When is one more urgently reminded of the emptiness of human glory and greatness? This nothingness fills the soul with melancholy when one thinks that soon these crumbling fragments will be razed and that soon one can say with the poet: The ruins themselves have perished, *Etiam periere ruinae!*[1]

---

[1] The ruins have since been removed. — TR.

IX.

W E have just studied the civil and the military household of the Emperor in 1805; let us now study the Empress's household at the same period.

The Empress's First Almoner was a bishop, a great lord, Ferdinand de Rohan. Her Maid of Honor was a relative of her first husband, the Duchess de La Rochefoucauld, called in the Imperial Almanack of 1805 simply Madame Chastulé de La Rochefoucauld. She was short and deformed, but distinguished for her intelligence, tact, and wit, void of ambition, with no taste for intrigue, who only reluctantly accepted the position of Maid of Honor, and often wanted to hand in her resignation. The Lady of the Bedchamber was Madame de Lavalette, a Beauharnais, an able and affectionate woman, who immortalized herself, in the early days of the Restoration, by saving her husband's life by her heroism.

To the four Ladies of the Palace at the beginning of the Empire, Madame de Luçay, Madame de Rémusat, Madame de Talhouët, Madame de Lauris-

ton, were added thirteen other ladies: Madame
Duchâtel, Madame de Séran, Madame de Colbert,
Madame Savary, Madame Octave de Ségur, Madame
de Turenne, Madame de Montalivet, Madame de
Bouillé, Madame de Vaux, Madame de Marescot.

The Maid of Honor was for the Empress what the
Grand Chamberlain was for the Emperor. The Lady
of the Bedchamber's duties corresponded to those of
the Keeper of the Wardrobe. The Ladies of the
Palace were, so to speak, female chamberlains.

"We were all," said the Duchess of Abrantès, "at
that time radiant with a sort of glory which women
seek as eagerly as men do theirs, that of elegance
and beauty. Among the young women composing
the court of the Empress and that of the Princesses
it would have been hard to find a single ill-favored
woman, and there were very many whose beauty
made, with no exaggeration, the greatest ornament
of the festivities held every day in that fairy-like
time."

All the Ladies of the Palace were young, and
almost all were remarkable for their beauty. Among
the most conspicuous was Madame Ney, a niece of
Madame Campan; Madame Lannes, whose face recalled the most charming pictures of Raphael, and
above all, the wife of an already aged Councillor of
State, Madame Duchâtel (whose son was Minister of
the Interior in the reign of Louis Philippe, and
whose grandson was Ambassador of the Republic at
Vienna). The Duchess of Abrantès thus describes

this famous beauty: " There is one woman in the Imperial court who made her appearance in society shortly before the coronation, whose portrait is drawn in all the contemporary memoirs, especially in those written by a woman, and that is Madame Duchâtel. Madame Duchâtel would not serve as a model for a sculptor, because her features lack the regularity which his art requires. The indefinable charm of her face, a charm which words are unable to convey, lay in dark blue eyes, with long, silken lashes, in a delicate, gracious, refined smile, which disclosed teeth of ivory whiteness, and, moreover, beautiful light hair, small hands and feet, a general elegance which matched a really remarkable mind. All these things formed a combination which first attracted and then attached every one to her."

Josephine's First Chamberlain, in 1805, was the General of Division Nansouty ; the chamberlain who introduced the ambassadors was M. de Beaumont; there were four ordinary chamberlains, MM. d'Aubusson-Lafeuillade, de Galard-Béarn, de Coutomer; de Gavre ; a First Equerry, Senator de Harville ; two equerries, Colonel Fowler and General Bonardy de Saint Sulpice ; a private secretary, M. Deschamps. The Council of the Empress's household was composed of the Maid of Honor, the Lady of the Bedchamber, the First Chamberlain, and the First Equerry. The private secretary was also the secretary of the Council. The Chief Steward of the household was also a member.

The Lady of the Bedchamber had under her orders a first woman of the bedchamber, Madame Aubert, who had whole charge of the wardrobe. Madame Saint-Hilaire held this place under Josephine, as Madame Campan had done under Marie Antoinette. Madame Saint-Hilaire's duties consisted in supervising the chamberwork, in receiving the Empress's orders about the hours of her rising, and of her morning and evening toilet. The first woman of the Bedchamber had what were called the honors of the service when the Maid of Honor and the Lady of the Bedchamber were absent. The Empress had also ushers and women who discharged the same duties, six ordinary chambermaids, a reader, the beautiful Madame Gazani; four ordinary valets de chambre, and two footmen, trusted men always in the antechamber. The ushers, who remained without the drawing-room where the Empress was, never opened both the doors to their full width except for the Princes and Princesses of the Imperial family; and they could not leave their posts except to ask the Maid of Honor the names of those who were waiting to be presented. There were two pages in the Empress's service; the older carried the train of her dress when she left her apartments, and got in or out of a carriage; the other walked before her.

The Empress's apartment consisted of an apartment of honor and an inner apartment. The first consisted of an ante-chamber, the first drawing-room, the second drawing-room, the dining-room, the music-room; the other, of the bedroom, the library, dressing-room, boudoir, bath-room. The entrance to the Empress's apartment was controlled by etiquette like that to the Emperor's.

Josephine played her part as sovereign as easily as if she had been born on the steps of the throne. "One of her charms," says the Duchess of Abrantès, "was not merely her graceful figure, but the way she held her head, and the gracious dignity with which she walked and turned. I have had the honor of being presented to many real princesses, as they are called in the Faubourg Saint Germain, and I can truly say that I have never seen one more imposing than Josephine. She combined elegance and majesty. Never did any queen so grace a throne without having been trained to it."

Josephine had all the qualities that are attractive in a sovereign : affability, gentleness, kindliness, generosity. She had a way of convincing every one of her personal interest. She had an excellent memory, and surprised those with whom she talked by the exactness with which she recalled the past, even to details they had themselves nearly forgotten. The sound of her gentle, penetrating, and sympathetic voice added to the courtesy and charm of her words. Every one listened to her with pleasure; she spoke with grace and listened courteously. She wanted no one to go away from her annoyed. She always appeared to be doing a kindness, and thus inspired affection and gratitude. Her courtiers and her suite

were her friends. Madame de Rémusat, who was
never too favorable, was forced to recognize the charm
which Josephine exercised over the court by her tact,
intelligence, and dignity. " The Empress," she says,
" is enchanted to be surrounded by a large suite, and
it gratifies her vanity. Her success in attaching
Madame de La Rochefoucauld to her person, her
pleasure in counting MM. d'Aubusson, de Lafeuillade
among her chamberlains, Madame d'Arbry, Madame
de Ségur, and the wives of the marshals among the
ladies of the palace, turned her head a little, but even
this feminine joy did not lessen her usual gracious-
ness; she always succeeded in maintaining her rank,
even when most deferential to those men and women
who lent it a new lustre by their brilliant names."
She was very kind, extremely soft-hearted, and always
overwhelming her companions with attentions and regards. Mademoiselle Avrillon, her reader, says : " I
do not believe that there ever lived a woman with a
better character, or with a less changeable disposition."
She never dared to utter a word of blame or reproach.
" If one of her ladies," said Constant, the Emperor's
valet de chambre, " ever gave her cause for dissatisfaction, the only punishment she inflicted was to
maintain absolute silence for one, two, three days,
a week, more or less, according to the seriousness
of the case. Well! this punishment, apparently so
slight, was for most of them very severe. The Empress knew so well how to make herself beloved !"

Her only fault was extravagance. She had an unbounded love of luxury and dress. The jewel-case which had belonged to Marie Antoinette was too small for Josephine. One day when she wanted to show some ladies all her jewels, a great table had to be arranged to hold the cases, and, since that was not enough, much more of the furniture was covered by them. Josephine had the fault that accompanies this quality, for generous persons are commonly lavish. Her extravagant expenditures came from her kindliness. She had not the heart to dismiss a tradesman without buying something of him, and it never entered her head to try to beat him down. Often she bought for vast sums things she did not want, simply to oblige the dealers. There was no limit to her liberality. She would have liked to own all the treasures of the earth in order to give them all away. She sought for opportunities for alms-giving. Many of the émigrés lived entirely on her bounty. She was always in active correspondence with the sisters of charity. She was the Providence of the poor, and did good with delicacy, tact, and discretion. Giving is not all; the art lies in knowing how to give. She seemed to be the debtor of those to whom she made gifts. Naturally, with this disposition, she got into debt. But Napoleon was there to help her; and since he was economical by nature, he grew angry and scolded his extravagant wife, and ended by paying.

In fact, Napoleon could refuse Josephine nothing, and she was really the only woman who had any influence over him. If he opposed her, she had an

infallible resource in her tears. She knew thoroughly
her husband's character. She knew how to speak to
that mind and heart. She busied herself with seeking what could please, with divining his wishes, with
anticipating his slightest desires. If he was the least
ailing or annoyed she was literally at his feet, and
then he could not live without her. He felt that
when misfortune came Josephine alone would be able
to console him. She had brought him happiness with
her gentleness, her tenderness, her devotion; she had
well deserved to receive the crown from his hands.

X.

NAPOLEON'S GALLANTRIES.

JOSEPHINE appeared to have every wish satisfied; her good fortune exceeded her wildest dreams; never had a more wonderful romance actually happened, and yet the Empress of the French, the Queen of Italy, was not happy. A cruel passion which brings no pleasures, but only cruel sufferings, disturbed her happiness and tormented her heart. This passion, jealousy, which had tortured Napoleon in the early days of his wedded life, now Josephine in her turn had to endure with all its keen anguish. She felt that for her, a woman of forty-one, to hold fast the affections of a man of thirty-five, covered with glory and full of charm, was a difficult task; but this reflection, far from consoling her, only disturbed her the more, and she made desperate efforts to triumph in an almost hopeless contest. As was said by Mademoiselle Avrillon, her reader, she seemed not to understand that if the highest rank is a safeguard for a woman, because few men are bold enough to pursue her, the same is not true of a sovereign whose glory dazzles the inexperience of the young, and whose slightest attention arouses coquetry and flatters vanity.

110

Josephine had not a moment's peace. In the hope of pleasing her, many women of the court, who were, so to speak, on the watch for the Emperor's attentions, hastened to torture her with their interested revelations. For several years now her beauty had been fading. Napoleon, on the other hand, had never been better looking. His health, which formerly had been delicate, had much improved. He had grown stouter, and this was very becoming. His head was like that of a Cæsar. Full of self-confidence, fortunate, flattered on every side, at the height of power, he imagined that in love, as in war, he had but to appear to say, *veni, vidi, vici,* "I came, I saw, I conquered." Many of the beauties of the time did their best to confirm him in this good opinion of himself, and as Madame de Rémusat says of him, he in his court was not unlike the Grand Turk in his harem.

"The Emperor," we read in Constant's Memoirs, "used to say that a good man was to be known by the way he treated his wife, his children, and his servants. He added that immorality was the most dangerous vice a sovereign could have, because it established a precedent for his subjects. What he meant by immorality, was giving scandalous publicity to relations which should have been kept secret; these relations he was by no means disposed to refuse when they presented themselves before him." The faithful valet de chambre goes on in an attempt to defend his master: "Others perhaps would have succumbed oftener. Heaven forbid that I should undertake to apologize for him; I will even acknowledge that he did not always practise what he preached, but it was none the less a good deal for a sovereign to hide his distractions from the public, to prevent scandal, and, what is worse imitation; and from his wife, to save her pain."

Napoleon was by no means so indifferent to women as he professed to be. He was averse to being ruled by them, but he was far from being insensible to their charms. Opposition exasperated him; all his caprices found many obsequious allies ready to further his suit, and more than one woman made a deep, if brief, impression upon him. His disdain of woman has, we are sure, been much exaggerated. At Saint Helena he declaimed against women, but his remarks were mere paradoxes, not meant to be taken seriously.

Count Las Cases, in the *Memorial*, reports these remarks of the Emperor to the ladies who shared his captivity. "We Occidentals," he said, with a smile full of malice, "have spoiled women by treating them too well. We have made the mistake of raising them almost to an equality with ourselves. The Orientals showed more intelligence and justice: they declared they were men's property; and, in fact, nature has made them our slaves, and it is only by our whimsicalness that they presume to be our sovereigns; they abuse their advantages to mislead and control us. For one who inspires us to our good there are a hundred who make us do stupid things." Then he went on to praise polygamy in a very unchivalrous and unsentimental way, saying ironically: " What cause of complaint do you have, after all? Have we not acknowledged that you have a soul? You know that there are philosophers who have weighed it. Do you claim equality? But that is absurd; women are our property, we are not theirs; for she gives us children, men give them none. So she is his property, as a fruit-tree is a gardener's property. Nothing but a lack of judgment, of common sense, and a defective education, can make a woman think that she is her husband's equal. And there is nothing degrading in the difference; each sex has its qualities and its duties: your qualities are beauty, grace, charm; your duties are dependence and submission."

Napoleon was often malicious with women; often he teased them; but at heart he honored faithful wives and good mothers. His ideas were far more moral than those of the men of the Directory, and his court was far purer than that of the kings of France. We will add that Josephine was the only woman he ever loved for a long time and seriously. The others appealed to his senses, not to his heart.

Fortunately for herself, Josephine had a shallow character; her impressions were keen, but evanescent. The pleasures of sovereignty outweighed the griefs. She felt that the crown was heavy at times, but it adorned her and kept her young; and in spite of the jealousy it gave rise to, the court satisfied her vanity and brought her sufficient consolation. To the satisfaction of her pride she found another purer and more lasting emotion, which she valued more, in the opportunity of doing good.   She had, besides, passed through so many vicissitudes in her life that nothing could surprise her, and her soul, accustomed to suffering, was prepared for the most violent emotions, the most terrible anguish.   She wept readily, but her tears were soon dried; the rainbow followed close upon the storm, and Josephine would smile through her tears.

XI.

WHILE Napoleon, proud in the possession of his new empire, was exhibiting at the Tuileries his vast power and grandeur, the same palace was inhabited by a holy old man, whose humility presented a marked contrast with the conqueror's haughty spirit. Pius VII., who was quartered in the Pavilion of Flora, led the life of an anchorite, with all the modesty and piety of an old monk, fasting every day as in his convent, and edifying even the impious by the nimbus that shone around his pale and mystic face. It was impossible to approach this worthy Vicar of Christ without a filial feeling of tenderness. The crimes of the French Revolution — the massacre or the execution of the priests, the profanation of the altars, the persecutions and blasphemies — had imprinted the stamp of melancholy on his face. It was easy to see that he lamented the barbarities of the times, and that his life had been full of anguish. He embodied all the sufferings of the Church. With his ascetic air, his deep-set eye, his complexion as pallid as ivory, his white robes tinged with red, the Sovereign Pontiff

115

had in his whole person something strange and imposing.   He occupied the apartment on the first floor
of the Pavilion of Flora, where Madame Elisabeth
had lived from October, 1789, to August 10, 1792.
The Abbé Proyart, the author of the letter to the
prisoner of the Temple, came to offer the Pope a
copy of this same life of Madame Louise of France,
which he had long since offered to the sister of
Louis XVI.

"I am living here," said Pius VII., "in the apartments of another saint." What singular vicissitudes!
The same place occupied in turn by Madame Elisabeth, the members of the Committee of Public
Safety, and by the Vicar of Christ!

The Pope had been very anxious before he started
for Paris.   His fears were so great that just as he
was leaving Rome, with a presentiment of the captivity that awaited him, he had left his abdication
in the hands of Cardinal Consalvi, in case he should
suffer any violence during his journey.   It was only
with trembling and prayer that he had set foot on
the volcanic soil of France, which, from a distance,
seemed alive with impiety and terror.   The unfail-
ing respect with which he had been treated had
comforted him somewhat.   Whenever he visited a
church, the Parisians followed him with mingled
curiosity, sympathy, and veneration: they knelt to
him as he passed them, and received with all deco-
rum his apostolic benediction.   Every day a large
crowd gathered under his windows.   He had found

his rooms arranged and furnished like those he occupied at the Vatican, and he had been very grateful
for this, which he called a really filial attention.

General de Ségur, at that time captain and aide of
the Grand Marshal of the Palace, was entrusted with
guarding the Pope's person. He says in his Memoirs:
" The same attention and respect was shown to the
Pope as to the Emperor himself. His rooms had been
so arranged and furnished as to recall Rome so far
as possible, and to suit his tastes. As for Napoleon,
we all noticed his ever gentle and grateful gaiety,
and his filial and affectionate deference to his guest.
When the Holy Father gave his blessing from his
window, and more especially at his audiences in the
gallery of the Louvre, which were always crowded,
precautions were taken against any outbreak of the
indiscretion or levity to which the French are prone.
We saw the atheist Lalande himself fall at the Pontiff's feet and kiss his slipper. In the public buildings which the Pope honored with his presence he
was received as a sovereign. No one dared to betray
more curiosity than piety ; and it often happened to
me to see this real saint, the successor of the Apos-
tles, whose venerable face bore the stamp of the
serenest gentleness, so frugal, simple, and austere for
himself alone, and so kindly indulgent to others,
deeply moved by the intense and holy impression he
made."

Every day the long gallery of the Louvre was
filled with two rows of men and women who had

come to ask his blessing.   Preceded by the governor
of the Louvre, and followed by the Italian cardinals
and nobles of his household, Pius VII. advanced
slowly between the two lines of the faithful, often
stopping to place his hand on some child's head, to
say some kind words to its mother, and to offer his
ring to be kissed.   One day, when he was surrounded
by a crowd of prostrate and respectful people, he saw
a man whose worn face bore traces of irreligious
passion, who was moving away as if to escape the
apostolic benediction.   The Holy Father approached
him, and said gently, " Do not run away ; an old
man's blessing has never done any one any harm."
This remark spread through Paris and made a most
favorable impression.   Pius VII. was not only respected, but, if we may use the worldly phrase, he
became the fashion.   Dealers in rosaries and chaplets
made much money all that winter.   In January alone
a shopkeeper in the rue Saint Denis who sold those
articles is said to have cleared forty thousand francs.
All who approached the Pope had chaplets blessed
for themselves, their relatives, and friends in Paris
and the provinces.   " The prolonged stay of the Holy
Father," says Bourrienne, " was not without influence in the return to religious ideas, so great was
the respect inspired by the Pope's gentle appearance
and kindly manners.   When the time came for him
to be persecuted, it would have been desirable that
Pius VII. had never come to Paris, for it was impossible to look upon him otherwise than as a man whose
holy gentleness was a matter of notoriety."

At Saint Helena, Napoleon spoke thus of this venerable Pope: "He was really a lamb, a thoroughly good and upright man, whom I greatly esteem and love, and who, I am sure, does not wholly hate me."

It has been asserted that the Pope made such an impression in Paris that the Emperor felt for the august old man a sort of secret jealousy. But even granting, what is by no means certain, that he suffered from this, he had at least skill to conceal it. Always the Pope was overwhelmed with flattering attentions. The President of the Legislative Body, M. de Fontanes, said to him November 30, 1804: "Everything else has changed; religion alone knows no change. It sees the families of kings, and those of subjects, perish; but resting on the ruins of thrones, it ever admires the successive manifestations of the eternal designs and obeys them with confidence. Never has the universe beheld a more imposing sight, never have its people received more important lessons. This is no longer the time of rivalry between the priesthood and the Empire. They have joined hands to repel the fatal doctrines which threatened Europe with total overthrow. May they yield forever to the double influence of politics and religion combined! Doubtless this wish will not be disappointed; never in France has there been so great a genius to control its policy, and never has the pontifical throne presented to the Christian world a more worthy and more touching model." The *Moniteur*, in its report of the coronation, spoke with the same official enthu-

siasm "of the most venerable apostolic virtues and of
the most astounding political genius crowned by the
highest destinies." David, the artist, once a member
of the Convention and a regicide, then an Imperialist, painted the portrait of Pius VII., and the *Moniteur*, in its number of March 30, 1805, thus praised
the picture and the sitter: "A large crowd gathered
in the gallery of the Senate, to see the portrait of His
Holiness by M. David, member of the Institute and
first painter to the Emperor. This portrait is in every
way worthy of the master's reputation. If the first
essential in a portrait is an exact likeness, this one
possesses it to a very high degree. The head, which
is admirably painted, expresses the indulgent and
wise character, the gentleness and reasonableness,
that are so conspicuous in the model; the eyes an
expression, affectionate and paternal; the expression
of the mouth is most striking; one feels that it can
utter only words of peace, consolation, and truth."

Josephine had for Pius VII. a feeling of veneration
full of gratitude. She was most grateful to him for
having persuaded Napoleon to have the religious
marriage for which she had long yearned. She, who
had preserved her faith in the midst of an irreligious
society, was happy to inhabit the same palace, to live
under the same roof, with the Vicar of Christ, and
firmly hoped thereby to secure good fortune for herself and her husband. For his part, Pius VII. appreciated Josephine's good qualities, especially her charity: he treated her as an indulgent father treats his
child.

The second son of Louis Bonaparte and Hortense
de Beauharnais was baptized by the Pope himself at
Saint Cloud, March 27, 1805. The ceremony was
most impressive. Eight Imperial carriages conveyed
thither Pius VII. and his suite. The gallery of the
palace had been turned into a chapel. In one of the
Empress's drawing-rooms had been placed, on a platform, beneath a canopy, a bed without posts. On the
foot of the bed had been spread a large cloak lined
with ermine, to cover the child. In the same room
were two tables on which were placed what were
called the child's *honors;* that is to say, the candle,
the chrisom-cap, and the salt-cellar, and the *honors* of
the godfather and godmother, — the basin, the ewer,
and the napkin. The towel was placed on a square of
golden brocade, and all the other things, except the
candle, on a gold tray. Preceded by the Grand Master of Ceremonies, and followed by a colonel-general of
the Guard, by the Grand Almoner, the Grand Chamberlain, and the Master of the Hounds, the Emperor,
who was godfather, and the godmother, Madame
Bonaparte, his mother, went to the room where the
ceremony was to be performed. The child was un-
covered by Madame de Villeneuve, Maid of Honor
to Princess Louis Bonaparte, and by Madame de
Boubers, who was serving as governess. The first
one lifted up the baby and handed him to the godfather, who gave him to Madame de Boubers to carry
to the font. The Grand Master of Ceremonies
handed the salt-cellar to Madame de Bouillé, the

chrisom-cap to Madame de Montalivet, the candle to Madame Lannes, the towel to Madame de Sérant, the ewer to Madame Savary, the basin to Madame de Talhouët. Then they went to the gallery, which had been turned into a chapel. Mesdames Bernadotte, Bessières, Davout, and Mortier held the corners of the Empress's cloak. The godmother was at the Emperor's left. After the baptism the child was carried back to his room with the same procession.

That evening *Athalie* was given, with choruses, at the court theatre. The company on their way thither passed through the orange house, which was aglow with colored lanterns.

All day the park of Saint Cloud had been open to the public; the fountains had been playing; shows of all sorts amused the crowd; the road to Paris was crowded with carriages and foot-passengers. In the evening there were fireworks; the palace and gardens were illuminated; there were bands playing, and rustic balls.

The Pope, who had reached Paris November 28, 1804, left April 4, 1805, just when the Emperor was starting for Italy, there to be crowned at Milan. Pius VII. had received some magnificent presents from the Emperor: a gold altar with chandeliers, and the sacred vessels of rich workmanship, a superb tiara, some gobelin tapestries, carpets from the Savonnerie, and a statue of Napoleon in Sèvres ware. The Empress had given him a valuable vase decorated by the best artists. The *Moniteur* thus announced the

Pope's departure: "To-day, April 4, at half-past twelve, His Holiness left Paris with the prelates and others of his suite. A crowd of both sexes and all ages assembled on the way he was to pass through, and received the Sovereign Pontiff's blessing; once more he was the object of expressions of the deepest veneration, and plainly manifested the emotions which these expressions called forth."

Yet Pius VII. was not wholly satisfied with his journey. He had received much homage, but he had not secured any real political concessions of any importance. He had been unable to settle the important matter of the organic statutes, and nothing had been done about the restoration of the legation on which he was so warmly set. Besides, he was much annoyed that he had not himself crowned Napoleon, as the Popes, his predecessors, had crowned emperors and kings. He, who later was to be a prisoner at Fontainebleau, went away distressed about the present, anxious for the future, and wondering whether his host might not say, with Voltaire, "It is all very well to kiss the Popes' feet, but it is better to have their hands tied first."

XII.

THE JOURNEY IN ITALY.

THE Pope had left Paris to return to Rome April 4, 1805. At almost the same time the Emperor and Empress had started from Fontainebleau to go to Milan, where Napoleon was to be crowned King of Italy. The code of etiquette that prevailed at the Tuileries was observed on journeys. The house in which the Emperor lodged at any stopping-place was the place where all who accompanied him were to meet. A great placard on which were written all the names, and where they were to be quartered, was pasted on the front door. In the villages where Napoleon spent but one night he received the local authorities, either before or after dinner. In the towns where he spent more than one day, after he had eaten his breakfast and held his receptions, he rode out to visit the fortifications and monuments. The evenings were generally taken up by the entertainments offered him.

The Emperor and Empress reached Troyes April 2. A letter dated the 3d was printed in the *Moniteur*. It said: "Everywhere the presence of the

124

Emperor has evoked the liveliest applause; the people seem astonished to see him wearing such a modest uniform, and conspicuous, in the midst of his court, by the plainness of his dress. The people of this department exhibit this joy all the more because it is here that was brought up the man who was destined to raise France to the highest glory and prosperity. It is at Brienne that the Emperor received his earliest instruction. His Majesty, being anxious to revisit the places that recall these agreeable memories, started at two o'clock to-day for Brienne."

On the steps of the castle in this town Napoleon found Madame de Brienne and Madame de Loménie, who had been the guardians of his childhood. He treated them with the greatest respect, and took pleasure in recalling happy and touching memories of the past. He recalled many anecdotes, and told them in his usual vivid, picturesque way. He accepted their invitation to dinner, played cards with them, and having found out their usual time of going to bed, asked to be shown at that hour to the room which had been prepared for him at his request. At dawn the next morning he went alone, without escort, to see some of his old walks in the neighborhood. He remembered a hut where he and his companions used to lunch, and recognizing the wood in which it was, he rode through the shady path that led to it.

It belonged to a woman who in old times used to serve nuts, cheese, and brownbread to the schoolboy of Brienne, the future Emperor. He was delighted to see her once more, and asked her for the same repast which had formerly been his delight. At first the poor woman did not recognize the stranger; but gradually he refreshed her memory by recalling many incidents of the past. Then she understood that she was in the presence of the all-powerful Emperor, and flung herself at his feet. Napoleon lifted her, and left her a purse of gold, promising as he left to provide for her old age.

The Emperor and Empress arrived at Lyons April 10. A quarter of a league from the city, on the Boucle road, stood a triumphal arch, on the top of which, as in the reign of Augustus, was perched an eagle supporting the conqueror's bust. On the two side doors were two bas-reliefs, one representing the union of the Empire and Liberty; the other, Wisdom, in the figure of Minerva distributing crosses of honor to soldiers, artists, and scholars. On these two bas-reliefs were statues of the Rhone and the Seine. At the top of the arch was a flattering inscription in verse.

April 12, the Empress held a reception. The *Bulletin of Lyons* thus described it: " The assembly was most brilliant. As our sovereign has exhibited in his audiences profundity, affability, exact and varied learning, and true greatness, so his august wife has shone with grace, courtesy, and gentleness. Thus we witness a revival of that old French urbanity and politeness of manners which have always dis-

tinguished our court, and have made it an example
and an object of admiration for all foreign courts."

The city offered Napoleon and Josephine an entertainment at the Grand Theatre. The back-scene
represented the Emperor, seated, clad in a long triumphal robe. Two allegoric figures, representing,
one, France, the other, Italy, with their feet resting
on clouds, held in their hands a roll bearing this
inscription : *Sublimi feriam sidera vertice*, "I shall
strike the stars with my lofty head "; with the other,
they each offered a crown to Napoleon. Thus did
flattery renew the apotheoses of the Cæsars of ancient
Rome.

There was sung a cantata entitled *Ossian's Dream*.
The young men of the National Guard of Lyons and
the leading ladies of the city waltzed before the
throne. Two young girls held each a basket into
which the dancers threw flowers as they passed by;
out of these flowers the girls wove two crowns which,
after the dance, they presented to the Emperor and
Empress.

April 29, Napoleon and Josephine were present at
a grand performance at the Grand Theatre in Turin.
They stayed at the castle of Stupinizi, just outside of
the city, where they bade farewell to Pius VII., who
had celebrated the Easter festival at Lyons, and was
on his way to Rome.

The Emperor and the Empress reached Alessandria
May 2, at ten in the morning, amid the roar of cannon and the ringing of church-bells. Napoleon spent

the day in revisiting the battle-field of Marengo, where he gave the Empress a mimic representation of the battle he had won five years before. From a throne he watched the manœuvres executed under the command of Murat, Lannes, and Bessières. He had had the coat and hat he wore on the day of the battle brought from Paris. The coat was somewhat moth-eaten, and the odd hat would have seemed very much out of date if it had not recalled such precious memories. But Napoleon liked to recall that eventful day when he had managed to grasp victory when apparently beaten. After the manœuvres he solemnly laid the corner-stone of a monument to the memory of Desaix and the other brave men who fell at Marengo.

At Alessandria, the next day, he had an interview with his brother Jerome, which in fact was a reconciliation. In 1803, after the breaking of the Peace of Amiens, Jerome Bonaparte, who then, a young man of twenty, was in the naval service, happened to be forced by an English cruiser to land in the United States. There he had fallen in love with the young and charming daughter of a rich merchant of Baltimore, Miss Elisabeth Paterson, and he married her. Napoleon was unwilling to recognize this marriage. No sooner had he ascended the throne than he at once exhibited all the feeling and prejudices of a monarch who belonged to a dynasty of the most venerable antiquity. He really believed that his brothers could marry only princesses, and that any other marriage was an unpardonable mésalliance.

If, possibly, Napoleon was able to condemn Lucien's wife for her past conduct, no such criticism could apply to the wife of Jerome, who was a young woman of conspicuous morality, intelligence, and amiability. But she was the daughter of a ship-owner, a merchant, and thus was not a proper match, he thought, for the brother of the powerful monarch who was already dreaming of restoring the vassal kingdoms and the whole vast imperial edifice of Charlemagne. He, the Emperor of the French, the King of Italy, did not like to remember that he had wedded a simple subject, and that he had been very proud of his marriage. He could not pardon his brother Jerome for making a love-match. He would not even listen to his defence of his young wife, soon to be a mother, and who deserved only respect and pity, and who, humiliated, abandoned, and broken-hearted, was about to be treated as a concubine, and driven away forever. Ambition had destroyed Napoleon's natural kindliness. Yet, if he had seen Jerome's wife, a devoted and interesting woman, warmly attached to her husband, and alive to her duties, probably he would have taken pity on her. Possibly he was himself aware of this, for he forbade the unhappy young woman to enter any part of the Empire, and compelled this innocent victim of political considerations to take refuge in England, as if she were a criminal.

February 22, 1805, Napoleon had compelled his mother, Madame Letitia, to place in the hands of a notary, Raguideau, a protest against Jerome's marriage, on the pretext that he, having been born November 15, 1784, was not yet twenty at the date of his marriage, and according to the law of September 20, 1792, a marriage contracted by any one under twenty without the consent of his father and mother was null and void. The *Moniteur* of the 13th Ventose, Year XIII. (March 4, 1805), had contained the following lines: "11th Ventose. By an act dated to-day, all the civil officers of the Empire are forbidden to receive on their registers a copy of the certificate of an alleged marriage contracted by M. Jerome Bonaparte in a foreign country, when under age, and without his mother's consent, and without previous publication in the place where he is domiciled." A few days later this appeared in the *Moniteur:* " M. Jerome Bonaparte has arrived at Lisbon in an American ship; in the passenger list were the names of Mr. and Miss Paterson. M. Jerome at once took port for Madrid. Mr. and Miss Paterson have re-embarked. They are supposed to be returning to America."

Jerome, in obedience to the Emperor's orders, started from Portugal for Italy, posting day and night at full speed, through Badajoz, Madrid, Perpignan, and Grenoble. He says in his Memoirs: "Amid the mountains of Estremadura, his modest carriage encountered the almost royal train of the French Ambassador to Portugal. It was Junot whom he had left a simple aide-de-camp of the First Consul, and saw again one of the first personages of the

Empire. Madame Junot, an old friend from childhood of Jerome, was with her husband. This interview was a most interesting one, partly from the deserted spot where they met, and partly from the great events that had occurred since their separation."

Junot and his wife found Jerome much improved. He had become more serious; a certain gravity had taken the place of his youthful bubbling high spirits. He spoke with emotion, respect, and affection of his young wife whose pathetic situation was made even more disturbing by the state of her health. He proposed to throw himself at his brother's feet, and by prayers and supplications to wring from him the consent he desired. " No one can doubt," he says in his Memoirs, " that his heart was torn by the keenest agitations, to say nothing of the anxiety about his wife; the mortification at two years of inactivity, during which his comrades, friends, and relatives had worked, fought, and become great; the regret for the lofty position he had lost; the hope of regaining it; his fear of his brother's wrath which he had ventured to arouse, and which made kings tremble on their thrones."

Napoleon was to be inflexible; he refused to admit that his brothers could be anything but members of the dynasty, future sovereigns. It was then that according to Miot de Mélito, he said: " What I have accomplished so far is nothing. There will be no peace in Europe until it is under a single head, an Emperor, who shall have his officers for kings and divide the kingdoms among his lieutenants; who shall make one King of Italy, another King of Bavaria, one Landemann of Switzerland, another Stadtholder of Holland, and all with high positions in the Imperial household, with titles as Grand Cupbearer, Grand Master of the Pantry, Grand Equerry, Grand Master of the Hounds, etc. It will be said that this plan is only an imitation of that on which the German Empire is established, and that these ideas are not new; but nothing is absolutely new; political institutions only revolve in a circle, and what has happened necessarily recurs." A man with such aspirations and so near to realizing them, could not endure the idea of being the brother-in-law of a simple shipowner.

Jerome arrived at Turin, April 24, 1805. Napoleon was then at Alessandria. Eleven days passed before the brothers met. The Emperor had announced his decision. He was absolutely determined not to meet Jerome until he had made perfect submission. The unhappy youth still ventured to hope against hope, but soon he had to recognize his mistake. Then his heart and soul were torn by a hot conflict: on one side were his love for his wife, family feeling, the thought of the child that was soon to be born, his respect for marriage and for his vows; on the other, ambition, love of power, the visions of the kingdoms that he might rule; on one side, the smiles and tears of the woman he loved; on the other, the influence and glory of the genius who filled the earth with his fame, and always exercised a powerful fascination. Jerome, who was less sentimental and less proud than Lucien, at last yielded to his terrible brother, and condemned himself out of ambition never to see again the woman whom he loved and cherished. May 6th he went to Alessandria, having first sent a letter of submission to the Emperor. Napoleon before receiving him, replied to it in these terms: —

"Alessandria, May 6, 1805. MY BROTHER: Your letter of this morning informs me of your arrival at Alessandria. There is no fault which cannot be effaced in my eyes by repentance. Your marriage with Miss Paterson is null in the eyes of both religion and law. Write to Miss Paterson to return to America. I will grant her a pension of sixty thousand francs for life, on condition that she shall never bear my name, a right which does not belong to her in the non-existence of the marriage. You must tell her that you could not and cannot change the nature of things. When your marriage is thus annulled by your own will, I will restore to you my friendship, and resume the feelings I have had for you since your infancy, hoping that you will show yourself worthy of them by the efforts you will make to win my gratitude and to acquire distinction in the army."

A few days later Napoleon wrote to the Minister of the Navy: "M. Décrès, M. Jerome has arrived. He has confessed his errors and disavows this person as his wife. He promises to do wonders. Meanwhile I have sent him to Genoa for some time."

After his reconciliation with Jerome, Napoleon went to Pavia, where the magistrates presented to him the homage of his new capital, and he entered that city, with the Empress, May 8, amid the roar of cannon and the ringing of bells.

XIII.

BY descent, by his physical, moral, and intellectual nature, by his imagination and genius, Napoleon was much more an Italian than a Frenchman. His father and mother were Italians, his ancestors were Italian, and Italian was his mother-tongue. His family and Christian names were Italian. His mother spoke French with the strongest Italian accent. He had loved Corsica before he loved France. As a child, he had felt the greatest enthusiasm for Paoli, the Corsican patriot, and had then looked upon the French as foreigners and oppressors. His face not only resembled that of an Italian, but that of an ancient Roman. By a singular coincidence, he had the head of a Cæsar. Italy was not only the home of his family, it was there that he laid the foundations of his glory. That unrivalled country, as one of our poets calls it, had brought him good fortune. There he wrote the famous bulletins of his first victories; there he began to impress the popular imagination; and it was through Italy that he subjugated France. There he felt at home. The people of

that peninsula greeted him as a fellow-countryman.
He liked to speak their language to them, charmed
by its harmony and sincerity.   His Southern genius
rejoiced in its bright skies which lent everything such
lustre, and well suited the conqueror's thoughts.   He
perhaps preferred Milan to Paris as a place to live in.

His formal entrance into the capital of his kingdom of Italy had been skilfully arranged.   Cardinal
Caprara, the Archbishop of that city, had great influence there, and he was never tired of speaking to his
flock about the services Napoleon had rendered to
the Catholic religion.   The Grand Master of Ceremonies, M. de Ségur, who reached Milan a few days
before the Emperor, charmed the best society of
Lombardy by his pleasant wit and delightful manners, and induced the most illustrious families to
solicit the honor of figuring among the ladies and
officers in waiting at the palace of the King and
Queen of Italy, as Napoleon and Josephine were
called at Milan.

The first visit which the King and Queen made
in this capital was to the famous Cathedral.   There
they fell on their knees, and the Milanese were much
touched by the spectacle.   The *Italian Journal*, in
its official account of Napoleon's entrance into Milan,
uttered these dithyrambics: "It is impossible to
imagine a more brilliant day than that which yesterday adorned our capital, when Bonaparte, the hero of
the age, our adored monarch, entered within our
walls.   This day will be forever memorable in the

chronicles of our history. Milan saw entering its
gates, bearing the proud name of King, the same
hero who had already been proclaimed conqueror,
liberator, peace-maker, and legislator, and who to-day,
under his august Empire, assures that greatness to
which his victories and his genius permit us to aspire.
The Emperor entered by the gate named after his
most glorious triumph, the Marengo Gate."

On reaching Milan, Napoleon exchanged the decorations of the Legion of Honor for the oldest orders
of chivalry in Europe. He received from the Minister of Prussia the Black and the Red Eagle; from
the Spanish Ambassador, the Golden Fleece; from the
Ministers of Bavaria and Portugal, the Orders of
Saint Hubert and Christ respectively; and he gave
them the broad ribbon of the Legion of Honor.
When he had received besides foreign decorations
for the principal men of the Empire, he granted an
equal number of his own. May 12, wearing the
broad ribbon of the Black Eagle, he went with the
Empress to the theatre of La Scala and saw the opera
of *Castor and Pollux.* The theatre, which was brilliantly lit, was crowded with the fair ladies of Milan,
resplendent in full dress and jewels. The elegance
and splendor of these deservedly famous beauties,
the brilliant diversity of the uniforms, the sumptu-
ousness of the Imperial box, and on the stage the
magnificence of the dresses and the scenery, the
skill of the singers, all combined to make the performance most memorable. That day, after mass,

Napoleon had ridden out, and had inspected the troops who paraded on the Place of the Cathedral.

The Empress's grace and affability aroused general admiration. At the reception of the upper clergy of Italy, May 25, she was thus complimented by the Archbishop of Bergamo: " Madame, If charity were to descend from heaven to relieve the woes of humanity, it would seek no other asylum than the heart of a Queen adored by her subjects. The feelings of love, gratitude, and respect which animate all your subjects are the same that lead to your feet all the bishops of the kingdom of Italy. Happy to find in your august spouse sublimity, glory, and genius, and in you all the charm of kindness, nothing is left for them but to pray for the happiness of your reign, and to offer thanks to heaven for having united in the souls of their sovereigns everything which can make supreme power loved and respected." This speech will suffice to show to what pitch the official flatteries were tuned.

The coronation took place May 26, in the Milan Cathedral, which is the largest church in Italy, with the single exception of Saint Peter's in Rome. The weather was magnificent. From early morning a numberless throng crowded the Place of the Cathedral, the court-yards of the palace, and the adjacent streets. Just as in Paris at the coronation, a wooden gallery had been built, connecting the Archbishop's Palace with Notre Dame, so here at Milan, a similar gallery led from the palace to the Cathedral. The

interior of the church was decorated with crimson
silk stuffs. As at Notre Dame, a large throne had
been built at the entrance to the nave, approached by
twenty-five steps. Four gilded statues, representing
victories, upheld like caryatides the canopy above the
throne. The four figures held in one hand palms;
in the other, the green velvet mantle falling from
the royal crown above the canopy. The Cathedral
was brilliantly lit by forty chandeliers hanging
from the roof, and as many candelabra fastened on
the columns.

Josephine, who had been crowned as Empress in
Paris, was not to be crowned at Milan, although she
bore the title of Queen of Italy. She watched the
ceremony from a gallery. At half-past eleven she
went to the Cathedral, preceded by her sister-in-law,
the Princess Bacciocchi, and was conducted beneath
a canopy to her gallery, amid loud applause. At
noon the Emperor and King left his palace, and
reached the Cathedral through the wooden gallery.
On his arrival there incense was burned, and he was
welcomed by an address from Cardinal Caprara, Archbishop of Milan, at the head of all his clergy. Preceded by the ushers, the heralds-at-arms, the pages,
the Grand Master and the masters of ceremonies, by
the seven ladies carrying offerings, and by the honors
of Charlemagne, of the Empire, and of Italy, he
appeared in most impressive pomp. On his head he
wore the crown; he carried in his hands the sceptre,
and the hand of justice of the kingdom; on his back

he wore the royal cloak, the skirts of which were carried by the two First Equerries of France and Italy. As he entered the Cathedral a march of triumph was played. He took his seat on the small throne in the choir, having on his right the honors of Italy, on his left, those of France. The Archbishop of Bologna, who held a place at the coronation of the King very like that of the Pope at the crowning of the Emperor, carried to the altar the iron crown of the old Lombard kings, and began the mass. After the gradual, he blessed the royal ornaments in the following order: the sword, the cloak, the ring, the crown. Napoleon received from the Archbishop's hands the sword, the cloak, and the ring, but he took himself the iron crown from the altar, and proudly placing it on his head, exclaimed, in a voice that thrilled all present: "*Dio me la diede, guai a chi la tocca!*" — "God has given it to me; woe to him who touches it!" Then, having replaced the iron crown on the altar, he took the crown of Italy and placed it on his head, amid unanimous applause. Preceded by the same officials who had conducted him to the chair, he walked down the nave and took his place on the great throne at the other end by the entrance. The first herald-at-arms shouted, "Napoleon, Emperor of the French and King of Italy, is crowned and enthroned. Long live the Emperor and King."

The same day, at half-past four in the afternoon, the King and the Queen drove in a state carriage, with a brilliant escort, to the church of Saint Ambrose, one of the most revered sanctuaries of Italy, and there they heard a *Te Deum* of thanksgiving.

Mademoiselle Avrillon, Josephine's reader, tells us that Napoleon, when he had returned to the palace, was full of the wildest gaiety. He rubbed his hands, and in his good humor said to the reader: " Well! Did you see the ceremony? Did you hear what I said when I placed the crown on my head?" Then he repeated, almost in the same tone that he had used in the Cathedral: "God has given it to me! Woe to him that touches it!" "I told him," says Mademoiselle Avrillon, "that nothing that had happened had escaped me. He was very kind to me, and I often noticed that when there was nothing to annoy the Emperor, he talked cheerfully and freely with us, as if we were his equals; but whenever he spoke to us he used to ask questions, and in order to avoid displeasing him, it was necessary to answer him without showing too much embarrassment. Sometimes he gave us a pat on the cheek, or pinched our ears; these were favors not accorded every one, and we could judge of his good humor by the way they hurt us. . . . Often he treated the Empress in the same way, with little pats preferably on the shoulders; it was no use her saying: 'Come, stop, Bonaparte!' he went on as long as he pleased."

The Emperor greatly enjoyed his stay in Milan, and breathed with rapture the incense burned in abundance before him. The *Italian Journal* in its account of the coronation reached lyric heights:

"The most brilliant day has lit up Milan; it has had no equal in the past, and it offers the happiest auguries for the future. . . . Old men themselves, accustomed as they are to praise the past, have exhibited the liveliest enthusiasm. It was in vain that night struggled to draw its veil over our city, it had to yield before the general and magnificent illumination which brought out in lines of fire the shape and admirable form of the Duomo. Most of the palaces and private houses were covered with devices and inscriptions. The first one of the days consecrated to the liveliest national rejoicing was ended by a vast exhibition of fireworks, which were set off on the spot where so many have perished at the stake."

The next day games were celebrated, in the manner of the ancients, in a circus rivalling the Roman amphitheatres in size. This was the occasion of a dithyrambic outburst inserted in the *Moniteur:* "The Italians have just offered Napoleon the same spectacle that their ancestors offered Marcus Aurelius and Trajan; but the presence of Napoleon has called forth more joy and admiration, because it has aroused greater admiration and higher hopes. They were but the preservers of Italian greatness; he is its creator and its father. In the pomp of the games, amid the tumultuous applause, the immense mass of people were to be seen turning their eyes towards him alone, as if they were saying to him: 'These festivities are but feeble expressions of the gratitude that all Italy vows to you for all the good you have done her; and

since you deign to accept it, since you like to sit
among us as our Prince and our father, these festivities become an augury to us of still greater benefit.
The day will perhaps come when Italy, restored to
this new life, may be able to adorn its circus with
the monuments of its own bravery which will also
be the monuments of your glory; and Italy, being
never doomed to perish, whatever great deeds may
be wrought by Italians in the course of centuries
will be due to the hero who has recalled them to
life.' After the races there was a balloon ascension.
The courageous wife of the aeronaut Garnerin accompanied him and threw down flowers to Napoleon
and Josephine. Thus," the *Moniteur* goes on, "in
a single day, at one show, the Italians have combined
the proudest pomp of the ancients and the boldest
invention of modern science, together with the
presence of a hero who excels both ancients and
moderns."

The 29th of May was devoted to popular festivities.
All the afternoon the public gardens were crowded
with musicians, singers, mountebanks, and pedlars.
In the evening the via della Riconoscenza, as far as
the East Gate, was lit by lampstands, and at the end
of a long row there was an eagle of fire holding on
his breast an iron crown.

Nothing was neglected to touch the national pride
of Italy. An article in the *Moniteur*, speaking of a
poem of Vincenzo Monti's, said: " What interest the
poet has aroused, in recalling the glorious titles of

ancient Italy, the disasters and degradation which followed this period of glory, in evoking the shades of those remote days, and after them, the shade of Dante who, by the wisdom of his maxims, is superior to the poets of other nations; of Dante, the most enthusiastic admirer of the former glory of the Italians, the severest censor of the corruption into which Italy had fallen in his time; of Dante, whose sole ambition was to prepare the new birth of Italy! And how did he prepare it? By preaching union to the inhabitants of the different countries of Italy, and to the public authorities the consecration of power modified by the laws."

June 3 Napoleon and Josephine went to visit an industrial and artistic exhibition at the Brera. There they saw Canova's Hebe, and his colossal statue of Clement XIII. " The desire of seeing and approaching the sovereign," says the *Moniteur*, " had made the crowd larger. An octogenarian who had in vain struggled to get to a staircase before him, was hustled and knocked down on the steps by the eager multitude. The Empress, who was following, ran to his aid. The Emperor turned back, questioned the old man, who was more disturbed by his joy than by his fall, asked him his name and a memorandum, and promised to look out for him. This scene produced a deep impression, and Their Majesties were led back amid universal applause and thanksgivings."

At Milan, Josephine, who had become Queen of Italy, inhabited, with the Emperor, the magnificent

Monza Palace. But, perhaps, in all the splendor of
the highest point of her good fortune, she regretted
the Serbelloni Palace, where, nine years before, she
exercised so beneficent an influence on her husband's
destiny, and had protected him with her affection,
as with a talisman. Doubtless the Empress and
Queen would have returned gladly to the time when
she was called simply Citizeness Bonaparte. Then,
instead of the imperial and royal diadem, she possessed youth, which is better than any crown, and
her husband gave her something preferable to any
throne — his love ! There the generals used to wear
less showy uniforms, more moderate salaries, but they
were more enthusiastic and unselfish. Then Bonaparte's glory was less famous, but purer. When she
saw Milan again, after many years' absence, Josephine
recalled all the happiness and all the misery that had
occurred meanwhile, all the grandeur and the tragedy
that had filled this period so brief, but so crowded
with marvellous events.

There were many happy memories, but also many
shadows ! This look backward was not without
melancholy. When she saw the approach of the
autumn of her amazing career, Josephine could not
think without secret sadness of the splendor of its
summer. While her husband proudly enjoyed his
satisfied ambition, she dreamed and pondered seriously. She desired once more to see the places
which recalled the pleasantest memories of her first
journey: the lake of Como, with the Villa Julia and

Islands; the palaces of the Isola Bella and the Isola Madre; all the enchanting spots which recalled the gracious memories of youth and love.

June 7 Napoleon appointed Eugene de Beauharnais Viceroy of the Kingdom of Italy, and three days later left Milan with Josephine. In all the principal cities of the Empire his coronation had been celebrated by public rejoicings. Murat had given a ball at his castle of Neuilly, about which the *Journal des Débats* had said: "At the same moment when the arts of ingenious Italy were displaying all their marvels under the eyes of Their Majesties, French gallantry and gaiety were rendering similar homage to the happy reign which had recalled them from a long exile." Aix-la-Chapelle inaugurated the statue of the great Carlovingian Emperor amid salvos of artillery and the applause of the Germanic populace, who saluted at the same time the names of Charlemagne and of Napoleon.

XIV.

THE FESTIVITIES AT GENOA.

THE Italian journey closed as brilliantly as it began. After leaving Milan, Napoleon approached the frontiers of Austria, against which he was to fight before the end of the year, visiting the celebrated quadrilateral, consisting of the four fortified towns: Mantua, Peschiera, Verona, and Legnago. He was present at a mimic representation of the battle of Castiglione, in which twenty-five thousand men took part on the field upon which that battle had been fought; then he went to Bologna, where the charms of his conversation were highly appreciated by the learned professors of its university. While he was there a deputation from Lucca visited him, asking him to take that little country under his protection. He gave it for Prince and Princess, his brother-in-law, Felix Bacciocchi, and his sister Elisa, to whom he had already entrusted the Duchy of Piombino. Lucca was thus elevated to a hereditary principality, a dependent of the French Empire, which should revert to the French crown in case the male line of the Bacciocchi should become extinct. It was a sort

of revival of the old Germanic fiefs. Evidently the
memory of Charlemagne continually filled Napoleon's
thoughts. Elisa thenceforth bore the title of Princess of Lucca and of Piombino. She was a well educated and able woman, of marked intelligence and
strong will. M. de Talleyrand used to call her "the
Semiramis of Lucca." After Bologna, Napoleon
visited Modena, Parma, and Piacenza. The cities
he passed through rivalled one another in flattery.
They voted him medals, statues, and even a temple,
which, however, the demi-god declined.

June 30 Napoleon and Josephine arrived at Genoa,
where they were to stay till July 7, amid unprecedented festivities celebrating the incorporation of the
old Republic with the French Empire. It was a singular sight, this enthusiastic reception of a Corsican
by the Genoese. While at Milan, the Emperor·had
received M. Durazzo, the last Doge of Genoa, who
had come to beg him to permit the illustrious Republic, famous for its historical splendor, to exchange
its independence for the honor of becoming a plain
French department. The offer was accepted. The
home of Andrea Doria, the city of marble palaces,
that municipality once called "the superb" had
begged as a favor to be stricken from the list of
independent states. It contented itself with being
the principal town in the twenty-seventh military
division, and its doge, dispossessed by his own desire,
went to swell the number of the Senators of the
Empire. Napoleon took formal possession of his

peaceful conquest, and slept in the palace, and in the bed of Charles V.

The night festivity, given in the harbor, July 2, was, in the way of picturesqueness, one of the most original and most beautiful ever seen. The sky was clear, the sea calm, the crowd of spectators enormous. Napoleon and Josephine, going down from the terrace in the garden of the Palazzo Doria, entered a large round temple, magnificently decorated, which was at once set in motion as if by magic, and transported by many oars to the middle of the harbor. Four rafts, covered with shrubbery, resembling floating islands, then drew up to the temple. The sovereigns were thus, in open sea, enclosed in a vast garden with trees, flowers, statues, and fountains. About this garden of Armida, thus radiant upon the waves, were a multitude of boats, under sail or propelled by oars, moving about, and their lights resembled the swarms of fireflies that in summer flutter above the fields of Lombardy. The mild temperature favored this joyous festival. The whole city, all the buildings, every vessel, were ablaze with a thousand lights, and the glassy sea reflected numberless flames. The darkness of night gave the signal for the illuminations. Magnificent fireworks were set off from the mole, the jetty, and the ships lining the entrance of the harbor. Music mingled with the joyous cries of the multitude. The temple in which were Napoleon and Josephine was rowed back to the terrace of the Palazzo Doria amid the applause of the crowd lining the shore.

The next day the Emperor and Empress were at a ball given in the old Ducal Palace. "The presence of Their Majesties in this superb building," says the *Moniteur*, "the kindness with which they deigned to speak to every one, gave this festivity a touching character. All who saw and heard our sovereigns, rejoiced in their new destinies. The concert was followed by a ball, and Their Majesties stayed through the several dances, leaving about midnight. Their path was lit by numberless candles. On their way they met a multitude, delighted even at that hour, to be able to discern some of our monarch's features."

In spite of all these splendid ceremonies Josephine, though idolized, was not happy. "In general," Mademoiselle Avrillon says with justice, "the public has a very faint knowledge of the real feelings of those in the highest station. Being often on show, they are obliged to assume a fictitious character, just as they dress themselves for great ceremonies. I have seen the Empress's sufferings, whom nothing could console for her separation from her children, whom she loved above everything. Ambitions were less to her than maternal love, her strongest feeling. The thought of leaving her son in Italy, the fear of never seeing him again, or the certainty of seeing him seldom, made her shed tears." One day when she was in more distress than usual, Napoleon said to her: "You are crying, Josephine; that's absurd; you are crying because you are going to be separated from

your son. If the absence of your children gives you
so much pain, judge what I must suffer. The affection you show them makes me feel most acutely my
unhappiness in having none." These words sounded
in Josephine's ears like a funeral knell. She saw the
spectre of divorce rising before her, and turned pale.

From Genoa they went to Turin. Napoleon heard
there of the coalition preparing against him, and left
suddenly for France with Josephine. Non-commis-
sioned officers of the Grenadiers and the Chasseurs of
the Guard served as escort, but they were unable to
keep up with the carriages, so the Emperor thanked
them for their zeal and pushed on without them. He
did not stop once for twenty-four hours. Josephine,
who never tormented her husband by complaining,
did not say a word about the fatigues of this quick
journey. After an absence of a hundred days, they
reached Fontainebleau, July 11. No one expected
them and no preparations had been made for their
reception. Their departure from Turin had been
so recent, and it resembled a flight. The Emperor
did not wish to be recognized on the way, and burst
into Fontainebleau like a bombshell. The palace porter was an old servant, named Guillot, who had been
Napoleon's cook in Egypt. "Well," the Emperor
said to him, "you must go back to your old business
and cook us some supper." Fortunately the porter
had in his sideboard some mutton-chops and eggs.
He set to work, and Napoleon ate this improvised
meal with great relish. Josephine borrowed some

linen from one of her old chambermaids.   The Emperor asked for a full account of everything that had happened in Paris during his absence, and began to draw up the plans which were to be accomplished at Austerlitz before the end of the year.   July 18, at one in the afternoon, he arrived at Saint Cloud, accompanied by the Empress, amid the roar of the cannon at the Invalides.   That evening they went into the city, called on Napoleon's mother, and went to the opera, where the *Prétendus* was given; the audience greeted them most warmly.   After all the splendor of the Italian festivities the time had come for military preparations and warlike thoughts.

XV.

AUSTERLITZ was to be for the Empire what Marengo had been for the Consulate: a consolidation. In spite of the pomps of the double coronation, Napoleon did not feel firmly established on his Imperial and Royal throne. Opinions varied with regard to the stability of the new régime. The Liberals missed the Republic, and the Royalists the Bourbons. If the army and the people showed confidence in the Emperor's star, the Parisian middle class was always cool, and business men observed with anxiety the hostility of England, Austria, Russia, and possibly Prussia. Paris was gloomy; business was dull; the absence of the court depressed the shop-keepers; the theatres were empty; in short, the winter was infinitely less gay than the one before. There was general uneasiness; wives feared for their husbands; mothers for their sons. Every one had become used to the peace which had lasted five years, and the renewal of war inspired the greatest anxiety.

As for Napoleon, he felt the need of some great stroke that should astonish and fascinate the world.

He understood that to maintain his fame he was condemned to work miracles. September 23, 1805, he
had exposed to the Senate the hostile conduct of
Austria, and had announced his speedy departure to
carry aid to the Elector of Bavaria, the ally of
France, whom the Austrians had just driven from
Munich. Five days later he had started, confident of
success, and certain that he would find his people at
his feet on his return. The Empress accompanied
him as far as Strassburg, and established herself there
to be near the scene of war and to receive earlier
news than was possible at Paris.

Napoleon's letters to Josephine during the Austerlitz campaign have been preserved; unfortunately,
we have not hers to him. The Emperor writes very
differently from General Bonaparte. His letters are
not the ardent, passionate, romantic epistles recalling
the fervid style and thought of the *Nouvelle Héloise.*
They are substantial letters, concise and interesting,
such as a good husband might write after ten years
of marriage, but not at all a lover's letters. Josephine,
who was quite observant, must have noticed the difference, but she had enough tact and prudence to
avoid complaint. 1805 was not 1796; Napoleon still
loved Josephine, but from habit, gratitude, and a
sense of duty, not with mad passion. He paid her
much attention, held her in high regard, felt sympathy with her, deference, and friendship, but scarcely
love. Beneath the vaulted roof of Notre Dame
Napoleon had given to Josephine the Imperial dia-

dem, but he had not given her the true crown,— love.

October 1 the Emperor took command of his army, which had assembled with wonderful promptness on the Rhine. The next day he wrote to the Empress from Marenheims: "I am still very well, and leaving for Strassburg, where I shall arrive this evening. The advance has begun. The armies of Würtemberg and of Baden are joining mine. I have a good position and love you." October 4 he wrote to her: "I am at Ludwigsberg, and leave to-night. There is no news. All the Bavarians have joined me. I am well. I hope in a few days to have something interesting to tell you. Keep well and believe that I love you. There is a very fine court here, a pretty bride, and the people are pleasant, even the Elector's wife, who seems very good, although she is a daughter of the King of England."

October 5 Napoleon sent another letter to Josephine from Ludwigsberg: "I have at once to continue my march. You will be five or six days without news of me; don't be anxious; it is on account of the operations we undertake. Are you as well as I could hope? Yesterday I was at the wedding of the son of the Elector of Würtemberg with a niece of the King of Prussia. I want to give her a present of from thirty-six to forty thousand francs. Have it made and send it by one of my chamberlains to the bride when the chamberlains are coming to me. Do this at once. Good by; I love and kiss you."

These five or six days of silence were taken up by the opening of hostilities on the road from Stuttgart to Ulm, the crossing of the Danube, and the occupation of Augsburg. From this city Napoleon wrote to Josephine October 10: "I spent last night with the former Elector of Treves, who has comfortable quarters. I have been on the move for a week. The campaign opens with noteworthy successes. I am very well though it rains nearly every day. Things have moved very quickly. I have sent to France four thousand prisoners, eight flags, and have captured fourteen cannon. Good by, my dear; I kiss you." Two days later the French army entered Munich in triumph, the Austrians having been driven out of Bavaria. The Emperor wrote to the Empress, October 12: "My army has entered Munich. The enemy is partly on the other side of the Inn; the other army of sixty thousand men I have blockaded on the Iller between Ulm and Memmingen. The enemy is lost, has completely lost its head, and everything promises the luckiest, shortest, and most brilliant campaign ever known. I leave in an hour for Burgau on the Iller. I am well; the weather is frightful. It rains so that I have to change my clothes twice a day. I love you."

The first successes of the campaign caused great excitement in Paris, as is shown by the letters of Madame de Rémusat, no great lover of military glory, to her husband, who had accompanied the Empress to Strassburg; every day this lady would jot down what had happened, and her interesting correspondence brings the period vividly before us. October 12, she wrote, the absence of the Empress leaving her time heavy on her hands: " How gloomy and ill we are in this odious Paris! Please tell M. de Talleyrand that it is really something pitiable. Not even a word of gossip! In short, we are as bored as we are virtuous. I don't know which is the cause and which the effect, but I do know that I am horribly bored. The solitude of this great city is really remarkable; the theatres are empty; I hardly ever go to them."

In two days there was a complete change. Paris woke up as if to a joyous trumpet-call, and Madame de Rémusat was full of happiness: " My dear, what good news!" she wrote October 14, ". . . This morning the cannon announced the victory to the city of Paris; it produced a great effect. Every one was inquiring about it in the street, and congratulating himself; in short, I send the Empress word, the Parisians were French. I have already written twenty notes, and received all the visits of congratulation. . . . But what a great victory! How proud I am of being a Frenchwoman! I couldn't sleep for joy. Perhaps by this time you have heard of others, and when we are rejoicing over the first victory, you have forgotten it with another. May Heaven continue to protect this noble army and its glorious leader!" This enthusiastic letter ends with these somewhat harsh criticisms of the Parisians: " This victory was necessary, for these sad Parisians had begun to complain. The

emptiness of Paris, its quiet, the lack of money which
continues to make itself felt, gave to the malevolent
a good opportunity to excite dissatisfaction, and they
did their best to spread it.   I was wondering this very
morning why in a nation so devoid of national feeling
there should be in the army such unity of action and
thought.   It seems to me that honor has a good deal
to do with this difference, and that it takes the place
of public spirit in many who in ordinary times are
too happy, too rich, and too careless to care for anything beyond their own belongings."

Napoleon went from one victory to another.   October 18, just before the capitulation of Ulm, he wrote
to Josephine from Elchingen : "I have been more
tired than I should have been; for a week getting wet
through every day, and cold feet, have done me a little
harm, but staying in to-day has rested me.   I have
carried out my plan and have destroyed the Austrian
army by simple marches.   I have taken sixty thousand
prisoners, one hundred and twenty cannon, more than
ninety flags, and more than thirty generals.   I am
going to attack the Russians ; they are lost.   I am
satisfied with my army.   I have lost only fifteen
hundred men, and two-thirds of these are but slightly
wounded.   Good by.   Remember me to every one.
Prince Charles is coming to cover Vienna.   I think
Masséna ought to be at Vienna at this time.   As soon
as I am easy about Italy I shall make Eugene fight.
My love to Hortense."

The capitulation of Ulm was arranged by Napoleon

with Prince Lichtenstein, Major-General of the Austrian army. A heavy rain fell without cessation, and
the prisoners were amazed to see the Emperor, who
had not taken off his boots for a week, wet through,
covered with mud, and more tired than the humblest
drummer. When some one spoke of it, he said
to Prince Lichtenstein : " Your Emperor wanted to
remind me that I was a soldier. I hope he will
acknowledge that the throne and the Imperial purple
have not made me forget my old trade." October
21, the day after the capitulation, Napoleon wrote
to Josephine : "I am very well, my dear. I leave at
once for Augsburg. I have made an army of thirty-
three thousand men surrender. I have taken from
sixty to seventy thousand prisoners, more than ninety
flags, and more than two hundred cannon. In the
military annals there is no such defeat. Keep well.
I am a little worried. For three days the weather
has been pleasant. The first column of prisoners
starts for France to-day. Each column contains six
thousand men." Never had war been fought with
such art. An army of eighty-five thousand men had
been destroyed almost without firing a gun ; its adver-
saries had lost only three thousand men. After this
great victory Napoleon's soldiers said, " The Emperor
beat the enemy with our legs, not with our bayonets."

These chronicles of war have a sad side even when
they commemorate the most brilliant victories. Even
while he counts the trophies the historian cannot
avoid melancholy reflections. What capitulations

awaited France sixty-five years after this capitulation
of Ulm! But in this intoxication of victory, people
have eyes only for their success. Were they reasonable, they would then reflect on the calamities of war.
Hortense, who was as kind as her mother, Josephine,
had this wisdom and pity. She said, " When I read
these accounts I am surprised to find myself ready to
weep even when I am happy at the victories." At
the same time Madame de Rémusat wrote to her husband: "Poor creatures that we are, how restless we
are on this sandhill, and too often only to hasten our
end! A good subject for the philosopher is this glory,
with which we adorn our eagerness in killing one
another." The triumphal music should not drown
the sobs and cries of the mothers; we should think of
the dead and wounded. But nations are like individuals: they never reflect.

Napoleon pushed on the war with real delight. He
felt about war as a good workman feels about his
work, as a great artist about his art. To war it was
that he owed his power and glory. Without it, he
said, he would have been nothing; by it, he was
everything. Hence he felt for it not merely love, but
gratitude; loving it both by instinct and calculation.
He preferred the bivouac to the Tuileries. Just as
the snipe-shooter prefers a marsh to a drawing-room,
he was more at home under a tent than in a palace.
To men who like the battle-field, war is the most
intense of pleasures. They love it as the gamester
loves play, with a real frenzy. They defeat the enemy,

not merely without feeling, but with a fierce joy, as if it were their prey. They feel the same emotions as the Romans in a circus, or the Spaniards at a bull-fight. `The rattle of drums, the blare of trumpets, shouts of soldiers, are what they hear ; their ears are deaf to the cries of the wounded and dying. `The varying chances of the combat, the uncertainties of fear and hope produce in them emotions that they prefer to all others, however poetic and charming. It is with a sort of intoxication that they inhale the smell of gunpowder, perpaps even that of blood. A hotly contested victory is more agreeable to them than one too easily gained. Fortune is, in their eyes, a difficult mistress, whose favors seem the dearer, the harder they are of attainment. What a satisfaction for a proud man to be absolute commander of an army which, before the fight, shouts like the ancient gladiators: *Ave, Cæsar, morituri te salutant!* "Hail, Cæsar, those about to die salute you!" an army in which even dying men shout applause, with their last breath, to their sovereign, their idol! And yet how petty is all this glory! Bossuet was right when he said: "What could you find on earth strong and dignified enough to bear the name of power? Open your eyes, pierce the dusk. All the power in the world can but take a man's life: is it then such a great thing to shorten by a few moments a life which is already hastening to its end?"

Josephine did not in the least share her husband's warlike tastes. Gentle, kindly, affectionate, full of pity for human woes, she would have liked to reconcile all parties, all nations, — to have universal peace. This woman, who had all the graces and charms of her sex, never inspired Napoleon with ambitious or haughty thoughts. While the war lasted, she was anxious, unhappy; waiting anxiously with bated breath for news, scarcely living.

Napoleon wrote to her from Augsburg, October 23: " The last two nights have rested me completely, and I leave for Munich to-morrow; I am summoning to me M. de Talleyrand and M. Maret; I shall see them for a short time, and then leave for the Inn, where I mean to attack Austria in its hereditary states. I should have been glad to see you, but don't expect me to summon you unless there should be an armistice, or we should go into winter quarters. Good by, my dear; a thousand kisses. Remember me to all the ladies." From Munich the Emperor wrote the following letter, dated October 27: " I have received your letter from Lamarois. I am sorry to see that you have been over-anxious. I have heard many details of your affection for me, but you should have more strength and confidence. Besides, I had told you I should not write for six days. To-morrow I expect the Elector. At noon I start to strengthen my movement on the Inn. My health is very fair. You mustn't think of crossing the Rhine in less than two or three weeks. You must be cheerful, and amuse yourself in the hope of our meeting before the end of the month (Brumaire). I am advancing on the Rus-

sian army. In a few days I shall have crossed the
Inn. Good by, my dear; much love to Hortense, to
Eugene, and to the two Napoleons. Keep the wedding present for some time yet. Yesterday I gave
a concert to the ladies of this court. The leader
is a worthy man. I have shot pheasants with the
Elector; you see I am not worn out. M. de Talleyrand has come." Again, from Haag, November 3,
1805: "I am advancing rapidly; the weather is very
cold; the snow is a foot deep. This is not pleasant.
Fortunately, we have an abundance of wood; we are
continually in the forests. I am fairly well. Everything goes on satisfactorily; the enemy has more
cause for anxiety than I. I am eager to hear from
you, and to know that your mind is easy. Good by,
my dear; I am going to bed."

Napoleon continued his operations with startling
rapidity. He wrote to Josephine November 5: "I
am at Linz. The weather is fine. We are within
twenty-eight leagues of Vienna. The Russians are
retreating without making a stand. The house of
Austria is much embarrassed; all the belongings of
the court have been removed from Vienna. You will
probably have some news in five or six days. I am
very anxious to see you. My health is good." The
Emperor of Austria, compelled to leave Vienna, had
sought refuge at Brunn, where he joined the Czar and
the second Russian army; and Napoleon entered the
capital whence the Emperor Francis had fled. He
wrote to Josephine November 15: "I have been for

two days in Vienna, a little tired. I have not yet seen the city by daylight, but have only passed through it by night. To-morrow I receive the authorities. Almost all my troops are beyond the Danube in pursuit of the Russians. Good by, dear Josephine; as soon as possible I shall arrange for you to come. I send much love." The next day he wrote again to the Empress from Vienna: "I am writing to M. de Narville to arrange for you to go to Baden, thence to Stuttgart, and thence to Munich. At Stuttgart you will give the present to the Princess Paul. Fifteen or twenty thousand francs will be enough for it; the rest will be enough for a present to the daughter of the Elector of Bavaria at Munich. All that you heard from Madame de Sérent is definitely arranged. Bring presents for the ladies and officers in waiting on you. Be pleasant, but receive all their homages; they owe you everything, and you owe them nothing, except in the way of politeness. The Electress of Würtemberg is a daughter of the King of England; you should treat her well, and especially without affectation. I shall be glad to see you as soon as business will permit. I am leaving for the front. The weather is admirable; there is much snow, but everything is in good condition. Good by, my dear one." On the receipt of this letter, Josephine, who was most anxious to see her husband, hastened away from Strassburg to go to Munich through Baden and Würtemberg. At the same time Napoleon set off to meet the Austrian and Russian armies, commanded by their respective Emperors, in Moravia.

We have in the Memoirs of General de Ségur, an eye-witness, an interesting account of the eve of Austerlitz. Late in the afternoon Napoleon entered a hut, and took his place at table in the best of spirits, along with Murat, Caulaincourt, Junot, Ségur, Rapp, and a few other guests. They thought that he would talk about the next day's battle. Not at all: he discussed literature with Junot, who was familiar with all the new tragedies; he had a good deal to say about Raynouard's *Templars*, about Racine, Corneille, and the fate of the ancient drama. Then, by a singular transition, he began to talk about his Egyptian campaign. "If I had captured Acre," he said, "I should have put my army into long trousers, and have made it my sacred battalion, my Immortals, and have finished my war against the Turks with Arabians, Greeks, and Armenians. Instead of fighting here in Moravia, I should be winning a battle of Issus, and be making myself Emperor of the West, returning to Paris through Constantinople."

After dinner Napoleon wished to make a final reconnoissance of the enemy's position by their bivouac fires; he mounted his horse and rode out between the lines. One moment he came near paying dear for his imprudence; he went too far forward and suddenly fell on a post of Cossacks, and had it not been for the devotion of the chasseurs who escorted him, he would have been killed or captured, and he was scarcely able to escape at full gallop. After crossing the stream which covered the front of the French army, he dismounted and returned to his bivouac, from one watch-fire to another, on foot. On his way he stumbled over the stump of a tree and fell to the ground. Then a grenadier took some straw, rolled it up to something like a torch, and lit it; other soldiers did the same thing; the camp was illuminated, and the face of the great conqueror was plainly to be seen. The next day was December 2, the anniversary of his coronation. "Emperor," shouted an old soldier, "I promise you in the name of the grenadiers of the army that you will have to fight only with your eyes, and that to-morrow we shall bring you the flags and artillery of the Russian army to celebrate the anniversary of your coronation." Every one shouted applause. Napoleon in vain tried to stop them. "Silence," he commanded, "until to-morrow! think of nothing but sharpening your bayonets!" Shouts of "Long live the Emperor!" were repeated. Along a line of two leagues blazed thousands of fires and flames. The Russians wondered what was the cause of this unusual brilliancy, and thought the French were retreating. Napoleon was at first annoyed by this rapturous demonstration, but at last he was touched by it, and passing through a number of bivouacs, all brightly lit, he expressed his gratitude to his soldiers, saying it was the happiest evening of his life. Then he went to his tent, snatched a little sleep, and when he rose in the morning, said, "Now, gentlemen, we are beginning a great day."

A moment later, the commanders of the different army corps, Murat, Lannes, Bernadotte, Soult, Davout, came galloping up the little mound which the soldiers called the Emperor's hill, to receive his final orders. It was a solemn, impressive moment. "If I were to live," says General de Ségur, "as long as the world shall last, I shall never forget that scene. . . . Times have changed quickly since then. Heavens! how great everything was then, how brave the men, how glorious the time, how imposing the appearance of fate!" Never was there a more brilliant triumph. "I have fought thirty battles like that," said the conqueror, "but I have never seen so decisive a victory, or one where the chances were so unevenly balanced." And then full of admiration for his soldiers, he exclaimed, "I am satisfied with you; you have covered your eagles with undying glory."

From a military point of view Austerlitz was Napoleon's greatest triumph. War, which he loved with all its risks and emotions, then showed him its most tempting side. He was always tempting fate, and fate had always favored him. The hour had not yet struck when he was to ask more of fortune than it could give. As Sainte-Beuve truly says, it was not till in the icy plain of Eylau, from the cemetery covered with blood-stained snow, that receiving the first warning of Providence, he had a sort of terrible vision of what the future held in store for him. Then he had before his eyes a sort of rehearsal of the

horrors awaiting him in Russia, and at the sight of
so many corpses, and the awful scene, he said with
deep melancholy, " This sight is one to fill kings with
love of peace and horror of war." But at Austerlitz
it was very different. The shrieks of the Russians
sinking through the holes torn in the ice by cannon-
balls were drowned in the shouts of the victors.
The bright sunlight of that day of triumph dispelled
all traces of gloom in the conqueror's heart.

December 3, Napoleon wrote thus to Josephine
about his victory : " I despatched Lebrun to you from
the battle-field. I have beaten the Russian and Austrian armies commanded by the two Emperors. I am
a little tired. I have bivouacked for a week in the
open air, and the nights have been cool. To-night
I am going to sleep in the castle of Prince Kaunitz,
where I shall get two or three hours' rest. The
Russian army is not merely defeated, but destroyed.
Much love." December 3, he had an interview in
his bivouac with the Emperor of Austria ; and as if
to apologize for the wretched quarters in which he
received him, he said, " This is the palace which
Your Majesty has compelled me to inhabit these three
months." The Emperor of Austria replied, " You
make such good use of it, that you certainly can't
blame me on that account." And then the two
Emperors embraced.

The next day Napoleon wrote to Josephine : " I
have made a truce. The Russians withdraw. The
battle of Austerlitz is the greatest I have won : forty·

five flags, more than one hundred and fifty cannon, the standards of the Russian guards, twenty generals, more than twenty thousand killed, — a horrid sight! The Emperor Alexander is in despair, and is leaving for Russia. Yesterday I saw the Emperor of Germany in my bivouac; we talked for two hours, and agreed on a speedy peace. The weather is not yet very bad. Now that the continent is at peace, we may hope for it everywhere: the English will be unable to face us. I shall see with pleasure the time that will restore me to you. For two days a little trouble with the eyes has been prevalent in the army. I have not yet been attacked. Good by, my dear. I am fairly well, and very anxious to see you." December 3, there was another letter, also from Austerlitz: "I have concluded an armistice, and peace will be made within a week. I am anxious to hear that you have reached Munich in good health. The Russians are going back after suffering immense losses: more than twenty thousand killed and thirty thousand captured; they have lost three-quarters of their army. Buxhövden, their commander-in-chief, is killed. I have three thousand wounded and seven or eight hundred killed. I have a little trouble with my eyes: an epidemic; it amounts to nothing. Good by; I am anxious to see you once more. To-night I sleep in Vienna."

Cambacérès said that the news of the victory of Austerlitz filled the populace with the wildest joy, which expressed itself in the most extravagant flattery. The Emperor was treated like a god,`and naturally a sovereign so flattered did not control his love of war. It was only on his deathbed that Louis XIV. said, "I have been over-fond of war!" He said nothing of the sort when the gates of Saint Martin and of Saint Denis were built in his honor, when his statue was put up in the Place des Victoires, when Lebrun painted the proud frescoes in the gallery at Versailles. Like Louis XIV., Napoleon reproached himself with excessive love of war; but it was not after Austerlitz, but after Waterloo. No man is worthy of adoration; it belongs to God alone. Woe to the princes who are fed on flattery! Extravagant laudation brings its punishment; even in this world pride has its fall.

The enthusiasm was universal; the victorious French could not contain themselves for joy, and wholly lost their heads. Thus even Madame de Rémusat, who, after the defeat, had shown herself so severe, one might almost say so cruel, towards Napoleon, wrote thus to her husband, December 18, 1805, after the news of Austerlitz: "You cannot imagine how excited every one is. Praise of the Emperor is on every one's lips; the most recalcitrant are obliged to lay down their arms, and to say with the Emperor of Russia, 'He is the man of destiny!' Day before yesterday I went to the theatre with Princess Louis to hear the different bulletins read. The crowd was enormous because the cannon in the morning had announced the arrival of news; every thing was listened to, and then applauded with cries such as I had never imagined. I wept copiously all the time. I was so moved that I believe if the Emperor had been present, I should have flung my arms about his neck, to beg for pardon afterwards at his feet. After this I supped out: every one plied me with questions. I knew the whole bulletin by heart, and kept repeating it; and was glad to be able to tell the news to so many people, to repeat those simple impressive words, with a feeling of owning them, which you can understand better than I can define. I missed you much in all my joy, which I should have gladly shared with you; but in your absence I tried to communicate my admiration to our son. Instead of making him finish the life of Alexander, which he has been reading for two days, it occurred to me to have him read aloud the *Moniteur*, and he was so much pleased that he said he thought it all much greater than Alexander."

Alas! thoughtful people should never forget how much greater is virtue than success. In this low world no one takes a lofty enough view of things. Not after defeat, but after victory, is the time to speak of war seriously and sadly. If Napoleon in the hour of triumph had not been flattered to excess, if at the proper moment the lessons of history, philosophy, and religion had been enforced upon him, he would not have rushed blindly into the gulf that finally swallowed him. Nothing is less humane, less Christian, than the extravagant praise lavished on the conquer-

ors of the earth.   Laymen and priests are equally to
blame, for the flatterers of conquerors bear perhaps a
heavier responsibility than the conquerors themselves.
In the ancient triumphs, at least there was a slave
charged with reminding the hero that he was but a
man ; in modern times, there is nothing of the sort;
the hero can imagine himself more than mortal. Why
does not the clergy, instead of intoning a *Te Deum*,
take the part of that slave?   Is it well to forget that
those nations who are most modest in success are
bravest and most resigned in misfortune?   Those
whose heads are turned by prosperity cannot endure
reverses.   For society, as for individuals, nothing is
more baneful than outbursts of joy and pride.   The
vaster a monarch's power, the greater his need to
meditate on the fickleness of fate; but the lessons of
wisdom are never recalled till they are useless; they
are whispered into his ears only when they can but
add a sting to defeat.

XVI.

BOTH before and after the battle of Austerlitz a great part of Germany was at Napoleon's feet. The Electors of Baden, Würtemberg, and Bavaria, the last two of whom were to become kings by the consent of the new Charlemagne, testified an enthusiastic admiration for him, and were all to profit by his victory. The petty princes who were about to enter the Confederation of the Rhine were his humble vassals, and paid obsequious court to his Minister of Foreign Affairs, M. de Talleyrand. The archives of our Ministry of Foreign Affairs would have to be consulted for an exact understanding of their servility and flattery. Moreover, the populace itself shared the feelings of their princes. The Bavarians regarded Napoleon as their liberator. French manners and ideas were more than ever prevalent on the banks of the Rhine, and Germanic patriotism pardoned France the possession of the left bank of this river. If Napoleon had not abused fortune, what grand and pacific things might he not have accomplished in concert with Germany, and what progress might not have been made for the harmony of nations, for civilization and humanity!

We quote a letter written before the battle of Austerlitz, November 26, 1805, by the Elector of Bavaria to M. de Talleyrand, then in Vienna: "You are the most amiable of men, my dear Talleyrand. Your two letters which I received last evening have given me the greatest pleasure. How grateful I am that you should have thought of me and of Munich when you are in the most beautiful city in Germany, and hearing every day the famous Crescentini! I do as much for you, Your Excellency, but the merit is not the same. Every evening I express my regret that you are not here. M. de Canisy has announced the arrival of the Emperor in a week. Six days have passed, and I am hoping to see him in three days at the outside, and the Empress, Saturday next. My wife arrived day before yesterday, very anxious, as is her chaste spouse, to pay our court to Their Imperial Majesties, and to offer them all the honors of Munich. Lay me before the feet of the hero to whom I owe my present and future existence, and speak to him often of my respect, of my enthusiasm for his virtues, and of my heartiest and incessant gratitude. I hope that the coalition will soon grow tired of war; in any event, the lessons the Emperor has given it the last two months are of a nature to inspire disgust with it."

November 10, 1805, Napoleon had written to Josephine to leave Strassburg for Munich, stopping at Carlsruhe and Stuttgart. In this letter he had said:

" Be pleasant, but receive all their homages ; they owe
you everything, and you owe them nothing, except in
the way of politeness." He was not mistaken. This
trip of the Empress's through Germany was to be one
series of festivities and ovations. Before she left
Strassburg she received a visit from the Elector of
Baden, whose grandson, the hereditary prince, was,
the next year, to marry Mademoiselle Stéphanie de
Beauharnais, in spite of the opposition of his mother,
the Margravine. M. Massias, chargé d'affaires of
France at Baden, wrote to M. de Talleyrand, November 13 : " My Lord, His Most Serene Highness
the Elector, has returned with his family from
Strassburg, where he was most kindly received by
Her Majesty the Empress and Queen. He invited
her to honor Carlsruhe with her presence, and to
accept quarters in his castle when she should go to
join His Majesty the Emperor and King. Her Majesty the Empress seemed pleased with the invitation
and promised to accept it if circumstances should
permit. Before his departure, the Elector sent the
Prince Electoral to the Margravine his mother, to
beg her to come to Strassburg to pay her respects to
Her Majesty the Empress. She replied that when
the Empress of Austria was at Frankfort and the
Queen of Prussia at Darmstadt, she had not left
Carlsruhe to visit them, and that if the Empress of
the French should pass through that town, she should
gladly pay her all the respect and honor due her rank
and character."

Charles Frederick, Elector of Baden, was then seventy-seven years old. He had lost his son, and his heir was his grandson, Charles Frederick Louis, Prince Electoral, then twenty years old. The mother of this young Prince, the Margravine of Baden, entertained no friendly feelings towards France; and he was the brother-in-law of the Emperor of Russia, who had married his sister, and was at war with Napoleon. His other sister, Frederica Caroline, had married the Elector of Bavaria, and he was betrothed to the step-daughter of this Electress, the young Princess Augusta. They were said to be much attached to each other, but their plans of happiness were destined to be sacrificed to Napoleon's imperious will, for he proposed to arrange the matches of the German Princes as he did those of his own brothers. The Electoral Prince of Baden and the old Elector, his grandfather, far from complaining, only showed to the Emperor most unbounded devotion.

We may judge of their attitude and their respect by this despatch of M. Massias, chargé d'affaires at Carlsruhe, addressed to Talleyrand, under date of November 23, 1805: " My Lord M. de Canisy reached here from headquarters at four o'clock this morning, and asked me to inform His Most Serene Highness the Elector that he had been sent by Her Majesty the Empress, who meant to come to Carlsruhe within two or three days. I promised to do this as soon as possible, and told him that great preparations had been made to receive Her Majesty in a suitable manner.

The Elector, to whom I communicated this news at seven in the morning, expressed the greatest satisfaction, and he has sent me word that in order to carry out his desire to give Her Majesty a proper reception, he wishes me to send a message to Strassburg to find out, 1, the exact day when she will arrive; 2, the number of persons in her suite, and how many horses she will need; 3, whether she desires to eat alone or with the principal persons of her own and the Electoral court; 4, to ask to have at once sent an official of the court to arrange the quarters and the ceremonies according to the Empress's wishes. At Kehl, Her Majesty will find a carriage and eight horses from the Elector's stables. Similar relays will be placed as far as the frontiers of Würtemberg. Her Majesty will be escorted by the Electoral cavalry. She herself will determine the etiquette to be observed at the court of Carlsruhe during her entire stay.

"His Most Serene Highness, the Prince Electoral, will go as far as Rastadt to meet Her Majesty. The Margrave Louis will meet her outside of Carlsruhe at the head of his body-guard. Bells will be rung wherever Her Majesty passes. The city will be brilliantly illuminated."

November 28, at six in the evening, the Empress formally entered Carlsruhe, which was amid a general illumination. At the Mühburger gate stood an arch of triumph under which she passsd. In front of the arch was this inscription: *Pro Imperatrice Josephina*;

on the other, *Votiva lumina ardent.*   At the entrance
of the castle gate stood a little temple bearing this
inscription: *Salve.*   In the middle of the garden was
a larger temple, in which was to be seen on a pedestal
the Emperor's bust, crowned with laurels and surrounded with palms.   The inscription ran: *Maximis
triumphis sacrum,* — " Consecrated to the greatest triumphs."   On two pyramids was to be read this
motto: " Love leads to glory."   November 29, there
was a grand reception and concert in her honor at
the court.   At nine o'clock in the morning of the
30th, she left Carlsruhe for Stuttgart, after an affectionate farewell to the Electoral family.

At seven that evening she made a similar formal
entrance into the capital of Würtemberg, passing
under an arch of triumph bearing her name surmounted by an Imperial crown.   Soldiers lined the
way from the gate to the Elector's castle.   The main
street was decorated with Egyptian altars, and was
brilliantly illuminated, as was the castle also.   The
Elector, his wife, a daughter of the King of England,
and all the court received the Empress at the castle
door and escorted her to her rooms, where she supped.
The next day she sat on a platform at a state dinner
in the white hall.   Afterwards the company went to
the Opera House, where *Achilles* was given.   After
they had returned to the castle there were some fine
fireworks.   These festivities continued until December 2, when *Romeo and Juliet* was given for the first
time, and the 3d, at seven in the morning, Josephine,

after bidding the family farewell, pushed on towards Munich, while the troops presented arms and cannon were fired.

The Empress was not to stop between Stuttgart and Munich, but on her way she saw many places that had just become famous in the war. As she drew near them she looked at the plain where, a few days before, the enemy's army had marched out before Napoleon and laid down its arms. From Augsburg to Munich everything made her journey most brilliant; arches of triumph, bands of music so numerous that often their notes mingled with one another, wreaths of leaves, successive guards of honor who joined her, composed of the Royal Guard of Italy, at nearly every parting station. As a letter in the *Moniteur* says, " Enthusiasm succeeded to fear, the whirl of festivities to the lamentation of battle; all that had been said of the Empress's benevolence seemed still to make part of her suite, and it was as if the Angel of Peace had come to visit these countries."

The Empress reached Munich December 5, eight days after leaving Strassburg. A salute of a hundred guns welcomed her. In almost every street even houses were draped, windows adorned with transparent and complimentary figures; the illuminations of private houses rivalled in expense and splendor those of the public buildings. State carriages were sent out to the city gates for the Empress and her suite, but Josephine did not get into any of them;

she kept on her travelling dress. This did not mar
the brilliancy of the entrance, which was conspicuous
for universal joy. December 7, she went to the
theatre, where Mozart's *Don Juan* was given, and
she was greeted with sound of trumpets and the
applause of the audience.

The Empress had scarcely reached Munich before
people began to talk about an early marriage between
her son, Eugene de Beauharnais, and the Princess
Augusta, the daughter of the Elector, but it was still
merely a faint rumor. The French minister, M. Otto,
wrote December 16, 1805, the following despatch on
the subject to M. de Talleyrand: "My Lord, —
Immediately after the arrival of Her Majesty the
Empress, the rumor spread that His Most Serene
Highness Prince Eugene was likewise on his way
to Munich, there to conclude a marriage with Princess Augusta of Bavaria. The rumor has taken
such shape in the last few days that a foreign lady,
who has been most kindly received by the Electoral
family, ventured to ask the Elector if she might
congratulate him on so desirable a marriage. This
Prince replied that he knew nothing about it; that
his daughter was promised to the Prince of Baden;
that the two young people had the strongest attachment for each other; and that only day before yesterday the Electress had received from Baden a most
affectionate letter on the subject; and that he loved
his daughter too much to wish to oppose her inclina-
tions. This is the first time that mention has been

made at court of a matter which the public supposed
settled quite differently. The Electress was present
at this conversation, and corroborated everything
that was said concerning her brother's attachment
to the Princess. This anecdote, which comes to me
straight from the castle, proves that the Baden
marriage is not broken, as has been said at Carlsruhe, unless the Elector wished to conceal the truth
from the lady who questioned him on this subject.
Inquisitive people have tried to make out the true
state of things by watching the conduct of Her
Majesty the Empress and the persons of her suite.
The relations of the two courts are confined to
politeness on each side, to social attentions, in which
Her Majesty exhibits all her natural amiability, which
wins every heart. Beyond that, there prevails the
greatest reserve."

Maximilian Joseph, Elector of Bavaria, was born in
1756, and was then fifty years old. He had lost his
first wife, who had borne him one daughter, the Princess Augusta Louisa, who was born in 1788. His
second wife, Caroline, a Princess of Baden, sister of
the hereditary Prince of Baden, to whom the Princess Augusta was betrothed, was then thirty years old.
Though not handsome, she was not devoid of charm,
her figure was good, her manners were amiable and
dignified. The young Princess Augusta was the
ornament of the Munich court. She had all the
freshness, brilliancy, and charm of a young German
girl of eighteen. As for the Elector, he was an

attractive, sympathetic man, who combined frank joviality with tact, wit, and delicacy. He was tall; his face was noble and regular. He liked the French, and they liked him; it was in France that he had spent many years of his youth. As a younger prince of the house of Deux Ponts he became Elector only by the extinction of the branch of his family that reigned in Bavaria. In his early life he had no fortune. In the reign of Louis XVI. he served in the French armies, commanding the regiment of Alsace. At the court of Versailles, as in the garrison at Strassburg, he had left behind him a reputation of good manners and chivalrous gallantry. His soldiers, who adored him, called him Prince Max. At that time he might have married a daughter of the Prince of Condé, but his father and his uncle objected to this match, because, since he was not rich, he would doubtless have been compelled to make some of his daughters canonesses, and certain chapters would have been unwilling to receive them on account of their illegitimate descent from Louis XIV. and Madame de Montespan. He was fond of recalling the last years of the old régime in France, and spoke most affectionately of that country, in which he had been very happy. He was worshipped by his family, his servants, and his subjects. There was never a kinder, more amiable prince. Often he would stroll unaccompanied through the streets of Munich, going to the markets, bargain over grain, enter the shops, talking to every one, especially to the children, whom he urged to go to their schools. He was at once familiar and full of dignity, and he was as much respected as loved. There were many points of resemblance between his character and that of the Empress Josephine, and they had a very strong sympathy for each other.

The Empress was ailing during a good part of her stay in Munich, and whether for this reason or because Napoleon, who was always moving from place to place, did not get his letters regularly, he was for some time without news from his wife. He wrote to her from Brunn, December 10, 1805: "It is a long time since I have heard from you. Have the grand festivities of Baden, Stuttgart, and Munich made you forget the poor soldier who lives covered with mud, rain, and blood? I am going to leave soon for Vienna. They are trying to make peace. The Russians have left and are fleeing far from here, going back to Russia badly beaten and sorely humiliated. I am anxious to be with you once more. Good by, my dear; my eyes are well again."

Napoleon wrote again December 19, renewing his complaint: "Great Empress, not a letter from you since I left Strassburg. You have passed through Baden, Stuttgart, Munich, without writing us a word. That is not very kind or very affectionate! I am still at Brunn. The Russians are gone; we have a truce. In a few days I shall see what is to become of me. Deign from the giddy height of your grandeur to interest yourself a little in your slaves."

From Schönbrunn he wrote to Josephine, December 20, 1805 (29th Frimaire, Year XIV.): "I have your letter of the 25th [Frimaire]. I am sorry to hear that you are not well; that is not a good preparation for a journey of a hundred leagues at this time of year. I don't know what I shall do; that depends on what happens. I have no will of my own; I am waiting to see how matters settle themselves. Stay at Munich, amuse yourself; that is not hard, amid so many pleasant people, in such a charming country. I am tolerably busy. In a few days I shall have made up my mind. Good by, my dear."

December 26, peace was signed at Pressburg between France and Austria. The treaty gave to the Kingdom of Italy, Istria, Dalmatia, and Friuli; to the Elector of Würtemberg, the title of King and the Suabian territory; to the Elector of Baden, the Breisgau, Ortenau, and the town of Constanz; to the Elector of Bavaria, the title of King, the Vorarlburg, and the Tyrol. But Napoleon had determined that these indemnifications should be paid for by three marriages, — that of his step-son, Prince Eugene, with the daughter of the King of Bavaria; that of a relative of his wife, Mademoiselle Stéphanie de Beauharnais, with the hereditary Prince of Baden; that of his brother Jerome with the daughter of the King of Würtemberg.

Napoleon, accompanied by Murat, entered Munich beneath an arch of triumph, December 31, 1805, at a quarter to two in the morning. This entrance in the night, lit up by torches, was very impressive. The next day, January 1, 1806, a herald-at-arms, escorted by numerous horsemen, passed through the different quarters of the city, and read the following proclamation, after a flourish of drums and trumpets, while an immense crowd gathering in every street and crossway loudly applauded: "By the grace of God, the dignity of the sovereign of Bavaria having recovered its old-time splendor, and this State having resumed the rank it formerly held for the happiness of its subjects and the glory of the country, be it known that His Most Serene Highness the powerful Prince and Lord Maximilian Joseph is, by these presents, solemnly proclaimed King of Bavaria and of all the countries on it dependent. Long live and happily Maximilian Joseph, our very gracious King! Long live, and happily, Caroline, our very gracious Queen!" That evening the whole city was full of joy, and the next day was celebrated as a national festivity.

Napoleon, having recaptured the twenty-nine cannon and the twenty-one Bavarian flags that had fallen into the hands of the Austrians by the chances of war and the occupation of the country, had decided to restore to his faithful allies the trophies which they had valiantly defended and whose loss they mourned. In the morning of January 2, all citizen soldiery was under arms, lining the streets through which was to pass the procession and their precious burden. The cannon were placed on carts adorned with fes-

toons and garlands, each cart was drawn by two horses
belonging to the citizens; the houses were also decorated with different colored ribbons. All the young
people in the city accompanied these carts. The
students of the Royal College of Cadets carried the
flags. When the procession reached the grand square,
a large chorus, accompanied by a large band, sang a
song of thanksgiving and victory. The populace and
the soldiers mingled their cheers with this song.
The procession then made its way to the Church of
Our Lady, where a *Te Deum* was sung with great
solemnity.

January 4, Napoleon wrote to Prince Eugene:
"My Cousin, — Within twelve hours at the most, after
the receipt of this letter, you will start with all speed
for Munich. Try to get here as soon as possible, so
that you may be sure to see me. Leave your command in the hands of the general of division whom
you judge to be most capable and upright. You
need not bring a large suite. Start at once, and
incognito, and so avoid both dangers and delays.
Send me a messenger to give me twenty-four hours'
notice of your arrival." The Emperor had decreed
the marriage of his step-son with Princess Augusta
of Bavaria, but he had to go through certain formalities to overcome the objections of the Queen of
Bavaria, who wanted her brother, the hereditary
Prince of Baden, to marry the young Princess. Her
family pride and her inmost feelings revolted against
the admission into her family of a young man whom

she looked on as an upstart. She sought for pretexts
and devices to delay, if not to prevent, this alliance.
No one would have dared to say at Munich that the
Emperor's step-son was not great enough to marry
a king's daughter, but she found fictitious excuses: it
was said that the young Princess was ailing, and at
another time that she was suffering from a sprain.
Napoleon, who sometimes played the diplomatist,
feigned to believe in these alleged ailments, and said
that he would send his own surgeon to heal her. He
would gladly have returned speedily to Paris, where
he deemed that his presence was necessary, but his
Chamberlain, M. de Thiard, whom his previous negotiations had made familiar with the secrets of the Bavarian court, advised him to stay in Munich until the
marriage was absolutely settled. " Very well," said
the Emperor; "but do you know that while I am
here, your Faubourg Saint Germain is making a run
on my bank, and that my stay in Munich costs me
fifteen hundred thousand francs a day?" M. de
Thiard insisted, and dared to show Napoleon the
Queen of Bavaria's ever-present recollection of the
Duke of Enghien, which was the secret cause of her
aversion to the projected alliance. But this opposition could hold out for only a few hours; no one
then dared to brave the Imperial wrath. The Queen,
fearing that Napoleon's surgeon would discover that
the Princess's alleged sufferings were only an excuse,
yielded to the wishes of the hero of Austerlitz. The
marriage was announced even before the couple had

met. Everything was done in military fashion. Orders were issued that they should love, and they loved.

There is this to be said in behalf of Napoleon: that in the whole matter he made no use of harsh words or rough manners. He appeared in an attractive, not in a threatening light, and by dint of appearing smitten with the Queen of Bavaria, even aroused Josephine's jealousy.

Prince Eugene arrived, as commanded, January 10. He had the good fortune to please; but even if he had not pleased it would have made no difference. As soon as he reached Munich, after travelling day and night, the Emperor took possession of him and never left him. The Empress was still in bed when her son's arrival was announced. She was much moved, and began to cry at the thought that his first visit was not to her. A moment later, while she was still agitated, she saw the Emperor burst into her room, holding the young Prince by the hand, and pushing him forward as he exclaimed: "Here, Madame, is your great booby of a son whom I'm bringing to you." Josephine burst into tears, and pressed her son to her heart.

Eugene de Beauharnais, a French Prince, and Viceroy of Italy, was then twenty-four years old. Mademoiselle Avrillon, reader to the Empress, thus draws his portrait: "Prince Eugene's face, although in no way remarkable, was rather well than ill favored; he was of medium height, well proportioned, and stoutly made. He excelled in all sorts of corporeal exercises, and was an accomplished dancer. Kind, frank, simple in his manners, without haughtiness or reserve, he was courteous to every one; and although he was not devoid of deep feelings, his most striking trait was persistent good spirits. He was very fond of music, and sang very well, especially Italian songs, which all his family preferred. As he was young, he naturally paid many women attention, as I have often seen, but he always treated them with great respect." Napoleon was very fond of him, and looked upon him as his pupil, as his own child. He was delighted with the way Eugene discharged his duties as Viceroy, and when he received his despatches he exclaimed in the presence of several marshals, "I knew very well to whom I had entrusted my sword in Italy." He often gratified Josephine by saying, "Eugene may serve as a model to all the young men of his age."

The young Prince showed great tact and intelligence in his first meetings with his future wife. He sought every means of pleasing her, paid her assiduous court, as if their marriage was still undetermined. He was able to overcome the Princess's prejudices, for she had given her consent only at the last moment, as a victim sacrificed for reasons of state. Her father, the King, dreading the excitement of an interview, had written to her a letter, in which he set out all the advantages of the match desired by the Emperor, vaunted the good qualities of the young and dashing Viceroy of Italy, and to prove that it was a brilliant match, revealed to her what was then unknown, that at Pressburg the Austrian Minister had offered to Napoleon for his step-son the hand of one of their Archduchesses. "Consider, dear Augusta, that a refusal would make the Emperor as much the enemy as he has been hitherto the friend of our house." And he ended his letter with a last appeal to his daughter's patriotic devotion. The young Princess replied by writing: "I place my fate in your hands; however cruel it may be, it will be softened by the knowledge that I am sacrificed for my father, my family, and my country. On her knees your daughter prays for your blessing; it will aid me to bear my sad lot with resignation." The girl's unhappiness soon gave way to joy. The Empress had spoken to her most warmly of Eugene's qualities, his bravery, loyalty, and gallantry, and the Princess found out that Josephine was right. She forgot her cousin, the Prince of Baden, fell instantaneously in love with Eugene, and this marriage for reasons of state turned out to be a love match. It was celebrated with great pomp in the Royal Chapel, January 14, four days after the bridegroom's arrival at Munich. The Emperor adopted Prince Eugene, and gave him in the marriage contract the name of Napoleon Eugene of France. This adoption wrought a great change in their correspondence; previously the Emperor when he wrote to the Viceroy addressed him as, "My Cousin"; henceforth he always wrote,

"My Son." Madame Murat, who was then at Munich, was pained to see that the new Vice-Queen, as wife of the Emperor's adopted son, took precedence of her at all ceremonies, and she feigned an illness to avoid what seemed to her an affront.

On her wedding day the Princess charmed every one by her grace. She was tall, well shaped, with the figure of a nymph, and a face in which sweetness was blended with dignity. Moreover, she was very well educated, was pious and modest, and the possessor of all the family virtues. In short, she was a model wife and mother. She wrote to the Emperor a letter of thanks that touched him. He answered it, January 27: "My Daughter, — Your letter is as amiable as you are yourself. My feelings for you will only grow from day to day; this I know from my pleasure in recalling your fine qualities, and from the need I feel for your frequent assurance that you are satisfied with every one and happy with your husband. Amid all I have to do, nothing will be dearer to me than the chance to assure my children's happiness. Be sure, Augusta, that I love you like a father, and that I count on a daughter's affection for me. Travel slowly, and be careful in the new climate when you get there, and take plenty of rest."

January 21, Prince Eugene left Munich with his young wife for Milan. The next day M. Otto, the French Minister, wrote to M. de Talleyrand: "His Imperial Highness Prince Eugene left yesterday morning with his young wife. The King escorted them to their carriage with every indication of affection. It was noticed that in taking leave of the Prince he embraced him several times. The separation cost the Princess some tears. Their departure was announced by firing a hundred guns. The best wishes of all good Bavarians accompanied the pair. The stay of the French court at Munich has left the deepest and most lasting impression. The Emperor's greatness and power were known, but the effect of his extreme kindness and magnificence had to be seen at a closer view to be appreciated. I feel able to assure His Majesty that the Bavarian nation will always be his faithful and devoted allies. So many happy memories are attached to this period of our history that His Majesty can flatter himself that he has accomplished the most difficult of all conquests, — that of the love of the people who have witnessed his successes."

While the Viceroy and Vice-Queen of Italy were proceeding towards Milan, the Emperor and the Empress were on their way to France, stopping at Stuttgart and Carlsruhe, where they were warmly greeted. January 20, 1806, they found an arch of triumph built on a Roman model at Entzberg, in Baden. It bore this inscription: *Imperatori Napoleoni triumphatori augusto.* The bas-relief represented the capture of Ulm and the delivery of the keys of Vienna. Columns and obelisks had been erected at Carlsruhe with these inscriptions: *Hostium victori. — Patriam servavit. — Pacem restituit.* In front of the castle had been built a temple of Peace. At the French frontier stood an arch of triumph with this inscription : *Heroi reduci Galliæ plaudunt,* — " Gaul applauds the returning hero." The bas-reliefs represented the battle of Austerlitz and the interview between the two Emperors. In the night of January 26, Napoleon and Josephine were back at the Tuileries. Prince Eugene's marriage put a happy ending to the campaign just finished. To create a king and to give to his step-son the hand of this king's daughter was a stroke of imagination on Napoleon's part that did honor to his omnipotence. The accounts of the triumphal festivities in Munich, Stuttgart, and Carlsruhe followed close upon the bulletins announcing the victories of the Grand Army, and produced a great impression in both Germany and France.

XVII.

NAPOLEON arranged his return with the utmost skill. His prolonged stay at Munich kept alive the impatience of the Parisians for his return, and meanwhile there was a constant stream of flattery and enthusiasm. January 1, 1806, had just put an end to the Republican calendar, which had existed for thirteen years, three months, and a few days. The Year XIV. found itself suddenly interrupted by the return to the Gregorian calendar. Thus vanished the last trace of the Republic. The same day the new year was inaugurated with a patriotic ceremony. The Tribune carried with great solemnity to the Senate the forty-four Russian and Austrian flags which the hero of Austerlitz had entrusted to its care. All the houses in the streets through which the procession was to pass were decorated. In front of many of them were to be seen the Emperor's bust crowned with laurels. The ever lyrical *Moniteur* said: " At the sight of these noble spoils, these startling proofs of the heroism of the French army, all hearts seemed to meet in a common feeling of admiration and grati-

tude which was but faintly expressed by the shouts
issuing from the crowd and from every window, of
'Long live the Emperor!' 'Hurrah for the Grand
Army!' 'Victory, victory!' 'Long live the Emperor!' It was in this way that the people of Paris,
of all classes, of both sexes, of all ages, manifested
in the most vivid and unanimous way their devotion and gratitude to His Majesty and his victorious
armies."

One Tribune, M. Joubert, exclaimed: "Is not Napoleon the man of history, the man of all ages? May
we not say that there is something supernatural in
him, since it is true that God disposes of the fate of
empires, and that Napoleon the Great gladly submits
everything to Providence and ascribes everything to
religion?" In their official enthusiasm the Tribunes,
as accomplished courtiers, made one motion after
another. One proposed that the Emperor on his
return should receive triumphal honors, like those of
ancient Rome, and the city of Paris should go to
meet him. Another suggested that the sword which
he wore at the battle of Austerlitz should be solemnly
consecrated and placed in some public monument.
Another expressed a desire that on one of the principal places in the city a column should be set up,
bearing the Emperor's statue, with this inscription:
" To Napoleon the Great, the grateful country." The
Senate, with similar zeal, hastened to carry out the
plan by a decree.

The Parisians, who always worship success of monarchs, generals, or artists, then felt the wildest admiration for the victorious Napoleon. The *Moniteur* was full of dithyrambic eulogies, in prose and verse. Flattery appeared as it had never appeared before. Bishops became conspicuous for their ardent praise; some phrases from their charges may be quoted. Thus the Bishop of Versailles said: "God says: 'No one shall resist him whom I have clothed with a special mission to re-establish my worship, to lead my chosen people; no one will resist him because I am with him, and he is with me. *Deus cum eo.*'"

The Bishop of Bayonne: "Behold our enemies once more defeated. Let incredulity be silent and the atheist confounded. Our annals will be the story of the wonders of Providence. . . . Widows, cease to bemoan the loss of a loved husband; you are not left alone; you belong to the country. Orphans, you have found another father; Napoleon has adopted you."

The Bishop of Rennes: "Did not those kings know, or did they forget in their delirium, that the French nation is now the first nation in the world? Did they not know that the man who governs it is the most astounding man in the world, and the greatest warrior history has ever known?"

The Bishop of Coutances: "The Almighty wishes Napoleon to attain this new glory and hence impresses upon him a sort of divine character. He wishes him to attain it on the same day and at the same hour that the Sovereign Pontiff, one year ago, poured on his brow the holy oil."

The Bishop of Montpellier: "Let the earth be shaken, and the mountains cast into the bosom of the seas; our God blesses the views, the wisdom, the talents, and the courage of our august monarch."

The Emperor, in dividing the flags which he had captured from Russia and Austria, had given fifty-four to the Senate, eight to the Tribunes, eight to the city of Paris, and fifty to the church of Notre Dame, which he wished to adorn with his trophies as the Marshal of Luxembourg had done in the reign of Louis XIV. The day when these fifty flags were given to the Cathedral the Cardinal Archbishop of France said, "O Posterity, when you read our history you will imagine that you are reading anew the fall of the walls of Jericho, and listening to the miraculous deeds of Joshua, David, and Judas Maccabæus. *Benedictus Dominus qui facit mirabilia solus.* . . . God of Marengo, you declare yourself the God of Auster-litz; and the German eagle, the Russian eagle, abandoned by you, became the prey of the French eagle, which you never cease to protect." A singular piece of flattery this, to call the Creator of the universe — of which this earth is not a millionth part — the God of a village, because near this village a man has wrought the death of many other men!

Paris seemed to have recovered its ardor of the first days of the Revolution in order to salute the triumphant hero. The day of his arrival, January 27, 1806, the managers of the bank, anxious that his presence should be the signal for public prosperity,

ordered the resumption of specie payments. The
Opera celebrated his return and that of the Empress
by a grand performance which took place February 4.
The bills announced the *Prétendus* and a divertisement. The public knew that this divertisement was
to be a sort of apotheosis in honor of the Imperial
glories. The house was crowded, and the passages
themselves were crammed by the enthusiastic crowd.
During the second act of the *Prétendus* there was
great excitement over the arrival of Napoleon and
Josephine. Applause resounded from every side.
Ladies distributed laurel branches, which all the
spectators waved, shouting, " Long live the Emperor!" Musicians played the chorus of the *Caravan*.
Meanwhile, the scenery of the *Prétendus* disappeared,
and applause began over the magnificent decorations
that took its place. It was a semicircular enclosure
with trophies forming a colonnade showing the course
of the Seine from the Pont Neuf to the western limit
of Paris, showing the Louvre, which Napoleon had
promised to complete, the Pont des Arts, the Palais
de la Monnaie, the Tuileries, and in the misty distance the Champs Elysées overlooking this fine view.
The interior of the enclosure was adorned with garlands and crowded with people, awaiting the return
of the Grand Army. This appeared with a military
march: the sappers in front with their axes and
white aprons; the grenadiers of the Guard with
their high fur caps; the artillerymen with their black
caps; the dragoons with their double armor; the

Mamelukes with their scimetars. Then came the
Bavarians, worthy comrades of Napoleon's soldiers.
The people applauded their defenders. Pupils of
the military schools sprang into the ranks to welcome their fathers, while old men embraced their
children. A general chorus was heard. Then a
warrior came to the front of the stage and celebrated
in a hymn the marvels of the campaign of Austerlitz.
This was followed by a ballet of foreign nations, in
which joined French peasants and girls in the dress
of their provinces, from Caux and Alsace, Provence,
Béarn, Auvergne, and the Alps. After the dances
came songs, — the words by Esménard, author of the
Navigation, the music by Stobelt. The marches,
evolutions, and ballet were arranged by Gardel. The
principal stanzas were sung by the most distinguished
artists, Lainez, Laïs, Madame Armand, Madame
Branchu. When it was all over, the Emperor and
the Empress withdrew amid applause, and there was
sung the *Vivat* of Abbé Rose which had made such
a success at Notre Dame on Coronation Day, and was
as warmly applauded at the Opera as it had been in
the Cathedral.

XVIII.

THE MARRIAGE OF THE PRINCE OF BADEN.

IF anything is capable of proving the admiration, terror, and fascination that the hero of Austerlitz exercised over Europe, and especially over Germany, in 1806, it is certainly the marriage of the hereditary Prince of Baden with Mademoiselle Stéphanie de Beauharnais. It was a curious sight! A Prince belonging to one of the oldest and most illustrious families in the world, whose three sisters had married, one, the Emperor of Russia; another, the King of Sweden; the third, the King of Bavaria; a Prince who might have allied himself with the oldest reigning houses had come to regard as an honor a marriage with the plain daughter of a French senator, — a girl not united by any ties of blood with Napoleon, but only by adoption; that is to say, by a whim. One might have supposed that the Empire of the new Charlemagne was centuries old, and the German Princes bowed before it like devoted vassals before their suzerain. What a vast power he had attained, and how easily he could have kept it, if he had limited his ambition, and put bounds to his power, and had not asked of docile Germany more than it could give him!

The marriage of Mademoiselle Stéphanie de Beauharnais with the hereditary Prince of Baden was at first warmly opposed by the Margravine, this Prince's mother. M. Massias, French chargé d'affaires at Baden, had written on this matter to M. de Talleyrand, Minister of Foreign Affairs, January 6, 1806: " My Lord, — For some days there has been a rumor quietly circulating among the principal persons of the court of Carlsruhe that the object of M. de Thiard's last journey was to arrange the marriage of the Electoral Prince of Baden with the daughter of Senator Beauharnais. Last evening arrived a messenger from the Electress of Bavaria for the Margravine, the mother of this Prince. I have learned by chance the contents of this missive to his mother. She says substantially that she has had a talk of more than an hour with the Emperor Napoleon; that His Majesty promised that the marriage of the Electoral Prince of Baden with Mademoiselle Beauharnais should never take place without the consent of the Margravine; and in case of her refusal of this consent, he would only reserve to himself the right of being consulted on the choice of the wife to be given to this young Prince. . . . The Electoral Prince called on his mother after she had received this despatch, and was with her alone for two hours; he came away in great dejection. When he got to his grandfather's, he exclaimed, involuntarily, ' That woman is lost; she wants to ruin herself!' "

The chargé d'affaires ended his letter with this sketch of the Margravine: " I have known the Margravine for six years, and I think I can say that if she judges the match in question opposed to the pride inspired by the first ideas of her education, no persuasion can move her. She possesses to a very marked degree the confident obstinacy of feeble and timid spirits. She does not dare to dismiss an incompetent footman; and when she has once made up her mind, which is only possible in matters about which her opinions are rigidly formed, neither force nor persuasion can modify her. That is my reading of her character, and I think it the true one."

The more the Margravine opposed this match which the Emperor had suggested, the more the young Prince of Baden and his grandfather, the Elector, desired it. M. Massias wrote again to M. de Talleyrand, January 9, 1806: " His Most Serene Highness, the Prince Electoral of Baden, is to leave tomorrow for Ulm and Augsburg, to invite, in his grandfather's name, His Majesty the Emperor and King to honor Carlsruhe with his presence, and to stay at the castle on his way back to France. But, he tells me himself, the main object of his journey is to convince His Majesty that the marriage of which I had the honor to speak to Your Excellency in my last letter, is far from opposing his desires ; and he hopes to dissipate without difficulty the doubts which it has been sought to raise regarding this in the mind of His Majesty, for whom he always manifested a profound devotion and a sincere attachment."

What was the origin of this young girl whose hand was thus sought by the hereditary Prince of Baden? The Marquis of Beauharnais, the father of the Viscount of Beauharnais, the first husband of the Empress Josephine, had a brother, Count Claude de Beauharnais, who was a commodore, and married Mademoiselle Fanny Mouchard. Countess Fanny, a friend of Dorat and Cubières, took much interest in literature and wrote many novels. She was a blue-stocking, and it was about her that Lebrun wrote the malicious epigram: —

> " Eglé, fair and a poetess, has then two slight faults:
> She makes her face and does not make her verses."

By her marriage with Count Claude de Beauharnais, the Countess Fanny (born in 1738, died in 1813) had one son, named Claude after his father, who married the daughter of the Count of Lezay-Marnésia. They had a daughter, Stéphanie de Beauharnais, born August 28, 1789, who was adopted by Napoleon, married the hereditary Prince of Baden, became the grandduchess of this country, and died in 1860, much loved by her family and the people of Baden. Her father, Claude de Beauharnais, was a senator in the Empire, a peer of France at the Restoration, and died in 1819.

During the childhood of Mademoiselle Stéphanie de Beauharnais no one would have predicted the lofty destiny that awaited her. Her father, having lost his wife, entrusted her to a pious old aunt, who lived at Montauban, and there she remained in obscurity until it occurred to her uncle, M. de Lezay-Marnésia, to take her to Paris, and present her to the wife of the First Consul. Josephine, her cousin once removed, thought her pretty and bright, became very fond of her, and sent her to finish her education at Madame Campan's boarding-school at Saint Germain. Madame Campan wrote to Madame Louis about her young pupil as follows: "I am certainly surprised at the way Mademoiselle Stéphanie has turned out since she returned from Saint Leu. She may become a very charming woman, but not if she stays at Saint Cloud. Royal palaces have never been good schools; pleasures, the taste for excitement and flattery, corrupt not merely those who are young, but even those who go there already matured, unless they are protected by the highest principles. If you have the power, do try to let me keep Stéphanie until she marries; you will thereby render her a great service, and to me, too; for the result will condemn me in the eyes of the Emperor, who will say, with a sharp glance, 'That's very bad'; and will not have time to ascertain the real reason. I can assure you that in a year she will be very charming, if I can only keep my hand on her."

In the same letter Madame Campan thus describes her pupil's character: "It is a curious compound of ease at learning, self-love, emulation, idleness, amiability, clear-mindedness, levity, haughtiness, and piety. There are a good many qualities to dispose of, and on this proper arrangement depends her happiness or unhappiness, and my success or failure."

In personal appearance Mademoiselle de Beauharnais was very charming; she had a good figure, an expressive countenance, a brilliant complexion, bright blue eyes, light hair, and an agreeable voice. Moreover, her manners were good, she had keen mother wit, much gaiety and enthusiasm, and was, in short, a very attractive young person.

The Emperor had a sort of infatuation for her, and treated her with exceptional kindness that did not fail to excite comment. Although her father was still living, he decided to adopt her, and this was thought a singular thing to do. The young Stéphanie became an Imperial Highness and took precedence of the Emperor's sisters, while her father was merely one of the herd of senators. In the decree of March 3, 1806, it was said: "Our intention being that our daughter the Princess Stéphanie Napoleon, shall enjoy all the prerogatives due to her rank; at receptions, festivities, and at table she shall sit at our side, and in our absence she shall take her place at the right of Her Majesty the Empress." Josephine possibly thought that her young relative was a little too well treated by the Emperor, and that his feelings for her were not wholly paternal. Evil tongues asserted that Napoleon was in love with his adopted daughter, but in spite of those malicious insinuations, no serious charge can be brought against her innocence. Her betrothed, the Prince of Baden, was madly in love with her, and showed by his conduct that it was he who was making a fine marriage.

Mademoiselle de Beauharnais from the moment that she assumed the name of Napoleon imagined that nothing was too good for her. It was only by con-descension that she married the son of an elector, for she was never tired of saying, to her adopted father's great delight, that an emperor's daughter could marry either a king or a king's son.

The marriage was celebrated with great pomp in the chapel of the Palace of the Tuileries, April 8, 1806, at eight in the evening. The witnesses for the bridegroom were the Crown Prince of Bavaria, Baron de Gueusau, and M. de Dalberg; those of the bride were M. de Talleyrand, M. de Champagny, and M. de Ségur. The procession went from the grand apartments to the chapel in the following order: the Empress, preceded by the officers of the Princesses, accompanied by the Prince of Baden, the Princesses, and the Crown Prince of Bavaria, and followed by the ladies of her household and of those of the Princesses; the Emperor, conducting the bride, and preceded by the officers of the Princes, his own officers, the Grand Dignitaries of the Empire, the Ministers, the High Officers of the Crown, and followed by the colonel-general of the guard on duty. At the chapel door the clergy received Napo-leon and Josephine beneath a canopy, and they took their places on two small thrones in front of the altar, while the Prince of Baden and the bride took their places on two stools at the foot of its steps. The ceremony began with the blessing of thirteen pieces of gold which the Cardinal Caprara, Legate *a latere*, gave to the Prince of Baden, who presented them to his bride. The Cardinal gave them the nuptial blessing. Meanwhile Monsignor Charier-Lavoche, Bishop of Versailles, the Emperor's First Almoner, and Monsignor de Broglie, Bishop of Acqui, his Almoner in Ordinary, were holding a canopy of silver brocade over the head of the kneeling Prince and Princess. These two prelates wore a camail and rochet. Cardinal Caprara and his assistant, Monsignor de Rohan, the Empress's Almoner, wore the golden cape.

During the ceremony, which lasted about an hour, the front of the Tuileries and the garden were illuminated. At nine o'clock there were fireworks on the Place de la Concorde, which the Emperor and Empress watched from the balcony of the Hall of the Marshals. As they appeared on the balcony with the young people, they were greeted with warm applause from the dense crowd in the garden. The Empress, who was clad in a dress embroidered with gold, wore on her head, besides the Imperial crown, a million francs' worth of pearls. Princess Stéphanie was charming in her white tulle dress, with silver stars, trimmed with orange flowers, and her diamond frontlet. After the fireworks came a concert and ballet in the Hall of the Marshals. But little attention was paid to the concert, although silence prevailed; the ballet, which was rendered by the best dancers from the Opera, was very successful. Then

the company went to the Gallery of Diana, where
tables had been set for two hundred ladies, and a
magnificent supper was served. The grace and
distinction of the bride aroused general admiration.
Her father, Senator Beauharnais, kept silence and
wept for joy.

Never had the court been more dazzling with its
glittering uniforms, gorgeous dresses, and sumptuous
pomp. The Emperor in his gala dress, the Empress
in her Imperial splendor, the Princesses vying in
luxury, the new Queen of Naples staggering under
her load of precious stones, the Princess Louis covered
with turquoises set in diamonds, Princess Caroline
Murat decked with a thousand rubies, Princess Pauline with all the Borghese diamonds besides her own,
the ambassadors, grand dignitaries, marshals, generals, with their coats covered with gold and decorations,
the chamberlains in red, the master of ceremonies
in violet, the masters of the hounds in green, the
equerries in blue, all the ladies in dresses with long
trains; the two fashionable women, Madame Maret
and Madame Savary, who each spent fifty thousand
francs a year in dress; Madame de Canisy, tall, black-
haired, bright-eyed, with her aquiline nose and her
impressive air; Madame Lannes, with her gentle face
like one of Raphael's Madonnas; Madame Duchâtel,
fair, with blue eyes; and that proud duchess of the
Faubourg Saint Germain, a lady of the palace in
spite of herself, the Duchess of Chevreuse, who, if
not the most beautiful woman there, had perhaps the

grandest air. It was a most animated festivity, with its flowers, lights, and splendor. The Hall of the Marshals was radiant with its military portraits, its chandeliers, and air of triumph. . . . Now consider the ruins of this palace of Cæsar, this Olympus of Jupiter, this sanctuary of glory, majesty, and dominion. See and reflect! Nothing is left of all that pomp and grandeur! The proudest buildings have vanished! Such is the end of human splendor!

XIX.

AT the beginning of 1804, Napoleon regarded himself the absolute master of fortune. His twofold title of Emperor of the French and King of Italy no longer sufficed him; he yearned for that of Emperor of the West. He created kings, grand dukes, sovereign princes. He made his brother Joseph King of the Two Sicilies; his brother-in-law Murat Grand Duke of Berg and Cleves; his sister Pauline Princess of Guastalla; he conferred the principality of Massa upon his sister Elisa, who was already in possession of the Duchy of Lucca; his Minister of Foreign Affairs, Talleyrand, became Prince of Benevento; his Major-General, Berthier, Prince of Neufchâtel; and his brother Joseph's brother-in-law, Bernadotte, Prince of Ponte Corvo. He also elevated members of his wife's family as well as of his own to high positions. Josephine's son was Viceroy and son-in-law of a king. Josephine's daughter was about to become a queen.

France, which, fourteen years before, had wanted to convert every monarchy into a republic, was now endeavoring to turn the oldest republics into monarchies. The illustrious republics of Genoa and Venice had become an integral part, the one of the French Empire, the other of the Kingdom of Italy. The Batavian Republic was about to be transformed into the Kingdom of Holland. When it became known in Paris that this new kingdom was to be created by the Emperor's will, people wondered who was to fill the throne; some were betting on Louis Bonaparte; others on his brother Jerome; still others on Murat. The Emperor, however, had settled the question, and without even consulting him, had decided that Louis was to be King of Holland.

This new monarch, who was born September 2, 1778, was then twenty-seven years old. Four years before he had married Josephine's daughter, Hortense de Beauharnais, but the marriage had been an unhappy one. As he himself wrote, his marriage was celebrated in sadness. The author of a very remarkable study, *Holland and King Louis*, M. Albert Réville, says with great truth: "Like Hortense, Louis had literary tastes; but there the resemblance ceases. It was not that there was nothing romantic in Hortense's character; she was among the first to become interested in the Middle Ages, the Gothic revival, the imitation of the troubadours; but her romanticism was wholly different from that of her husband. Her ideal was, perhaps, a young and handsome soldier, pensive when away from the lady of his thoughts, but not when in her company." M. Réville

goes on: "Such a character could not understand the
sensitiveness, the shrinking, morbid melancholy of
the husband thrust upon her. Her gaiety, her devotion to pleasure, the frivolity of her talk, could only
pain more and more a man of a gloomy temperament,
who took the greatest care of his health, who fretted
himself over the most trivial details, and whose distrust amounted to injustice."

Hortense was expansive, merry, ardent, enthusiastic, young in heart and mind, a thoroughly open
nature. Her husband, on the other hand, was of a
morose, sombre, melancholy, reserved nature.   In
spite of her superior intelligence Hortense had a sort
of childlike air; but Louis, though young in years,
had the character and appearance of an old man. As
much as Hortense loved liberty, her suspicious husband wished to hold firmly the reins of conjugal authority. He was prematurely afflicted with various
infirmities, almost always morbidly nervous and im-
pressionable, disposed to take a dark view of everything, and bore no resemblance to the type of hero
which Hortense had imagined. Moreover, the unhappy husband endured a hidden anguish which he
had to conceal from every one and which tortured his
heart; he imagined that his rival with his wife was
his own brother, Napoleon. Thiers says in discuss-
ing this delicate subject: "Louis, ill, puffed-up with
pride, assuming virtue and really upright, pretended
that he was sacrificed to the infamous necessity of
covering, by his marriage, the weakness of Hortense

THE QUEEN OF HOLLAND AND NAPOLEON III

de Beauharnais for Napoleon, — an odious calumny, invented by the émigrés, spread abroad in a thousand pamphlets, about which Louis did wrong to betray such anxiety that he seemed to believe it himself."

In a word, there existed between husband and wife a real incompatibility of temper, and the constraint of their position only added to the mutual repulsion which they felt for each other in private, though they did not dare confess it through fear of Napoleon's reproaches. They were married January 4, 1802, and had a son born the next October, whom their enemies asserted was the son of the Emperor, and the greater the interest and affection the Emperor showed to this child, the more freely were calumnies circulated. Louis Bonaparte imagined his honor tainted, and suffered tortures.

As for Hortense, she was unhappy, but she had consolations. Her mother's love, the society of her old schoolmates, her interest in art, worldly successes, the distractions of Paris life, made her forget some of her domestic troubles. The thought of leaving that congenial spot to live alone with her husband in the cold dampness of Holland filled her with gloom. She did not care for a throne, for she felt that a royal palace would be for her nothing but a prison.

Louis, too, seemed devoid of ambition for the crown that was held before him. Annoyed at not being consulted in the negotiations on which depended his call to the throne, he maintained a passive attitude. But as he was accustomed to comply with every wish of a brother who had taken charge of his education, and thereby acquired special authority over him, he invariably obeyed his orders. The Batavian deputation, of which the most important member was Admiral Verhuel, had just arrived in Paris, and with it the Emperor was settling the fate of Holland. Baron Ducasse, in an interesting paper in the *Revue Historique* for February, 1880, has recounted all the unfortunate Louis Bonaparte's attempts to escape having royalty forced upon him. He gave as a pretext for his reluctance, the rights of the old Stadtholder. The Batavian deputation in reply announced to him the death of that official. "The hereditary Prince," they said, "has received in compensation Fulda; hence you can have no reasonable objection. We come, in accordance with the votes of nine-tenths of the nation, to beg of you to ally your fate with ours, and to prevent our falling into other hands." Napoleon used even plainer language. He declared to his brother without beating the bush that he had accepted for him, and that, even if he had not consulted him, a subject could not refuse obedience.

A few days later, Talleyrand, the Minister of Foreign Affairs, went to Saint Cloud and read to Louis and Hortense the treaty with Holland, and the constitution of that country. It was of no use for the King to say that he could not judge such important documents from a simple reading, he was not granted a moment's reflection. In vain he pleaded his health, which could not fail to suffer from the damp climate of Holland. Napoleon was inflexible, and said, "It is better to die on a throne than to live a French Prince." There was nothing for him to do but to give his consent.

The new King's proclamation was delivered at the Palace of the Tuileries in the Throne Room, June 5, 1806. Early in the same day, the Emperor had formally received Mahib Effendi, Ambassador of the Sultan Selim. The Oriental diplomatist had greeted him as "the first and greatest of Christian monarchs, the bright star of glory of the western nations, the one who held in a firm hand the sword of valor and the sceptre of justice." Napoleon had replied: "Whatever good or bad fortune may befall the Ottomans will be fortunate or unfortunate for France. Report, I beg of you, my words to the Sultan Selim. Bid him never to forget that my enemies, who are also his, would like to get at him. He has nothing to fear from me; united with me, he need not fear the power of any of his enemies." When the audience was over, the Ambassador made three deep bows and withdrew, but stopped in the next room, where the presents of the Grand Porte were set out on a table; they consisted of an aigret of diamonds, and a costly box set with gems and adorned with the monogram of the Sultan. Mahib Effendi, after offering the presents to the Emperor, showed him those sent to the Empress. They were a pearl necklace, perfumes, and Oriental stuffs. Napoleon examined them, and then went to the window to see some superbly har-

nessed Arabian horses, presented to him in the name
of the Sultan.

The proclamation of the King of Holland was read
a few moments later. Admiral Verhuel took the
floor and began to speak of the happiness assured to
his country when it should have made fast the ties
that bound it to the "immense and immortal Empire." The Emperor said to the Dutch representatives: "France has been so generous as to renounce
all the rights over you which were given it by the
events of the war, but I cannot confide the fortresses
that guard my northern frontiers to any unfaithful
or even uncertain hands. Representatives of the
Batavian people, I grant the prayer you present to
me, and proclaim Prince Louis King of Holland."
Then turning to his brother, he said: "You, Prince,
reign over this people; their fathers acquired their
independence only by the constant aid of France.
Since then Holland was the ally of England; it was
conquered; and still owes its existence to us. She
will owe to us the kings who protect its laws, its lib-
erties, its religion! But do not ever cease to be a
Frenchman. The dignity of Constable of the Empire
will ever belong to you and to your descendants; it
will define for you your duties towards me and the
importance I attach to the guard of the fortresses
protecting the north of my states, which I confide to
you. Prince, maintain among your troops that spirit
which I have seen in them on the field of battle.
Encourage in your new subjects the feelings of union

and love which they ought always to have for France. Be the terror of evil-doers and the father of the upright; that is the character of a great king."

The vassalage of the new monarch was thus definitely established; he remained Constable of the Empire; he was ordered to be French and not Dutch. His first duties were to the Emperor, his brother and suzerain. He respectfully approached the throne, and said with evident emotion: "Sire, I have made it my highest ambition to sacrifice my life to Your Majesty's service. I have made my happiness consist in admiring all those qualities which make you so dear to those who, like me, have so often witnessed the power and the effects of your genius; I may then be permitted to express my regrets in leaving, but my life and my wishes belong to you. I shall go to reign over Holland, since that nation desires it and Your Majesty commands it. I shall be proud to reign over it; but, however glorious may be the career thus opened to me, the assurance of Your Majesty's constant protection, the love and patriotism of my new subjects, can alone inspire me with the hope of healing the wounds of the many wars and events that have crowded into a few years." After the royal speech the usher threw open the door, and as in the time of Louis XIV., at the acceptation of the Spanish accession, the new King was announced to the assembled crowd.

As M. Albert Réville says, no one in France regretted the Batavian Republic when it was stricken from the roll of history by the will of a despot; or, rather, the Parisians, in their occasionally exaggerated infatuation, fancied that the Dutch would be overjoyed to have a French court.

The next day, after breakfast, the Emperor was playing with the new King's oldest son, the little Napoleon, who was only three years and a half old, but was very bright for his age, and already knew by heart La Fontaine's fables. The Emperor made him recite the fable about the frogs who wanted a king, and listened to it, laughing loudly. He pinched the Queen's ear, and asked her, "What do you say to that, Hortense?" The allusions to the poor king and to his poor people were only too clear. The melancholy monarch, or rather, the crowned monarch, was to be, according to the Emperor's plan, a mere tool in the hands of his powerful brother. He was condemned to discharge the functions of receiver of dues and of recruiting officer in the Emperor's service. He had a presentiment of this degraded position, and took his departure with much anxiety.

For Hortense, leaving was sadder. No exile ever turned towards foreign parts with heavier sorrow. Her diadem was a crown of thorns. Her mother's grief augmented her own. Without her children, Josephine, naturally unambitious, found no consolation in the thought that her son was a Viceroy, her daughter a Queen. Before she left Paris Hortense, in terror before the thought that the Emperor would no longer be near to defend her, told her all her domestic unhappiness, and said that if her husband treated her too ill, she would abandon her throne for a convent.

Nevertheless she had to obey. June 15, 1806, Louis started from Saint Leu to go to his kingdom. He was accompanied by his wife and his two sons, the elder, Charles Napoleon, who died in Holland the 5th of the next May, and the other, Louis Napoleon, who died at Forte, in 1831, in the insurrection of the States of the Church against the Pope. His third son, later Napoleon III., was born in 1808. The new King entered The Hague June 23, 1806. He countermanded a body of French troops which the Emperor had designed for his escort at his entrance into the capital, being unwilling to appear before his subjects as a sovereign imposed upon them by actual force. "You may be sure," he said to them, "that from the moment I set foot on the soil of this kingdom, I became a Dutchman." The same day General Dupont Chaumont, French Minister at The Hague, wrote to Prince Talleyrand: "To-day, June 23, His Majesty made his formal entrance into his capital. He went to the Assembly where he recieved the oath of the representatives of the people and made a speech which was much applauded. The French camp obtained permission from the Governor of the Palace to surprise Their Majesties by fireworks and military music. These festivities naturally put a stop to all business, except for His Majesty, who finds time to examine and decide the most urgent

matters, the ease with which he works greatly sur-
prising a nation unaccustomed to such activity.
Already the King and Queen are spoken of most
enthusiastically by those who have had the honor to
be presented to Their Majesties. The satisfaction
will be general, when many shall have had the opportunity to approach the throne."

In spite of the optimisms of this despatch, the new
King was to have an unhappy reign. His loyal and
upright intentions were to be shattered against the
inflexible will of his formidable brother. Louis was
a just man and sincerely devoted to his people. He
was called, and is still called, " the good King Louis ";
but the Emperor, who ironically reproached him with
trying to win the affection of shopkeepers, was to
write to him in 1807: " A monarch who is called a
good king, is a king that's ruined." As for Queen
Hortense, more and more tormented by her husband's
suspicions, with her health impaired by the moist
climate, and her ever-growing melancholy, she was
to feel like a condemned exile in her kingdom. No
woman ever gave a completer lie to the expression,
" As happy as a queen."

XX.

IN spite of all the honors that encompassed her, the Empress was ever more and more unhappy. The departure of her daughter Hortense left a void in her life that nothing could fill. She wrote to the new Queen from Saint Cloud, July 15, 1806: "Since you left I have been ill, sad, and unhappy; I have even been feverish and have had to keep my bed. I am now well again, but my sorrow remains. How could it be otherwise when I am separated from a daughter like you, loving, gentle, and amiable, who was the charm of my life? . . . How is your husband? Are my grandchildren well? Heavens, how sad it makes me not to see them! and how is your health, dear Hortense? If you are ever ill, let me know, and I will hasten to you at once. . . . Good by, my dear Hortense, think often of your mother, and be sure that never was a daughter more loved than you are. Many kind messages to your husband; kiss the children for me. It would be very kind of you to send me some of your songs."

Josephine was about to have another cause for

grief. A new war was imminent, but the Empress
hid her uneasiness in order not to distance Hortense.
"All your letters," she wrote to her, "are charming,
and you are kind to write so often. I have heard
from Eugene and his wife; they are evidently very
happy, and so am I, for I am going with the Emperor,
and am already packing. I assure you, that even if
this war breaks out, I have no fear; the nearer I am
to the Emperor, the less I shall care, and I feel that
I should die if I stayed here. Another joy to me is
our meeting at Mayence. The Emperor has bidden
me tell you that he has just given to the King of
Holland an army of eighty thousand men, and his
command will extend to Mayence. He thinks that
you can come then and stay with me. Is not that an
agreeable bit of news for a mother who loves you so
dearly? Every day we shall have news of the Emperor and your husband; we will be happy together.
The Grand Duke of Berg spoke to me about you and
the children; kiss them for me till I can kiss them
for myself, as well as my daughter; this will be
soon, I hope. My best regards to the King."

Napoleon was about to begin a gigantic war against
Prussia and Russia. In spite of his confidence in his
star, he was not without some apprehensions, and he
left reluctantly. A cloud seemed to hang over Saint
Cloud. "Why are you so gloomy?" the Emperor
asked Madame de Rémusat, whose husband, the First
Chamberlain, had just been sent to Mayence to prepare the Emperor's quarters. "I am gloomy," she

replied, "because my husband has left me." And
as Napoleon sneered at her conjugal devotion, she
added: "Sire, I take no part in heroic joys, and for
my part, I had placed my glory in happiness." Then
the Emperor burst out laughing and said: "Happiness? Oh yes, happiness has a great deal to do with
this century!"

The Empress hoped to accompany her husband as
far as Mayence, and remain there during the war,
with her daughter. At the last moment she came
near missing even this. Napoleon wanted to go off
alone, but she wept so much, besought him so
earnestly, that he took pity on her and gave her
leave to enter his carriage; she had but a single
chambermaid with her. Her household was to join
her some days later.

Napoleon and Josephine left Saint Cloud in the
night of September 24, 1806. After stopping for
some hours at Metz, they reached Mayence the 28th.
The Emperor started again, October 2, at nine in the
evening, for the head of the army. At this moment
he had an access of affection and a revival of his old
tenderness for the woman who long since had inspired
him with much love. Seeing that she was weeping
bitterly, he, too, shed tears, and was even attacked by
convulsions. They made him sit down and gave him
a few drops of orange-flower water. In a few moments he controlled his emotion, gave Josephine a
farewell kiss, and said: "The carriages are ready, are
they not? Tell those gentlemen and let us be off."

The Empress remained at Mayence. Napoleon wrote to her October 5, 1806: " There is no reason why the Princess of Baden should not go to Mayence. I don't know why you are so distressed; it is wrong of you to grieve so much. Hortense is inclined to pedantry; she is liberal with advice. She wrote to me, and I answered her. She should be happy and gay. Courage and gaiety, that is the recipe." It is plain that the Emperor's gloom had been of brief duration. When he was once more at war, in his element, he had quickly resumed his customary eagerness. He wrote to his wife from Bamberg, October 7: " I leave this evening for Kronach. The whole army is in motion. All goes on well; my health is perfect. I have not yet received any letters from you, but I have heard from Eugene and Hortense. Stéphanie ought to be with you. Her husband [the Prince of Baden] wishes to take part in the war; he is with me. Good by. A thousand kisses and good health!" Again, October 18: " To-day I am at Gera. Everything goes on as well as I could hope. With God's aid, the poor King of Prussia will be in a lamentable state, I think. I am personally sorry for him, because he is a good man. The Queen is at Erfurt with the King. If she wants to see a battle, she will have that cruel pleasure. I am wonderfully well, and have gained flesh since I left; and yet I go twenty or twenty-five leagues every day, on horseback or in a carriage, — in every possible way. I go to bed at eight and get up at midnight, sometimes, I think, before you have gone to bed. Ever yours."

In these campaigns Napoleon was not yet surrounded by the comforts which later made war less fatiguing for him, perhaps too easy. He endured all the toil and privation of a private soldier. In five minutes his table, his coffee, his bed were prepared. Often in less time than that the bodies of men and horses had to be removed to make room for his tent. His longest meal lasted no more than eight or ten minutes. The Emperor would then call for horses and leave in company with Berthier, one or two riders, and Roustan, his faithful Mameluke. At night, when lying on his little iron bed, he took but little rest. Hardly had he fallen asleep when he would call his valet de chambre who slept in the same tent: " Constant!" " Sire." " See what aide-de-camp is on duty." " Sire, it is so-and-so." " Tell him to come and speak to me." The aide-de-camp would arrive: " You must go to such a corps, commanded by Marshal so-and-so; you will tell him to place such a regiment in such a position; you will ascertain the position of the enemy, then you will report to me." The Emperor seemed to fall asleep again, but in a few moments he was calling again: " Constant!" " Sire." " Summon the Prince of Neufchâtel." The Major-General would appear in a great hurry, and Napoleon would dictate some orders to him. That is the way his nights were passed.

The night before the battle of Jena was an exception, and the Emperor slept soundly. "Yet," says General de Ségur, "our position was so perilous that some of us said the enemy could have thrown a bullet across all our lines with the hand. This was so true that the first cannon-ball fired the next day passed over our heads and killed a cook at his canteen far behind us." At about five o'clock Napoleon asked of Marshal Soult: "Shall we beat them?" "Yes, if they are there," answered the Marshal; "I am only afraid they have left." At that moment, the first musketry fire was heard. "There they are!" said the Emperor, joyfully; "there they are! the business is beginning." Then he went to address the infantry, encouraging them to crush the famous Prussian cavalry. "This cavalry," he said, "must be destroyed here, before our squares, as we crushed the Russian infantry at Austerlitz." The victory was overwhelming. Napoleon thus recounted it in a letter to the Empress, dated Jena, October 15, at three in the morning: "My dear, I have done some good manœuvring against the Prussians. Yesterday I gained a great victory. They were one hundred and fifty thousand men; I have made twenty thousand prisoners, captured one hundred cannon and flags. I was facing the King of Prussia and very near him; I just missed capturing him and the Queen. I have been bivouacking for two days. I am wonderfully well. Good by, my dear, keep well and love me. If Hortense is at Mayence, give her a kiss as well as Napoleon and the little one." And again from Weimar,

October 16 : " M. Talleyrand will have shown you the bulletin and you will have seen our success. Everything has turned out as I planned, and never was an army more thoroughly beaten and destroyed. I will only add that I am well ; that fatigue, watching, and the bivouac have made me stouter. Good by, my dear, much love to Hortense and the great Napoleon."

Hortense had joined her mother at Mayence with her two sons, meeting there her relative, Princess Stéphanie of Baden, the Princess of Nassau and her daughters, many generals' wives, who had desired to be near the scene of war to get early news. With what impatience tidings were awaited ! With what curiosity and respect were read and discussed the two or three words scrawled by the hand of the Emperor or of his lieutenants ! A lookout had been placed a league away on the high-road, who announced the coming of a messenger by blowing on a horn. At the same time the files of prisoners were seen passing on their way to France. Josephine, ever kind and pitiful, tried to soften their lot and gave aid and comfort to officers and soldiers.

Meanwhile Napoleon continued his triumphal march. From Wittenberg he wrote to his wife, October 23 : " I have received a number of letters from you. I write but a word: everything goes on well. To-morrow I shall be at Potsdam, the 25th at Berlin. I am perfectly well ; fatigue agrees with me. I am glad to hear of you in company together with

Hortense and Stéphanie. The weather has so far been very pleasant. Much love to Stéphanie and to every one, including M. Napoleon. Good by, my dear. Ever yours."

At Potsdam the Emperor visited the celebrated palace of Sans Souci and found the room of Frederick the Great as it had been in his lifetime, and guarded by one of his old servants. He then went to the Protestant church which contained the hero's tomb. "The door of the monument was open," says General de Ségur. "Napoleon paused at the entrance, in a grave and respectful attitude. He gazed into the shadow enclosing the hero's ashes, and stood thus for nearly ten minutes, motionless, silent, as if buried in deep thought. There were five or six of us with him: Duroc, Caulaincourt, an aide-de-camp, and I. We gazed at this solemn and extraordinary scene, imagining the two great men face to face, identifying ourselves with the thoughts we ascribed to our Emperor before that other genius whose glory survived the overthrow of his work, who was as great in extreme adversity as in success." The eighteenth bulletin said of this tomb: "The great man's remains are enclosed in a wooden coffin covered with copper, and are placed in a vault, with no ornaments, trophies, or other distinction recalling his great actions." The Emperor presented to the Invalides in Paris Frederick's sword, his ribbon of the Black Eagle, his general's sash, as well as the flags carried by his guard in the Seven Years' War. The old veterans of the army of Hanover received with religious respect everything which had belonged to one of the first captains whose memory is recorded in history." When he saw that the Prussian court had not thought of making those relics safe from invasion, the hero of Jena, who on this occasion abused his victory, exclaimed as he pointed to the famous sword: "I prefer that to twenty millions." In his letters to Josephine, Napoleon made no mention of his impressions in the house of Frederick. He simply wrote, October 24: "I have been at Potsdam since yesterday, and shall spend to-day here. I continue to be satisfied with everything. My health is good; the weather is fine. I find Sans Souci very agreeable. Good by, my dear. Much love to Hortense and M. Napoleon."

October 27, 1806, the Emperor made his formal entrance into Berlin, surrounded by his guard and followed by the cuirassiers of the divisions of Hautpoul and Nansouty. He proceeded in triumph from the Charlottenburger gate to the King's Palace, of which he was to take possession. The populace crowded the streets, but uttered no cries of hate or flattery for the conqueror. "Prussia was happy," says Thiers, "at not being divided, and at retaining its dignity in its disasters. The enemy's entrance was not first the overthrow of one party and the triumph of another; it contained no unworthy faction, indulging in odious joy and applauding the presence of foreign soldiers! We Frenchmen, unhappier in our defeats, have known this abominable joy; for we have seen everything in this century: the extremes of victory and of defeat, of grandeur and of abasement, of the purest devotion and of the blackest treachery!" Alas! What Frenchman could have foretold in 1806 the disasters of 1814 and 1815? The army deemed itself invincible and was wild with joyful pride. Davout, whose men the Emperor had just congratulated, wrote to him in great enthusiasm: "Sire, we are your tenth legion. Everywhere and at all times the third corps will be for you what that legion was for Cæsar." Never did soldiers have greater enthusiasm or more confidence in their leader.

One might have said that Josephine, amid all these triumphs, had a presentiment of the future. Victories could not dispel her sadness. Her husband wrote to her November 1: "Talleyrand has come, and tells me that you do nothing but cry. But what do you want? You have your daughters, your grandchildren, and good news; certainly you have the materials for happiness and content. The weather here is superb; not a drop of rain has fallen in the whole campaign. I am in good health, and everything is progressing favorably. Good by. I have received a letter from M. Napoleon; I don't think it is from him but from Hortense. Love to all."

Napoleon was not modest in his triumph. He pur-sued with sarcasms the nobility of Prussia and Queen Louise who had warmly counselled war. This fair sovereign, the mother of the late Emperor William, was then thirty years old; she was the daughter of a Duke of Mecklenburg-Strelitz and of a Princess of Hesse-Darmstadt. She was a most thorough German, hated France, and especially the French Revolution. She was a fearless horsewoman, and had been seen facing great dangers at the battle of Jena. When she rode before her troops in her helmet of polished steel, shaded by a plume, in her glittering golden cuirass, her tunic of silver stuff, her red boots with gold spurs, she resembled Tasso's heroines. The soldiers burst into cries of enthusiasm, as they saw their warlike Queen; before her were bowed the flags she had embroidered with her own hands, and the old, torn, and battle-stained standards of Frederick the Great. After the battle she was obliged to take flight, at full gallop, to avoid being captured by the French hussars.

In his bulletins the Emperor had made the serious blunder of speaking of Queen Louise in a manner wanting in proper respect for a woman, and especially for a woman in misfortune. Josephine, who was full of tact, was much pained by this lack of generosity, and reproached her husband for it. Napoleon sought to excuse himself, writing, November 6: "I have received your letter in which you seem pained by the evil I say of women. It is true that I hate, more than anything, intriguing women. I am used to kindly, gentle, conciliating women; those are the ones I love. If they have spoiled me, it is not my fault, but yours. Now I will show you that I have been very good for one who has shown herself sensible and kind, Madame Hatzfeld. When I showed her her husband's letter, bursting into tears, she said to me with great emotion and simplicity: 'It is certainly his hand-writing!' As she read it, her accent touched my heart and gave me real distress. I said to her: 'Well, Madame, throw that letter into the fire, I shall not be strong enough to punish your husband.' She burned the letter and seemed to be very happy. Her husband has ever since been very calm; two hours more, and he would have been a ruined man. You see then that I love kind, simple, gentle women; but it's because they are like you. Good by, my dear, I am well."

The kingdom of Prussia was conquered, but the war was not over. After fighting the Prussians he had to fight the Russians; the war in Poland was beginning. Napoleon wrote to the King of Prussia: "Your Majesty has announced to me that you have thrown yourself into the arms of the Russians. The future will decide whether this is the best and wisest choice. You have taken the dice-box and thrown the dice; the dice will decide it." At Paris, in spite of the splendors of the Imperial glory, there existed a vague uneasiness. Peace had been expected after Jena, and some apprehension was felt about the renewal of the struggle in the northern steppes. Madame de Rémusat wrote, November 9, to her husband, who was at Mayence with the Empress, "There is something in the Emperor's career which confounds ordinary calculations, and, so to speak, goes beyond them. It is most impressive, and, I might say, alarming, and yet he seems so far above customary conditions that there is no need of fear about the points to which he exposes himself, and still less, draw the line at which he shall stop. But I shudder to think how far he is from us at this moment. May God be with him, I am ever praying, and preserve him! While this great part of the French nation which is under his orders, is marching to great victories, we are vegetating here in complete dulness. There is very little society, and no houses are open."

Josephine was very anxious to join her husband who held it before her as a possibility, but never permitted it. He had written to her, November 16: "I am glad to see that my views please you. You were wrong to think I was flattering; I spoke of you as you seem to me. I am sorry to think that you are bored at Mayence. If the journey was not so long you might come here, for the enemy has left, and is beyond the Vistula; that is to say, one hundred and twenty leagues from here. I will await your decision. I shall be glad to see M. Napoleon. Good by, my dear. Ever yours." And November 22: "Be satisfied and happy in my friendship, in all I feel for you. In a few days I shall decide to summon you or to send you to Paris. Good by. You may go now, if you wish, to Darmstadt and Frankfort; that will amuse you. Much love to Hortense." After signing the decree establishing the continental blockade, Napoleon had left Berlin November 25. The next day he again held before Josephine the prospect of a speedy meeting. "I am at Custrin," he said in his letter, "to make some reconnoissances; I shall see you in two days if you are to come. You can hold yourself in readiness. I shall be glad to have the Queen of Holland come too. The Grand Duchess of Baden must write to her husband about coming. It is two o'clock in the morning; I have just got up. That is the way at war. Much love to you and every one." A letter from Meseritz, March 27, was still more explicit: "I am going to make a trip through Poland; this is the most important city here. I shall be at Posen this evening, after which I summon you to Berlin, that you may arrive there the same day. My health is good, the weather rather bad; it has been raining for three days. Matters are in a good condition. The Russians are in flight." Josephine, who had trembled with joy at the thought of seeing her husband, fell into great gloom when she saw that she had been deceived by a vain hope. The tortures of, alas! too well-founded jealousy were to be added to her sufferings!

Napoleon reached Posen November 28, and wrote the next day to his wife: "I am at Posen, the capital of Great Poland. The cold is beginning; I am well. I am going to make a trip in Poland. My troops are at the gates of Warsaw. Good by, my dear, much love. I kiss you with all my heart.

To-day is the anniversary of Austerlitz. I have been at a ball given by the city. It is raining. I am well. I love you and long for you. My troops are at Warsaw. It has not yet been cold. All the Polish women are Frenchwomen, but there is only one woman for me. Do you know her? I should draw her portrait for you; but I should have to flatter it too much for you to recognize it; neverthe-less, to tell the truth, my heart would have only good things to tell you. I find the nights long in my solitude. Ever yours." Perhaps Napoleon would not have been so amiable to Josephine had it not been that he was going to be very unfaithful to her in Poland, and in a movement of pity wanted to console her in advance. From there he sent her, December 3, two letters, one at noon, the other at six in the evening. This is the first: "I have your letter of November 26. I notice two things: you say, don't read your letters; that is unjust. I am sorry for your bad opinion. You tell me you are not jealous. I have long observed that people who are angry always say that they are not angry, that people who are afraid say they are not afraid; so you are convicted of jealousy; I am delighted! Besides, you are mistaken, and in the deserts of fair Poland one thinks but little about pretty women. Yesterday I was at a ball of the nobility of the province; rather pretty women, rather rich, rather ill dressed, although in the Paris fashion." Perhaps Napoleon said that to reassure the Empress; I imagine that the Polish women, with all their elegance and grace, were scarcely so ill-dressed as he pretended.

This is the second letter, dated December 3, 6 P.M.: "I have your letter of November 27, and I see that your little head is much excited. I remember the line: 'A woman's wish is a devouring flame,' and I must calm you. I wrote to you that I was in Poland, that when we should have got into winterquarters you might come; so you must wait a few days. The greater one becomes, the less will one must have; one depends on events and circumstances. You may go to Frankfort or Darmstadt. I hope to summon you in a few days, but events must decide. The warmth of your letter convinces me that you pretty women take no account of obstacles; what you want must be; but I must say that I am the greatest slave that lives; my master has no heart, and this master is the nature of things." Napoleon should have said: Providence. Man proposes, but God disposes.

Napoleon again spoke a little of having Josephine come. He wrote to her December 10: "An officer has brought me a rug from you; it is a little short and narrow, but I am no less grateful to you for it. I am fairly well. The weather is very changeable. Everything is in good condition. I love you and am very anxious to see you. Good by, my dear; I shall write to you to come with more pleasure than you will come."

December 12 he spoke once more of this projected journey which became ever more and more remote, like a mirage in the desert: "My health is good, the weather very mild; the bad season has not begun, but the roads are bad in a country where there are no highways. So Hortense will come with Napoleon; I am delighted. I am impatient to have things settle themselves so that you can come. I have made peace with Saxony. The Elector is King and belongs to the confederation. Good by, my dearest Josephine. Yours ever. A kiss to Hortense, to Napoleon, and to Stéphanie. Paër, the famous musician, his wife, whom you saw at Milan twelve years ago, and Brizzi, are here; they give me some music every evening." Napoleon left Posen in the middle of December. The evening before his departure he wrote a letter to his wife which showed the unlikelihood of her joining him, as she hoped to do; "I am leaving for Warsaw, and shall be back in a fortnight. I hope then to have you here. Still, if that is too long I should be glad to have you return to Paris where you are needed. You know that I have to depend on events." The unhappy Josephine already had a foreboding of his devotion to a great Polish lady.

Napoleon reached Warsaw December 18, 1806. He was to stay there till the 23d, return there January 2, 1807, and not to go away till the 31st of that month. He was greeted there with enthusiasm. He had said to his soldiers in his proclamation on entering Poland: "The French eagle is soaring above the

Vistula. The brave and unfortunate Pole, when he
sees you, imagines that he sees the legions of Sobieski
returning from their memorable expedition." No one
understood better than the Emperor how to impress
the imagination of a people. At sight of him the
inhabitants of Warsaw were thrilled with patriotic
joy. It seemed to them that their grand nation was
rising from the tomb. The Polish women, with their
lively, poetic, ardent nature, regarded Napoleon as a
sort of Messiah. In the intoxication of their ecstatic
admiration, the most beautiful of them — and Poland
is the country of beauty — turned towards him, like
sirens, their most seductive smiles. This coquetry
they regarded as a patriotic duty. Josephine had
good grounds for jealousy.

Napoleon was in the field during the last days
of December. War at that time was particularly
fatiguing. The dampness, worse than any cold, sad-
dened the eyes and wearied the body. The temperature was forever changing between frost and thaw.
Fighting took place in the most unfavorable conditions. But the Emperor, pitiless for himself and
every one else, uttered no complaint. He wrote from
Golimin to the Empress, December 29, at five in the
morning: "I write but a word, from a wretched barn.
I have beaten the Russians, captured thirty cannon,
their baggage, and six thousand prisoners; but the
weather is frightful; it pours, and we are knee deep
in mud." And from Pultusk, December 31: "I
have laughed a good deal over your last two let-

ters. You have formed a very inaccurate notion of the beautiful Polish women. Two or three days I have had great pleasure in hearing Paër and two women who have given me some very good music. I received your letter in a wretched barn, with mud, wind, and straw for my only bed." In spite of what her husband said, Josephine was right about the charm of the Polish ladies, and Napoleon, on his return to Warsaw, January 2, 1807, was to become seriously interested in one of them.

Soon there was no question of sending for the Empress, who would only have been in the way. Napoleon wrote to her, January 3: "I have received your letter. Your regret touches me, but we must submit to events. It is too long a journey from Mayence to Warsaw; we must wait till events permit my going to Berlin before I can write for you to come. Meanwhile, the enemy is withdrawing, defeated, but I have a good many things to settle here. I should advise your returning to Paris, where you are needed. Send back those ladies who have anything to do there; you will be better for getting rid of people who tire you. I am well; the weather is bad. I love you much." The Emperor, utterly taken up by his love for the Polish lady, was anxious that Josephine, instead of coming to him, should at once return promptly to France. "My dear," he wrote to her, January 7, "I am touched by all you say, but the cold season, the bad, unsafe roads prevent my giving my consent to your facing so many fatigues. Return to Paris for the winter. Go to the Tuileries, hold your receptions, and live as you do when I am there; that is my wish. Perhaps I shall join you there without delay; but you must give up the plan of travelling three hundred leagues at this season, through hostile countries, in the rear of the army. Be sure that it is more painful to me than to you to postpone for a few weeks the pleasure of seeing you; but this is commanded by events and the state of affairs. Good by, my dear, be happy and brave." The next day he wrote again on the same subject: "I have yours of the 27th, with those of Hortense and M. Napoleon enclosed. I have asked you to go back to Paris; the season is too bad, the roads too insecure and detestable, the distance too great for me to allow you to come so far to me when my affairs detain me. It would take you at least a month to get here. You would be sick when you got here, and then, perhaps, you would have to start back; it would be madness. Your sojourn at Mayence is too dull. Paris calls for you; go there; that is my desire. I am more disappointed than you; but we must bow to circumstances." In a letter of January 11, he says: "I see very few people here." But he saw the Polish lady, and that was enough

Josephine, who suspected a rival, was in despair. Her husband wrote to console her, January 16: "I have received yours of January 5. All that you say of your disappointment saddens me. Why these tears and lamentations? Have you not more courage?

I shall soon see you; do not doubt my feelings, and if you wish to be still dearer to me, show character and strength of soul. I am humiliated to think that my wife can doubt my destinies. Good by, my dear, I love you and long to see you, and want to hear that you are contented and happy." In another letter, January 18, Napoleon tried to cheer up Josephine, who was even more anxious and uneasy: "I fear you are unhappy about our separation which must last some weeks yet, and about returning to Paris. I beg of you to have more courage. I hear that you are always crying. Fie, that is very bad! Your letter of January 7 gives me much pain. Be worthy of me and show more character. Make a proper appearance at Paris, and above all, be contented. I am very well, and I love you much; but if you are always in tears, I shall think you have no courage and no character. I do not love cowards; an Empress ought to have some spirit."

Napoleon's will was not to be altered. Josephine was forced to leave her daughter and to return to Paris. Her husband wrote to her from Warsaw: " I have your letter of January 15. It is impossible for me to let women undertake such a journey: bad roads, unsafe, and a slough of mud. Go back to Paris; be happy and contented there; perhaps I shall be there soon. I laugh at what you say, that you married to be with your husband. I had thought in my igno-rance that the wife was created for the husband, the husband for the country, the family, and glory. For-

give my ignorance. Good by, my dear, believe that
I regret that I cannot have you come. Say to yourself, 'It is a proof how dear I am to him.'" All these
fine words could not console Josephine, who knew
from experience that Napoleon, like many unfaithful
husbands, had a smooth tongue when he needed for-
giveness. In vain she had waited four months at
Mayence for permission to rejoin her husband. She
at last found herself obliged to leave this town where
she had no other pleasure than the sight of her
daughter and her grandchildren, from whom she
parted with pain. January 27 she was at Strassburg,
and the 31st, at Paris.

XXI.

THE Empress Josephine was much loved in France, and especially in Paris, where her gentleness, amiability, and great kindliness had won for her all sympathies, even those of people who were hostile to the Emperor. Her return to the capital was greeted with pleasure, and her presence awakened it from its previous gloom. The *Moniteur* thus describes her passage through the chief town of the department of the Lower Rhine. "Strassburg, January 28, 1807. Her Majesty the Empress and Queen arrived within our walls yesterday, the 27th, on her way from Mayence to Paris. Her Majesty having consented to notify the Counsellor of State, Prefect Shée, that she would accept a modest entertainment, this news spread lively joy throughout this city. This proof of the Empress's kindness, accompanied by the gracious memory she wished to testify for the people of Strassburg, made the preparations for this impromptu event easy, and in spite of the brief time between the announcement and the arrival of Her Majesty, a numerous and brilliant company was soon

243

assembled at the Prefecture. The hall was elegantly
decorated; the emblems and mottoes recalled the
object of the festivity. After a square dance and a
waltz, Her Majesty passed through the company,
addressing a kind word to every lady present." The
next day, January 28, at seven in the morning, the
Empress started, amid cries of "Long live Josephine!" She reached the Tuileries January 31, at
eight in the evening. The next day, at noon, guns
were fired at the Invalides, to announce her return.
The great bodies of the state solicited the honor of
offering her their homages. She was a little tired by
her journey, and was unable to receive them till
February 5.

At this reception she was the object of almost as
much flattery as was the Emperor. We quote a few
of the phrases: —

M. Monge, President of the Senate: "Madame, the
Senate lays at the feet of Your Imperial and Royal
Majesty the tribute of its profound respect and the
homage of the administration with which it is animated for all your virtues. . . . It congratulates
itself on seeing again, in the capital, the august
spouse to whom our adored ruler has given all his
confidence and who deserves it in so many ways."

M. de Fontanes, President of the Legislative Body:
"Half of our wishes are granted. The presence of
Your Majesty will make us attend less impatiently
another return that the French desire with you. . . .
Paris consoles itself for not seeing him who gives

such glory to the throne, by finding in you her who has always lent to Sovereignty so much charm, so much gentleness and kindness."

M. Fabre, President of the Tribunal: "Madame, your return has aroused the keenest joy. The memory of that delicate kindness which knew how to temper so many woes; of that active beneficence which repaired so many misfortunes, is imprinted on every heart. Every one says: 'Providence in giving to us the hero, whose vast designs are crowned with the most constant and prompt success, desired to complete his kindness, by placing near him her to whom every stricken heart turns, who is the most agreeable object of gratitude, and who, moreover, throughout France is called the friend of misfortune.'"

M. Lejeas, First Vicar-General of the Chapter of Notre Dame (speaking in the place of the Cardinal Archbishop of Paris, who was ill): "Madame, His Eminence the Archbishop, our worthy prelate, has commanded me to convey to Your Imperial and Royal Majesty his regrets at not being able himself to present to you the chapter and clergy of Paris. 'Go,' that venerable old man said to me, 'and assure the benevolent Empress from me that I thoroughly share the joy which every one feels at her return. Tell her that never a moment passes that I do not address to Heaven the most fervent prayers for the happiness of France and of our invincible Emperor, and for the success of his arms. The Lord has deigned to grant my prayers; in a very short

time astounding prodigies have been wrought by
Napoleon, and I offer my thanks.'   The chapter and
the clergy of Paris pray for Your Majesty to be sure
that their feelings for your sacred person and for
that of your august husband are like those of His
Eminence."

The Prefect of the Seine: "You are far from the
Emperor, Madame, but Paris, too, is far from him.
Well, to mitigate this separation, equally painful for
Paris and for Your Majesty, Paris and Your Majesty
will talk to one another much about the Emperor.
You will take pleasure in hearing that his subjects of
the good city of Paris are ever faithful to him; that
they are prepared for every act of devotion which
may be demanded by his glory, the honor of the Empire, and the resolution he has formed of not laying
down his arms until he has assured the peace of
nations.   You will take pleasure in seeing us follow
in thought, even to the most distant climes, his ever
victorious eagles.   In short, Madame, at every exploit
of the Grand Army, you will be glad to hear the loud
applause which we have often wished could reach you,
even in the camps of the founder of the Empire, and
then touched by the sincerity of our prayers, you will
deign to listen to them, and sometimes even to be
their interpreter."

In spite of these official flatteries, and more or less
interested compliments, the Empress was far from
happy.   Possibly she imagined that soon, even in her
lifetime, the same homage would be addressed by the

same persons, in the same palace, to another woman. Besides this, however, she had many causes for distress. She suffered from the absence of her children, from her daughter's domestic unhappiness, from the Emperor's remoteness, his infidelities in Poland, from the dangers threatening him in this relentless and distant war. She wrote to her daughter February 3: "I got here, dear Hortense, the evening of the 31st, as I expected. My journey was pleasant, if I can call it so when it separated me further from the Emperor. I have received five letters from him since my departure. I need to hear from you now that you are no longer with me to console me. Tell me how you are; write to me about your husband and children. Although I see more people here than at Mayence, I am quite as lonely, and you will seem to be with me if you write. Good by, my dear, I love you tenderly." Josephine yearned all the more eagerly for happiness as a mother, because as wife she suffered cruelly, and the torments of jealousy were added to her grief at the Emperor's absence.

To one of the last letters his wife had written from Mayence Napoleon answered in an undated letter which she received in Paris: "My dear, your letter of January 20, has pained me much; it is too sad. That is the result of excessive piety! You tell me that your happiness makes your glory. That is ungenerous; you ought to say, the happiness of others makes my glory. It is not like a mother; you ought to say, the happiness of my children is my glory. It is not like a wife; you ought to say, my husband's happiness makes my glory. Now, since the nation, your husband, your children cannot be happy without a little glory, you should not despise it. Josephine, you have a good heart, but a weak head; your feelings are most admirable; you reason less well. But that is enough squabbling; I want you to be merry, content with your lot, and to obey, not grumbling and crying, but cheerfully and happily. Good by, my dear. I'm off to-night, to inspect my outposts." It must be confessed that to be as merry as the Emperor demanded, Josephine would have needed a very exceptional character. Her husband was at the other end of Europe, never interrupting the intense emotions and great risks of a colossal struggle except for brief distractions, which, however, could not be agreeable, so suspicious and jealous as she was.

Constant, the Emperor's valet de chambre, has recounted in his Memoirs, the passion with which a beautiful Polish lady inspired his master, early in 1807. Napoleon spent the whole month of January at Warsaw in a great palace. The Polish nobility gave him magnificent balls, and at one of them he noticed a young woman of twenty-two, Madame V., who had recently married an old nobleman, a most worthy man of stern principles and severe nature. By the side of her aged husband, this young woman, whose sadness and melancholy only added to her beauty, was like a victim in waiting for a consoler.

She was a charming person, with light hair, blue eyes, a brilliant complexion, a graceful figure, and dignified carriage. The Emperor went up to her, addressed her, and was soon delighted by her conversation. He imagined that she was unhappily married and he at once conceived a warm love for her, intenser and far more serious than any he had ever felt for one of his favorites. The next day he was noticeably restless. He would get up and walk about, then sit down only to get on his feet again. "I thought," Constant goes on, "that I should never get him dressed that day. Immediately after breakfast he despatched a great personage, whose name I shall not give, to pay a visit to Madame V., and carry his regards and entreaties. She proudly refused to listen to his propositions, possibly on account of their suddenness, or, it may be, by natural coquetry. The hero had pleased her; the thought of having a lover resplendent with power and glory fascinated her, but she had no idea of yielding without a struggle. The grand personage returned in great surprise and compassion at the failure of his negotiation."

Constant says that he found his master the next morning very busy. The Emperor had written many letters the previous evening to the Polish lady, who had made no reply. His pride was wounded by a resistance to which he had not been accustomed since he had become great. At last, however, he had written so many, and such ardent and touching letters, that she consented to visit him one evening between ten and eleven.   The grand personage who had tried to make the negotiations, was ordered to go to a remote spot and receive the lady in a carriage. Napoleon paced the room while awaiting her, betraying emotion and impatience.   "At last Madame V. arrived," says Constant, whose master kept asking him what time it was.   " She was in a most pitiable condition, pale, silent, her eyes full of tears.   As soon as she appeared, I led her to the Emperor's room. She could scarcely stand and she was trembling as she leaned on my arm.   Then I withdrew with the great personage who had brought her.   During her interview with the Emperor, Madame V. wept and sobbed so that I could overhear her even at a great distance.   At about two in the morning, the Emperor called me.   I went to him and saw Madame V. going away, with her handkerchief at her eyes, weeping freely.   The same personage carried her away.   I thought she would never come back."   But, contrary to his expectations, Madame V. came back two or three days later at about the same hour ; she seemed calmer, her eyes were less red, her face not so pale, and she continued her visits during the Emperor's stay.   Evidently Josephine had good grounds for jealousy.

Napoleon interrupted these distractions by going forth to fight the battle of Eylau, one of the bloodiest and most obstinate combats known to history.   He described it in two letters to the Empress, written in the same day.   This is the first : —

"Eylau, February 9, 1803, 3 A.M.   MY DEAR:
We had a great battle yesterday.   I was victorious,
but our loss was heavy; that of the enemy, which
was even greàter, is no consolation for me.   I write
you these few lines myself, though I am very tired,
to tell you that I am well and love you.   Ever
yours."

This is the second: —

"Eylau, February 9, 6 P.M.   I write a word lest
you should be anxious.   The evening lost the battle;
forty cannon, ten flags, twelve thousand prisoners,
suffering horribly.   I lost sixteen hundred killed
and three to four thousand wounded.   Your cousin,
Tascher, is unhurt.   I have placed him on my staff
as artillery officer.   Corbineau was killed by a shell.
I was exceedingly attached to him; he was an excellent officer, and I am deeply distressed.   My Horse
Guard covered itself with glory.   D'Allemagne is
dangerously wounded.   Good by, my dear."

The Emperor did not tell everything to Josephine;
he said nothing about the terrible vicissitudes of the
battle, a victory scarcely to be distinguished from a
defeat; he kept silence about the cruel sufferings of
his army which, without having eaten, had fought
amid blinding snow beneath a leaden sky; he said no
word about the regiments destroyed, one in particu-
lar, from colonel to drummers, all killed or wounded;
he did not mention his own danger in the cemetery
on the hill, where he had stood surrounded by his
Guard, his last resource, anxiously watching the

fight from its beginning, slashing the snow with his whip, and exclaiming at the approach of the Russian Grenadiers as they advanced towards him, " What audacity!" He did not say that after the terrible and fruitless bloodshed, which both armies claimed as a victory, he had been obliged to withdraw, and that Bennigsen had taken possession of the hotly dis- puted battle-field. He did not say what he was about to say in his bulletins: " Imagine, on a space a league square, nine or ten thousand corpses; four or five thousand dead horses; lines of Russian knapsacks; fragments of guns and sabres; the earth covered with bullets, shells, supplies; twenty-four cannon sur- rounded by their artillery-men, slain just as they were trying to take their guns away; and all that in plain- est relief on the stretch of snow." He did not quote the words he uttered in the biting frost, in face of thousands of dead and dying, when the gloomy day was sinking into a night of anguish: " This sight is one to fill rulers with a love of peace and a horror of war." No; the Emperor did not tell her everything.

In another letter, dated Eylau, February 11, 3 A.M., the Emperor tried to reassure the Empress: "I send you a line; you must have been very anxious. I fought the enemy on a memorable day which cost me many brave men. The bad weather drove me into winter quarters. Do not distress yourself, I beg of you; it will all be over soon, and my delight at seeing you once more will soon make me forget my fatigue. Besides, I have never been better. Little

Tascher, of the fourth of the line, did well; and he had a hard experience. I have given him a place near me, in the artillery; so his troubles are over. The young man interests me. Good by, my dear; a thousand kisses."

From this moment the Emperor's letters to his wife became cold, short, dull, and utterly insignificant; speaking of nothing but the rain, or the good weather, and perpetually bidding her to be cheerful. A clear-witted person ought to see readily that Napoleon, who was otherwise occupied, wrote to the Empress only from a sense of duty. Here are four letters; the first from Landsberg, the other three from Liebstadt. February 18: "I write a line. I am well. I am busy putting the army into winter quarters. It is raining and thawing like April. We have not yet had a cold day. Good by, my dear. Yours ever." February 20: "I write a line that you may not be anxious. My health is good, and everything is in good condition. I have put the army into winter quarters. It is a curious season, freezing and thawing, damp and changeable. Good by, my dear." February 21: "I have yours of February 4, and am glad to hear that you are well. Paris will give you cheerfulness and rest; the return to your usual habits will restore your health. I am wonderfully well. The weather and the country are wretched. Everything is in good condition; it freezes and thaws every day; it is a most singular winter. Good by, my dear. I think of you, and am anxious to hear that you are contented, cheerful, and happy. Ever yours." February 22: "I have your letter of the 8th. I am glad to hear that you have been to the Opera, and that you mean to receive every week. Go to the theatre occasionally, and always sit in the grand box. I am pleased with the festivities given to you. I am very well. The weather continues unsettled, freezing and thawing. I have put the army into winter quarters to rest it. Don't be sad, and believe that I love you."

Towards the end of February Napoleon had established his headquarters at Osterode, where he lived in a sort of barn, from which he governed his Empire and controlled Europe. He wrote to his brother Joseph, March 1, about the sufferings of this severe campaign in Poland. " The staff-officers have not taken off their clothes for two months, and some not for four. I have myself been a fortnight without taking off my boots. . . . We are deep in the snow and mud, without wine, brandy, or bread, living on meat and potatoes, making long marches and counter-marches, without any comforts, and generally fighting with the bayonets under grape-shot ; the wounded have to be carried in open sleighs for fifty leagues. . . . We are making war in all its excitement and horror." It is easy to see that Josephine, who knew all this, had good grounds for anxiety. Paris was empty and gloomy ; every face was sad. France is easily tired of everything, even of glory. The auditors of the Council of State, who were sent to Osterode to carry to the Emperor the reports of the different

ministers, returned to Paris in deep distress at the
sights they had seen, and spread alarm in official
circles. Napoleon consequently decided that those
reports should be brought to him by staff-officers, who
were more inured to scenes of distress.

From headquarters at Osterode the Emperor sent
eleven letters to the Empress between February 23
and April 1, 1807, but he said nothing of importance
in them. Thus: " Try to pass your time agreeably ;
don't be anxious. I am in a wretched village where
I shall be some time; it's not so pleasant as a large
city. I tell you again, I have never been so well;
you will find me much stouter. . . . I have ordered
what you want for Malmaison; be happy and cheerful; that's what I desire. I am waiting for good
weather, which must come soon. I love you, and
want to hear that you are contented and cheerful.
You will hear a good deal of nonsense about the
battle of Eylau; the bulletin tells everything; its
report of the losses is rather exaggerated than cut
down." At the same time he somewhat reproved his
wife: " I am sorry to hear that there is a renewal of
the mischievous talk such as there was in your drawing-room at Mayence; put a stop to it. I shall be
much annoyed if you don't find some clue. You let
yourself be distressed by the talk of people who
ought to cheer you up. I recommend to you a little
firmness, and to learn how to put everybody in his
place. My dear, you must not go to the small
theatres in private boxes; it does not suit your rank;

you ought to go only to the four large theatres and always sit in the Imperial box. If you want to please me, you must live as you did when I was in Paris. Then you did not go to the small theatres or such places. You ought always to go to the Imperial box. For your life at home, you must have regular receptions; that is the only way of winning my approval. Greatness has its inconveniences. An Empress can't go about everywhere like a commoner."

The greatness which the Emperor spoke about was no consolation to Josephine. She was unhappier beneath the gilded ceilings of the Tuileries than a peasant woman in a hovel. She besought her husband to let her join him in Poland, and wrote to him despairing letters.

Napoleon answered from Osterode, March 27: "My dear, I am much pained by your letters. You must not die; you are well and have no real cause of grief. I think you ought to go to Saint Cloud in May, but you ought to spend April in Paris. . . . You must not think of travelling this summer; all that is impossible. You couldn't be racing through inns and camps. I am as anxious as you can be to see you and be quiet. I understand other things than war; but duty is before everything. All my life I have sacrificed everything — peace, interest, happiness — to my destiny." These phrases in no way consoled Josephine who knew very well that her husband, in spite of his assumption of Spartan austerity, occasionally indulged in distractions.

In the month of March something occurred which somewhat moderated the Empress's sufferings. Her daughter-in-law, the Vice-Queen of Italy, gave birth at Milan, on the 17th, to a daughter who was named Josephine Maximilienne Augusta. She it was who was to marry, in 1827, Oscar, Crown Prince and later King of Sweden. "You will hear with pleasure," the Empress wrote Queen Hortense, " of the Princess Augusta's happy delivery. Eugene is delighted with his daughter; his only complaint is that she sleeps too much, so that he can't see her as much as he would like." Josephine would gladly have gone to Milan to congratulate her son and to kiss her granddaughter, but her grandeur kept her in Paris, where the prolongation of her husband's absence and the torments of too well justified jealousy plunged her into the deepest gloom.

Napoleon became tired of the monotonous and excessively disagreeable stay at Osterode, where he could not receive the Polish lady to whom he became continually more and more attached. Early in April he installed himself at Finkenstein, in a pretty castle belonging to a Prussian crown official, and there he was very comfortably quartered with his staff and military household. It was from thence that he wrote, April 2, the following short letter to Josephine : " My dear, I send you a line. I have just moved my headquarters to a very pretty castle, like that of Bessières, where I have a number of open fireplaces, which is very pleasant for me, as I get up often in the night; I like to see the fire. My health is perfect; the weather is fine, but still cold. The thermometer is but a few degrees from freezing. Good by, my dear. Ever yours." As soon as Napoleon was settled in this castle his first thought was to send for the Polish lady, for whom he had fitted up an apartment near his own. She left at Warsaw her old husband, who never consented to see her again, and spent three weeks with the Emperor. " They took all their meals together," says Constant. " I was the only one in attendance, so I was able to overhear their talk which was always amiable, lively, and eager on the part of the Emperor, always tender, affectionate and melancholy on the part of Madame V. When His Majesty was away Madame V. spent all her time in reading or looking through the blinds of the Emperor's room at the parades and drills going on in the courtyard of the castle, which he often directed in person." Constant, who felt bound to admire his master's choice, adds with some feeling: " The Emperor appeared to appreciate perfectly the interesting qualities of this angelic woman, whose gentle, unselfish character left on me an impression that can never fade. . . . Her life, like her nature, was calm and uniform. Her character fascinated the Emperor and bound him down to her." This loving idyl, a sort of interlude in the tragedy of war, may have suited Constant's taste, but it was hardly of a nature to please Josephine, who, like most jealous people, knew almost always what she wanted to know, and from the Tuileries found means to watch what was going on in this distant castle.

Napoleon's letters to Josephine during the reign of Madame V. were shorter and more stupid than usual. They were merely a few lines on the weather, the Emperor's health, or his desire to hear that his wife was " cheerful and happy." But, alas! cheerfulness and happiness were not for her! Too astute to be hoodwinked, she understood that her husband still had a friendly feeling for her but that his love was dead. In the eyes of a jealous woman, friendship is a slight thing. What does she care for the esteem and attentions of a friend who was once her lover? To all the good services of friendship she would a thousand times prefer the anger, fury, violence, of love.

XXII.

QUEEN HORTENSE was no happier in her Holland palaces than was the Empress in the Tuileries. She had to endure all the grief, deception, and misery of an ill-assorted marriage. The incompatibility of disposition which existed between her husband and herself from the first days of their married life, made itself continually more felt. King Louis blamed his wife not merely for her faults, but also for her good qualities. He was sometimes annoyed because she was gracious, amiable, charming; and the general sympathy she aroused in Holland, as in France, excited the fears of this irritable and sullen husband. Hortense looked upon herself as a victim. She had a lively imagination, and exaggerated her grief to herself, suffering more keenly on acconnt of her excitement, which was often very great. One day she said to Madame de Rémusat, her intimate and admiring friend, that her life was so painful and apparently so hopeless that when she was at one of her villas near the sea, and looked out on the ocean where were the English fleets blockading her ports, she wished that chance might bring a ship to where she was, and she might be carried off a prisoner.

The conjugal infelicities of Louis and his wife attracted the attention of the Emperor, who kept as strict a guard over his family as over his Empire, and was as prompt to exercise control in private, as in political matters. He wanted his brother to obey him, both as King and husband, and in his discontent at seeing his orders disobeyed, he wrote to him, from the depths of Poland, April 4, 1807, this reproachful letter, which is a real reprimand: "Your quarrels with the Queen have become public. Show, then, in private life some of that paternal and effeminate character which you display in matters of government, and in business the same rigor you exercise in your household. You treat a young woman as we treat a regiment. . . . You have an excellent and most virtuous wife and you make her unhappy. Let her dance as much as she pleases; she is young. My wife is forty; I wrote to her from the battle-field to go to a ball. And you want a young woman of twenty, who sees her life flitting, and has every illusion, to live in a cloister, or to be always washing her baby like a nurse. You are too much *you* in your household, and not enough in your administration. I should not say all this to you except for the interest I have for you. Make the mother of your children happy; you have one way to do this: that is, by showing her esteem and confidence. Unfortunately your wife is too virtuous; if you had married a coquette she would lead you by the end of your nose. But you have a proud wife who is afflicted and distressed by the mere thought that you may have a bad opinion of her. You ought to have married any one of a number of women whom I know in Paris; she would have had no difficulty in getting ahead of you and would have kept you at her feet. It is not my fault, I have often told your wife so." Thus the Emperor, by taking part in behalf of his daughter-in-law and against his brother, took a position as arbiter in their domestic quarrels. This interference was all the more galling to Louis, — who would have liked to be master in both his own kingdom and in his own house, — that calumny, as he well knew, persisted in representing the Emperor as his rival in Hortense's love, and as the father of the Crown Prince.

This child was named Napoleon Charles. He was born in Paris, October 10, 1802. His grandmother, Josephine, nourished the hope that some day he might be heir to the Empire, and she regarded his birth as a pledge of final reconciliation between the Bonapartes and the Beauharnaises. She believed that his cradle saved her from divorce. The Emperor, who always liked children, was especially fond of his nephew. He watched his growth with the keenest interest, admiring his amiability, his precocity, his excellent disposition. The boy was really remarkable for intelligence and beauty. His large blue eyes reflected every mood of his mind. Good, loving, frank, and merry, he needed only to appear and all sadness was banished. His mother had brought him up to revere the Emperor. His father, the King, gave him new toys every day, choosing those he thought most attractive. The boy preferred those he received from his uncle, and when his father said, "But just see, Napoleon, those are ugly; mine are prettier." "No," said the young Prince, "those are very pretty, my uncle gave them to me." One morning on his way to see the Emperor, he passed through a drawing-room where happened to be among others, Murat, then Grand Duke of Berg. The young Napoleon walked straight ahead without paying attention to any one, and when Murat stopped him and said, "Don't you mean to say good-morning to me?" the child replied, "No; not before my uncle the Emperor." Who knows? if this little Prince had lived the Emperor might have desired no other heir, and perhaps the divorce would never have taken place.

This boy was his mother's hope and pride, her joy and consolation. His father, too, loved him much. He was a light in the darkness, a rainbow after the storm. Sometimes when his parents were quarrelling he succeeded in reconciling them. He used to take his father by the hand, who gladly let himself be led by this little angel, and then he would say in a caressing tone: "Kiss her, papa, I beg of you"; then he was perfectly happy when his father and mother exchanged a kiss of peace.

The little Prince had a sudden attack of croup in

the night of May 4, 1807. He was thought to be lost, but in the morning he was a little better, and the physicians had some hope of saving him. The improvement lasted but a few minutes. In the course of the day he was given some English powders, which lent him a feverish strength, so that at six in the evening he asked for some cards and pictures to play with, but the fever only gave way to his death agony. Towards ten in the evening the child drew his last breath.

No words can describe the unhappy Queen's despair; she became stony with grief, and fears were felt for her reason. Josephine's grief was boundless. She did not dare to leave the Empire without the Emperor's authorization, and so did not go to The Hague, but went in all haste to the Castle of Laeken, near Brussels, whence she wrote to Hortense in the evening of May 14: " I have just reached the Castle of Laeken, my dear daughter, and await you here. Come and give me life; your presence is necessary for me, and you must have need of seeing me and of weeping with your mother. I should have liked to go further, but I was too weak, and besides I had not time to send word to the Emperor. I have summoned courage to come thus far; I hope that you will have enough to come to your mother. Good by, my dear daughter. I am worn out with fatigue and especially with grief." In the evening of May 15, Hortense arrived at the Castle of Laeken, accompanied by her husband and her sole surviving son. She was motionless,

apathetic, the figure of despair. M. de Rémusat, who
was with the Empress, wrote the next day to his wife:
" The Queen has but one thought, the loss she has suffered; she speaks of only one thing, of *him*. Not a
tear, but a cold calm, an almost absolute silence about
everything, and when she speaks she wrings every
one's heart. If she sees any one whom she has ever
seen with her son, she looks at him with kindliness
and interest, and says, 'You know he is dead.'
When she first saw her mother, she said to her:
'It's not long since he was here with me. I held
him on my knees thus.' Seeing me a few minutes
later, she made a sign for me to come forward. 'Do
you remember Mayence? He acted with us.' She
heard ten o'clock strike; she turned to one of the
ladies and said, 'You know it was at ten that he
died.' That is the only way she breaks her almost
continual silence. With all that, she is kind, sensible, perfectly reasonable; she thoroughly understands
her condition, and even speaks of it. She says she
is glad that she has fallen into this numb state,
otherwise her sufferings would have been too intense.
Some one asked her if she was much moved when
she saw her mother: 'No,' she answered; 'but I am
very glad to have seen her.' Mention was made of
Josephine's surprise at her lack of emotion on seeing
her; 'Oh, Heavens!' she said, 'she must not mind
it; that's the way I am.' To anything that is asked
her on any other subject, she says, 'It's all the same
to me; do as you please.'"

A messenger had been sent to carry the news to the Emperor, who was much affected by hearing it. He wrote to Josephine, May 14: "I can well imagine the grief which Napoleon's death must cause. You can understand what I suffer. I should like to be with you, that you might be moderate and discreet in your grief. You were happy enough never to lose a child, but that is one of the conditions and penalties attached to our human misery. Let me hear that you are calm and well! Do you want to add to my regret? Good by, my dear."

May 17 an imposing ceremony took place in Paris —the carrying of the sword of Frederick the Great to the Tuileries. A triumphal chariot, richly decorated, carried the one hundred and eighty flags captured in the last campaign. Marshal Moncey, on horseback, held the hero's sword. The chariot proceeded to the iron gate of the Invalides, which it was too lofty to pass under. Then the veterans came to take the flags and to carry them into the church. The ceremony began with a song of triumph. Marshal Sérurier, Governor of the Invalides, spoke: "We are here," he said, "to the number of more than nine hundred of those who fought against the great king whose warlike spoils our children have just won. At that time fortune did not always smile upon our valor. The fathers were no less brave than their sons, but they had not the same leader. Yet we can only recall with pride the words of that great man: 'If I were at the head of the French people, not a cannon would be

fired in Europe without my permission ' — honorable
proof of his esteem for the soldiers who were fighting
him.   But it was in the reign of a sovereign even
greater by his genius, his feats, his moderation, that
the French people was to rise to such a height of
power and glory.   We swear faithfully to guard the
treasure which his Imperial and Royal Majesty has
entrusted to us."   Then the old church echoed with
cries of " We swear it ! "

At this ceremony, the eloquent President of the
Legislative Body, M. de Fontanes, made a fine speech
full of enthusiasm for Napoleon, but respectful to the
memory of the great Frederick and to the misfortunes
of his successor.   He closed with a few words on the
grief that the death of the Crown Prince must have
caused the Emperor : " Perhaps, at this moment," he
said, " the hero who has saved us is weeping in his
tent at the head of three hundred thousand victorious
French, and of all the confederate kings and princes
who march under his banner.   He weeps, and neither
the trophies heaped about him, nor the glory of the
twenty sceptres he holds so firmly, which even Charlemagne failed to grasp, can distract his thoughts
from the coffin of that boy, whose first steps he aided
with his triumphant hands, whose promising intelligence he hoped one day to guide.   Let him not forget that his domestic woes have been felt like a
public calamity, and may a tender expression of the
national interest bring him some slight consolation.
All our alarm for the future is a more ardent expres-

sion of our homage. May fortune be satisfied with this one victim, and while she always favors the plans of the greatest of monarchs, may she not make him pay for his glory by similar misfortunes!"

Doubtless the death of this young child altered the face of things. If he had lived, it would have been for him, and not his brother, to bear the name of Napoleon III., or possibly even of Napoleon II., and apparently the destiny of the world would have been very different. Kingdoms and empires, on what does their fate depend! May 5 was to be a fatal date; the young Prince died May 5, 1807, and fourteen years later to a day his uncle was to die on the rock of Saint Helena.

XXIII.

THE END OF THE WAR.

THE Empress brought her daughter Hortense and her grandson Napoleon Louis, a boy a little over two, back to Paris with her, but she had not long the consolation of their presence; before the end of May Hortense was obliged to leave for Cauterets to repair her shattered health. Her mother wrote to her from Saint Cloud, May 27: "I have wept much since your departure; this separation is very painful for me, and the only thing that could enable me to bear it would be the certainty that you are getting some good from your trip. I have heard of you from Madame de Broc. I beg of you to thank her for this attention and to ask her to write to me when you are unable. I heard news, too, of your son; he is at Laeken, very well, and awaits the King's arrival. The Emperor has written to me again; he shares our sorrow. I needed this consolation, the only one I have received since your departure. I am always alone, every moment recalls our loss, my tears never cease flowing. Good by, my dear daughter, take care of yourself for your mother's sake, who loves you most tenderly."

Napoleon, who forbade his wife and daughter-in-law to be gloomy, — an order more easily given than obeyed, — thought their mourning excessive. His expressions of sympathy were very singular. He wrote from Finkenstein to Queen Hortense, May 20, 1807 : —

"MY DAUGHTER: Everything I hear from The Hague tells me you are not reasonable. However legitimate your grief, it should have some bounds. Do not ruin your health; seek some distractions, and remember that life is so full of dangers and evils that death is not the worst thing that can befall one." In his letter of May 24 to the Empress, the Emperor spoke of the unhappy Queen with a severity that amounted to brutality: " Hortense is unreasonable and does not deserve to be loved since she does not love any one but her children. Try to calm her and do not make trouble for me. For every hopeless evil, consolation must be found." He wrote to her again, May 26: "I have your letter of the 16th. I am glad Hortense has gone to Laeken. I am sorry to hear what you say about the sort of stupor she is in. She might show courage and self-control. I can't understand why she should be sent to the baths; she could find more distractions in Paris. Control yourself; be cheerful, and keep well. My health is excellent. Good by. I share your sufferings, and am sorry not to be with you."

In her bitter grief Hortense lacked courage to write to the Emperor, who was annoyed by her silence. ⟨" My dear," he wrote to Josephine, June 2, " I hear that you have arrived at Malmaison. I have no letters from you. I am vexed with Hortense; she has not written me a word. All you tell me about her distresses me. Why could you not distract her a little? You are always in tears! I hope you will show some self-control, that I may not find you sad. I have been for two days at Dantzic; the weather is fine; I am well. I think of you more than you think of an absent man. Good by; much love. Forward to Hortense this letter." This is the severe epistle which Josephine was bidden to send to Hortense: — ⟨ "June 2. MY DAUGHTER: You have not written me a word in your great and natural grief. You have forgotten everything, as if you had not still losses to endure. I hear that you love nothing, are indifferent to everything; this is plain from your silence. That is not right, Hortense. It is not what you promised us. Your son was everything for you? Are your mother and I nothing? Had I been at Malmaison I should have shared your sorrow, but I should have wanted you to listen to your best friends. Good by, my daughter; be cheerful; you must be resigned. My wife is much distressed at your condition; do not give her further pain. Your affectionate father."

It is easily seen that such letters were ill adapted to allay the anguish of an inconsolable mother mourning for her child.

Josephine's letters to her daughter showed very different feelings. The kind Empress did her best to persuade her that the Emperor sympathized with her grief. She wrote from Saint Cloud, June 4: "Your letter, my dear Hortense, gives me much consolation, and what I hear from your ladies about your health makes me easier. The Emperor was much distressed; in every letter he tries to give me courage, but I know that this unhappy event was a great blow to him. The King arrived at Saint Leu last evening; he has sent me word that he meant to call on me to-day, and he must leave the boy here during his absence. You know how much I love the child, and how careful I shall be of him. I want the King to take the same route as you; it will be a consolation for you both to meet. All his letters since you left are full of love for you. He has too tender a heart not to be touched. Good by, my dear daughter; take care of your health; mine will improve only when I don't have to suffer for those I love." This letter shows all the kindness and gentleness of Josephine's character. She was conciliating and benevolent, and did her best to smooth over Napoleon's blame and to reconcile Hortense with her husband. She wrote again from Saint Cloud, June 11: "Your boy is very well, and amuses me a great deal; he is so gentle; I think he has all the ways of the poor boy we mourn." Josephine understood consolation better than the Emperor.

What could be more touching, more maternal, than this letter from the Empress? "Your letter moved me deeply; I see your grief is ever fresh and I per-

ceive this better by my own sufferings. We have
lost what was most worthy to be loved; my tears
flow as they did the first day. Those regrets are too
natural to be repressed by reason, although it should
moderate them. You are not alone in the world.
You have left a husband, an interesting child, and
you are too tender for that to be strange and indifferent to you. Think of us, my dear daughter, and let
this calm your natural sorrow. I rely on your love
for me and on your reasonableness. I hope that the
trip and the waters will do you good. Your son is
very well, and is charming. My health is a little
better, but you know it depends on yours. Good
by. Many kisses."

The character of this loving mother and grandmother manifests itself in every one of her letters.
Her style was simple and affectionate, like herself.
Her letters, full of the gentlest, best, and most touching feeling, might make one say, " The style is the
woman."

While Josephine and Hortense were weeping, Napoleon was bringing a terrible campaign to a brilliant
end. June 15 he thus announced to his wife the
great victory of Friedland: "My dear: I write but
a word, for I am very tired; I have been bivouacking
for several days. My children have been worthily
celebrating the battle of Marengo. The battle of
Friedland will be quite as famous and glorious for
my people. The whole Russian army routed; eighty
cannon; thirty thousand men captured or killed;

twenty-five Russian generals killed, wounded, or cap-tured; the Russian Guard wiped out; it is a worthy sister of Marengo, Austerlitz, Jena. The bulletin will tell you the rest. My losses are not serious; I succeeded in outmanœuvring the enemy. Be calm and contented. Good by, my dear, my horse is wait-ing." The next day he wrote another letter to Jo-sephine: "My dear, yesterday I sent Moustache to you with news of the battle of Friedland. Since then I have continued to pursue the enemy. Königsberg, a city of eighty thousand inhabitants, is in my power. I have found there many cannon, stores, and finally sixty thousand muskets just come from England. Good by, my dear, my health is perfect, although I have a cold from the rain and cold of the bivouac. Be cheerful and contented. Ever yours." From Tilsitt Napoleon wrote to his wife, June 19: "I have sent Tascher to you to allay your anxiety. Every-thing goes on admirably here. The battle of Fried-land decided everything. The enemy is confounded, cast down, and extremely enfeebled. My health is excellent, my army superb. Good by; be cheerful and contented." Be cheerful and contented — he was always saying it.

June 25, at one in the afternoon, a great sight was to be seen in the middle of the Niemen. A raft had been placed midstream in plain view from both banks of the river. All the rich stuffs that could be found in the little town of Tilsitt had been taken to make a pavilion on a part of this raft for the reception of

the Emperors of France and Russia. ⌒ From one
bank Napoleon embarked with Murat, Berthier, Bessières, Duroc, and Caulaincourt; and from the other,
Alexander, with the Grand Duke Constantine, Generals Bennigsen and Ouvaroff, the Prince of Labanoff,
and the Count of Lieven. The two armies were
drawn up on the two banks, and the country people
of the neighborhood were present to watch one of
the most memorable interviews known to history.
When they reached the raft, the two sovereigns, who
had just been fighting so bitterly, and had sent so
many thousand men to death, fell into each other's
arms with emotion. The same day Napoleon wrote
to Josephine: "I have just seen the Emperor Alexander, and am much pleased with him; he is a very
fine-looking, good young Emperor; he has more intelligence than is generally supposed. He is going
to move into Tilsitt to-morrow. Good by; keep well
and be contented. My health is excellent." The
two monarchs became very intimate. "My dear,"
Napoleon wrote to his wife July 3, "M. de Turenne
will give you all the details about what is going on
here; everything is moving smoothly. I think I told
you that the Emperor of Russia drank to your health
with great kindness. He and the King of Prussia
dine with me every day. I want you to be contented.
Good by; much love." And July 6: "I have yours
of June 25. I am sorry you are so egoistic, and that
my success gives you no pleasure. The beautiful
Queen of Prussia is to dine with me to-day. I am

well and anxious to see you again when fate permits. Still it will probably be soon."

The Queen of Prussia was one of the most beautiful and most brilliant women of her time. An hour after her arrival at Tilsitt, Napoleon called on her, and that evening, when she came to dine with him, he went to the door of the house in which he lived to receive her with all respect. But in spite of all her efforts to modify the conditions of the peace imposed on Prussia, her gracious and obstinate endeavors were fruitless. Napoleon, July 7, thus described to Josephine the dinner of the evening before to the charming Queen: " My dear, the Queen of Prussia dined with me yesterday. I was obliged to refuse her some concessions she wanted me to make to her husband; but I was polite, and also kept to my plan. She is very amiable. When I see you I will give you all the details which would be too long to write now. When you read this letter, peace will have been concluded with Russia and Prussia, and Jerome will have been recognized as King of Westphalia with a population of three millions. This piece of news is for you alone. Good by, my dear; I want to hear that you are contented and cheerful." The story runs that the Queen of Prussia, who held a beautiful rose in her hand, offered it to Napoleon, saying with a gracious smile: " Take it, Sire, but in exchange for Magdeburg." The hero of Jena made a mistake not to make the exchange. He did too much or too little for the Prussian monarchy. Since he could not or would not wipe it out, he ought to have let it live, and become a friendly power. Who can tell? Perhaps his acceptance of the rose would have warded off many acts of vengeance, many disasters. On such slight things does the world's destiny depend!

Josephine wrote to her daughter from Saint Cloud, July 10: "I often hear from the Emperor, who speaks a great deal about the Emperor Alexander, with whom he seems well satisfied. He sent M. de Monaco and M. de Montesquiou to give me details of all they had seen. They say the first view was a magnificent sight. The two armies were on the two banks of the Niemen. The Emperor was the first to arrive at a raft built in the middle of the river; the Emperor Alexander's boat found some difficulty in approaching, which gave him a chance to speak of his eagerness thwarted by the stream. They tell me that when the two Emperors kissed, wide-spread applause arose from both banks. What most interests me in all this good news is my hope of soon seeing the Emperor again. Why is this happiness troubled by sad memories that can never be destroyed? Your boy is perfectly well; his complexion has entirely changed. I hope the waters will do both you and the King good; remember me to him, and believe in my constant love."

Before leaving Tilsitt, where he had signed a glorious peace, Napoleon had the bravest soldier of the Russian Guard presented to him, and he gave him the eagle of the Legion of Honor. He gave his portrait to Platou, the hetman of the Cossacks, and some

Baschirs gave him a concert after the custom of their country.   July 9, at eleven in the morning, wearing the grand cordon of Saint Andrew, he called on the Emperor Alexander, who wore the broad ribbon of the Legion of Honor.   The two sovereigns passed three hours together, then mounted their horses, and rode towards the Niemen.   Then they got down and embraced for the last time.   The Czar then embarked, and Napoleon waited on the river-bank until his new friend had landed on the other shore.   He returned to Königsberg and from there to Dresden, whence he wrote to Josephine, July 18 : " My dear, I reached here yesterday afternoon at five, very well, though I had been posting one hundred hours without stopping. I am staying with the King of Saxony, whom I like very much.   I have more than half my journey to you behind me.   I warn you that I may burst in on you at Saint Cloud one of these nights, like a jealous husband.   Good by, my dear; I shall be very glad to see you again.   Ever yours."   Napoleon spoke of jealousy.   The days of the first Italian campaign were very distant.   Everything had changed.   It was no longer he who had to be jealous of Josephine : it was Josephine who was jealous of him, and with good reason.   After an absence of nearly a year, the Emperor reached Saint Cloud, July 27, 1807, at six o'clock in the morning.

XXIV.

THE EMPEROR'S RETURN.

JULY 28, 1807, the Emperor, who had arrived at Saint Cloud the day before, received the great bodies of the State. It would be hard to form an exact idea of the flatteries addressed to him. Let us quote a few taken at random. M. Séguier, First President of the Court of Appeal, said to the hero of Friedland: "Napoleon is above admiration; only love can rise to him." The Cardinal Archbishop of Paris, speaking in the name of his clergy, was perhaps even more enthusiastic: "The God of armies," he said, "has dictated and directed all your plans; nothing could resist the swiftness of so many wonders. . . . Have confidence, Sire, in our zeal, and instruct the people in the submission and obedience they owe to all of Your Majesty's decrees and orders." But it was Councillor of State Trochot, Prefect of the Seine, who deserves the prize in this competition of adulation. Here is a fragment of his speech: "Sire, now that at last Paris receives you once more after so long an absence and such prodigious feats, it would gladly express to you all its intense admiration, and yet it can only speak to you of its love. And, indeed, if it tried to contemplate in you the conqueror of so many kings, the law-maker of so many peoples, the controller of so many events, the arbiter of so many destinies, how could it dare to approach Your Majesty, and in what language could it address you? Should it speak to you of triumphs? But can any one but a Cæsar himself speak of what Cæsar has done? Of glory? but for ten years it has been impossible to speak of all you have won. Of genius? but who can speak of all the marvels yours has wrought, before which we are dumb and confounded. Sire, all these things are beyond us, and since they command admiration, even silence, the silence of astonishment which admiration imposes seems to be our sole manner of expressing it." More had not been said to Louis XIV., the Sun King.

In allusion to the illuminations in Paris the evening before, the Prefect of the Seine added: "Why could not you, Sire, have been an eye-witness of the joy which the announcement of Your Majesty's return spread yesterday throughout the capital of your Empire! Why could not you have heard the applause with which your faithful subjects rent the welkin during the festivity which they gave on this occasion until well into the night!" The Prefect closed by a prophecy, alas! not too accurate: "The august Emperor Napoleon will render war between nations impossible, and the world's happiness will date from his reign."

The hero of Austerlitz, of Jena, of Friedland, then thought nothing impossible. His direct or indirect sway extended from the Straits of Gibraltar to the Vistula, from the mountains of Bohemia to the North Sea. Charlemagne was outstripped. Josephine saw her husband again with joy, but also with anxiety and terror. He returned so infatuated by his wonderful fortune, he was so flattered and deified by his courtiers, in his whole Imperial and royal person there was something so formidable and majestic, that his gentle and timid wife was, as it were, dazzled by the rays of a sun, too brilliant for her to look at.

Josephine had now become afraid to address him as thou, and to call him simply Bonaparte as she had done before. When she spoke to him, she often called him Sire. She did not dare to reproach him with his infidelities at Warsaw or the Castle of Finkenstein, or to show that she noticed his attentions to many ladies of the court, notably to a beautiful Italian woman, a friend of Talleyrand's, who was one of her readers and a prominent object of Napoleon's attentions. She saw rising before her the vision of divorce, the phantom which had haunted her imagination since the expedition to Egypt. Fearful of giving her husband the slightest pretext for discontent or annoyance, she was humbler, more submissive, more obedient than ever.

So long as the oldest son of Louis and Hortense had lived, Josephine felt comparatively secure, because she knew that this boy, a special favorite of

Napoleon's, was intended by his uncle to be the heir of his Empire. But his surviving brother, the little Napoleon Louis, born October 11, 1804, did not give the Empress the same confidence. The Emperor was less intimate with this child; he had not played with him as he had done with the other; he had not become attached to him. The little Napoleon Louis was staying with Josephine when the Emperor returned. She did all she could to make him love him.

Moreover, it was not an easy thing to hold the affections of a man like Napoleon. Six years younger than his wife, he was but thirty-eight, and in all the flower and prime of his Cæsar-like beauty. He liked to make a conquest of beauties as well as of provinces. The thought of resistance exasperated him. In everything he demanded success, triumph, dominion. The celebration of his birthday, August 15, 1807, which was accompanied with unusual pomp and splendor, was of the nature of a deification. He made Josephine share his triumph, and held her by the hand when he appeared on a balcony of the Tuileries, in the enclosure, amid the applause of the multitude assembled in the gardens.

King Jerome's marriage with the young Princess Catherine of Würtemberg added to the animation of the already brilliant court. The annulment of the young Prince's marriage with Miss Paterson had caused Napoleon much difficulty. When this marriage had been contracted at Baltimore, December 8, 1803, he had been only First Consul, and Jerome, a

simple naval officer, was in no way under the control
of the decree of the Senate, which was later to determine the civil conditions of the new Imperial
family. But in his haste to marry the young and
beautiful American girl, Jerome, who was but nineteen years old, had neglected, in spite of the advice of
the French Consul, to demand the permission of his
mother, Madame Letitia Bonaparte. This omission
had not prevented the Bishop of Baltimore from celebrating the marriage. Napoleon, however, regarded
it as null and void. It was not till February 22,
1805, that he obtained his mother's protest, and the
21st of the next March, by an Imperial decree, he
annulled the marriage which displeased him, by his
own authority. Yet, in the eyes of religion, this
union still existed. The Emperor asked the Pope to
pronounce it null, but Pius VII. gave the request a
formal refusal, writing in June, 1805 : " It is beyond
our power in the present state of things, to pronounce
it null. If we should usurp an authority we do not
possess, we should render ourselves guilty of an abuse
abominable before the throne of God ; and Your
Majesty himself, in his justice, would blame us for
pronouncing a sentence contrary to the testimony of
our conscience, and to the invariable principles of the
church. . . . That is why we earnestly hope that
Your Majesty will be convinced that the desire with
which we are always animated to second his designs,
so far as depends on us, particularly in a matter so
closely concerning his august person, has been ren-

dered idle by the absolute absence of power, and we entreat him to receive this sincere declaration as testimony of our really paternal affection." This was the beginning of the quarrel between the Pope and the Emperor. Pius VII. would not yield; but Napoleon found greater servility in the metropolitan officialty of Paris; and October 6, 1806, he secured a sentence pronouncing the nullity of his brother Jerome's marriage with Miss Paterson.

The King of Würtemberg, in the hope that a close alliance with the Imperial family would strengthen his throne, and procure him accession of land and power, had prepared to give to the Emperor's young brother the hand of his daughter, Princess Catherine. As soon as the King had formed this decision, he would not listen to a word of criticism from his family, who were already accustomed never to discuss his ideas. The King of Würtemberg was a real giant. He was so stout that a broad, deep hollow had to be cut out of his dining-table; for otherwise he would not have been able to reach his plate. He was fond of riding, but it was not easy to find a horse strong enough to carry his enormous weight. The horse had to be gradually accustomed to it, and to accomplish this, the equerry who had to prepare the royal steed used to wear a band full of lead, to which he would add new pieces every day, until he was as heavy as the King. This monarch, who was highly respected, though greatly feared, by his subjects, had some eccentricities. Thus he demanded that his

wife should be up and fully dressed by seven in the
morning; and insisted that at whatever hour of the
day or evening it should please him to enter her apartment, he should find her ready to accompany him
wherever he might want to go. The Queen, who
was his second wife, — Princess Catherine was a
child by his first marriage, — was a daughter of the
King of England, and consequently she was averse
to seeing her step-daughter marry the brother of
England's greatest enemy; but she took good care
not to make any objections. The King of Würtemberg was severe to his family and to his subjects,
but he was well educated, intelligent, and energetic.
Napoleon set great store by him, and regarded him as
a loyal and faithful ally.

Jerome, who had been made King of Westphalia
by the treaty of Tilsitt, was the youngest of the
Emperor's brothers. He was born at Ajaccio, November 15, 1784, and was not yet twenty-three when he
married Princess Catherine of Würtemberg, who was
nearly two years older than he, having been born
February 2, 1783. This Princess had much charm;
she was tall, handsome, her expression was noble and
kindly; she inspired every one with sympathy and
respect. She was a woman remarkable for intelligence, virtue, and affection. She was to be a model
wife and mother. She it was who, in 1814, refused
to get a divorce and to abandon an unfortunate husband, a dethroned king. She it was who wrote to
her father this admirable letter, without fear of his

anger: "Having been forced by reasons of state to marry the King, my husband, it has been granted me by fate to be the happiest woman in the world. I feel for my husband love, tenderness, esteem, combined; at this painful moment would the best of fathers desire to destroy my domestic happiness, the only sort left to me? I venture to tell you, my dear father, you and all the family, that you do not know the King, my husband. A time will come, I hope, when you will be convinced that you have misjudged him and then you will always find him and me the most respectful and most loving children." She was the courageous woman, the faithful wife, the devoted mother, of whom Napoleon said at Saint Helena: "Princess Catherine of Würtemberg has with her own hands written her name in history."

Jerome's marriage was an event of great ceremony. It was first celebrated, by proxy, at Stuttgart, the Princess's brother representing the bridegroom. The Emperor sent presents to his future sister-in-law, among other things a set of diamonds worth three hundred thousand francs. A detachment from the Emperor's household and many of the Empress's ladies of the bedchamber went to the frontiers to meet the Princess. She reached the Castle of Raincy, August 20, 1807, and there saw her betrothed for the first time, and the 21st, Napoleon received her at the Tuileries on the first step of the great staircase. As she bowed before him, he folded her in his arms, then he presented her to the Empress, before the

whole court and the deputies of the new kingdom
of Westphalia, who had been summoned to Paris to
be present at the marriage of their young sovereign
with a Princess belonging to one of the oldest and
most illustrious families of Germany.

Saturday, August 22, the signature of the marriage
contract and the civil wedding took place at the
Tuileries, in the Gallery of Diana, in presence of the
Emperor, the Empress, the ladies and officers of their
households and the great personages of the Empire.
M. Regnault de Saint-Jean d'Angély, Secretary of
State of the Imperial family, read the marriage-con-
tract, which was then signed by the Emperor, the
Empress, the young couple, the Princes and Princesses, the Prince Primate of the Confederation of
the Rhine, the Prince's high dignitaries of the
Empire, and the witnesses of the marriage. The
witnesses were, for the court of France: Prince
Borghese, Prince Murat, Grand Duke of Berg, and
Marshal Berthier, Prince of Neufchâtel; for the court
of Würtemberg: the Prince of Baden; the Prince
of Nassau; and the Count of Winzingerode, the
Minister of Würtemberg. Prince Cambacérès, Archchancellor of the Empire, then received the consent
of the couple and pronounced the formula of the
civil marriage.

The next day, Sunday, August 23, 1807, at eight
in the evening, the religious marriage was celebrated
in the chapel of the Tuileries, the galleries being
filled with the diplomatic bodies, the foreign princes

and noblemen and invited guests. The procession was brilliant. On entering the chapel, Napoleon gave his hand to the Princess Catherine, and Jerome his to the Empress. The Prince Primate of the Confederation of the Rhine, Archbishop of Regensburg, Sovereign Prince of that city, of Aschaffenburg, of Frankfort, etc., surrounded by his clergy and his court, stood at the chapel door. He gave holy water to the Emperor and the Empress, who at once went to their praying-chairs; then he gave the nuptial blessing to the young couple, while the canopy was held by the Bishop of Ghent and the Abbé of Boulogne, the Emperor's Almoners. After the ceremony, they all went back from the chapel to the grand apartments, where followed a concert, a ballet, and a reception in the Hall of the Marshals. Twice Napoleon appeared on the balcony, showing the newly married pair the vast throng filling the garden of the Tuileries. Unfortunately, a sudden storm prevented the display of fireworks.

While the thunder was roaring and the rain pouring down, the Empress, at her young brother-in-law's marriage, was the prey to sad reflections. She thought of the deserted American wife, who, far away, was weeping, while her husband, the father of her children, was joyfully leading another wife to the altar. Josephine doubtless thought that soon perhaps her lot would be the same as that of the unhappy Miss Paterson; that she would be sacrificed, abandoned, repudiated in the very same way.

The Empress had another cause of grief. At the
Pyrenees her daughter Hortense had become reconciled with Louis, and was soon to be the mother of
the child afterwards known as Napoleon III. But in
a few weeks the incongeniality of their dispositions,
for a moment forgotten in their common grief, asserted itself anew. On their return to Paris, at the
end of August, the discord between the King and the
Queen of Holland was as violent as ever. The King,
more uneasy and suspicious than ever before, wanted
to carry his wife to Holland, but the Queen had an
aversion to the country where she had suffered so
much, and to its fatal climate. She feared that if she
should return there she might lose her second son
like the first. Her health was wretched; she feared
that her lungs were affected. In France she felt that
the Emperor protected her from her husband's anger.
Holland seemed to her a gloomy, damp, melancholy
prison, of which the King, her husband, would be the
jailor. Louis Bonaparte was furious at his wife's resistance, all the more that he was obliged to hide his
feelings. Napoleon, who held his family, like his
Empire, in absolute control, gave Louis, as well as his
other brothers, orders which they had to obey without
a word or a murmur. The King of Holland returned
to his kingdom alone, his wife stayed in France, but
in the gloomiest spirits, with mind and body disor-
dered, disenchanted about all human things. "From
that time," she said later, "I understood that my misfortunes were beyond cure; I looked upon my life as

destroyed; I conceived a horror of grandeur, of a throne; I often cursed what so many called my good fortune; I felt lost to all enjoyment of life, shorn of all illusions, nearly dead to everything going on about me." Under other conditions, the Empress would have been delighted to have her daughter with her, but she found her so dejected, so morose, and so unhappy, that her presence was quite as much a grief as a comfort for her. These were the feelings of the Empress of the French and of the Queen of Holland when they went to Fontainebleau with the court at the end of September, 1807. There the Emperor lived more splendidly than ever, surrounding himself with all the pomp and majesty of monarchy.

XXV.

THE court arrived at the Palace of Fontainebleau September 21, 1807, and stayed there until November 15. Napoleon felt the need of displaying unprecedented luxury. He wanted to have the Diplomatic Corps send to foreign powers the account of magnificent festivities. This splendid palace, with its proud memories of the old French monarchy, was a residence that pleased him. He liked to be surrounded by great persons, whether foreigners or Frenchmen, who rivalled one another in flattery, zeal, and homage towards him. In his opinion, festivities and battles added to the glory of the throne. Desiring to be in everything first, he was very anxious for his court to be esteemed the most brilliant in Europe.

There were various types among the guests at Fontainebleau. There was Napoleon's mother, rather Italian than French by birth, and in face and accent. She recalled the characters of antiquity, unspoiled by prosperity, austere in her life, simple in her taste, rigidly economical, less from avarice than a distrust of the continuance of her son's good fortune. There was the beautiful Princess Borghese, Duchess of Guastalla, more elegant, more fashionable, more attractive than ever; then Madame Murat, rich in freshness and brilliancy, not satisfied with being a French Princess and Grand Duchess of Berg, but yearning to be a Queen; the Queen of Holland, on the other hand, in despair at having ascended the throne, and plunged in a deep melancholy in marked contrast with the splendors surrounding her in spite of herself. Then Joseph Bonaparte's wife, the Queen of Naples, whose tastes were modest, and who preferred Paris to her Italian kingdom. There were many Princes and great lords in the crowd of courtiers, the satellites of the Imperial sun. In the Gallery of Henry II. were to be distinguished a cluster of German Princes: the Grand Duke of Würzburg, who did not seem to sigh for his Grand Duchy of Tuscany, finding ample consolation in singing Italian pieces, for music was his passion; the Prince Primate of the Confederation of the Rhine, Archbishop of Regensburg, Sovereign Prince of that city and of Frankfort, who, in spite of his position in the church, joined the Emperor's hunt; Prince William of Prussia, who hoped by his devotion to alleviate the troubles of his country, and to modify the demands of the hero of Jena; the Prince of Mecklenburg-Schwerin, conspicuous for his formal German politeness; the young Prince of Mecklenburg-Strelitz, brother of the Queen of Prussia, less interested in

FONTAINEBLEAU

the patriotic grievances of his sister, than in his assiduous court to the Empress Josephine, whose respectful platonic lover he was; the Prince of Baden, who, although the brother-in-law of the Emperor of Russia, the King of Bavaria, and the King of Sweden, was proud to have married a Mademoiselle de Beauharnais, daughter of a simple Senator of the Empire, with but one regret — that his wife did not love him enough; Jerome, the young and brilliant King of Westphalia, apparently forgetful of Elisabeth Paterson, and full of mad love for his new wife, Princess Catherine of Würtemberg.

In the Gallery of Henry II. was also to be seen Murat, who, after his triumphal entry into Warsaw, thought of nothing but crowns, anxiously wondering whether he was to be King of Poland, or of Portugal, of Spain, or of Naples. There were the high dignitaries of the Empire, the foreign ambassadors, the marshals, the ministers; M. de Talleyrand with his enormous salary, his high position as Grand Chamberlain and Vice-Elector, his title of Prince of Benevento, always sparkling with the cold, sceptical, politely contemptuous wit that distinguished those who belonged to the old régime — Talleyrand, who, in the Emperor's closet possibly spoke to him with a certain freedom, but in the Gallery of Henry II. resembled the other courtiers and kept a profound silence as his master drew near. Then the Count of Ségur, Grand Master of Ceremonies, as attractive in the court of Napoleon as he had been in that of

Catherine II. as ambassador of Louis XVI.; Marshal
Berthier, Grand Master of the Horse, Vice-Constable,
Sovereign Prince of Neufchâtel, as devoted to Madame
Visconti as if he were a youth of twenty; Count Tol-
stoi, the brilliant ambassador of the Emperor Alex-
ander; M. de Metternich, the fascinating and skilful
Austrian Ambassador, conspicuous by his admiration
for Princess Murat.

When the Emperor entered, all eyes were turned
towards him alone; about him centred all interest,
all intrigues, all ambitions. He appeared as the
dispenser of fortune, the arbiter of destiny, the
exceptional being on whom depended individuals,
kingdoms, empires. He filled it all with his presence;
every one semed to live only for and by the Emperor.
A smile, a word, the slightest mark of attention on
his part, seemed a precious reward, a marked honor.
As soon as he entered, a quiver of admiration and
of terror seemed to run through the air. Every one
bowed like a horse who sniffs the approach of his
master; they almost prostrated themselves before
him. Any one to whom he spoke, stammered, feared
to reply, turned pale and red; and he, rejoicing in
their embarrassment, gloried in the wide gulf he had
set between himself and all other human beings.
Even foreigners seemed to be his subjects. Whatever their position, whatever their coat-of-arms, by
his side they were vulgar supernumeraries. His
power appeared to be limitless, like his genius; and
believing everything possible, looking upon himself

as a prodigy, a living miracle, he exulted proudly and majestically in his glory.

Under the second Empire, what were called the *series* of Compiègne and of Fontainebleau were much less ceremonious than under the first. All the guests of Napoleon III. breakfasted and dined at his table, — in the morning in frock-coat, in the evening in black coat and knee breeches; no uniforms were to be seen. Women appeared at breakfast in morning dress; they wore no especial dress at the hunt. Before dinner the Empress used to receive a few specially invited guests to drink tea. All day the Emperor left the company perfectly free. In the evening there was dancing to the music of a piano like a hand-organ, of which a chamberlain turned the handle. The Emperor was treated with great deference, but no one feared him, because his words were always marked by great affability. Napoleon I., on the other hand, was perhaps more feared than admired. Those who were charged with organizing his entertainments were perfectly happy if he was silent; for he almost never gave a word of praise and often criticised. It was a conspicuous and rare honor, even for Princes, to dine with him. There were besides at Fontainebleau, in 1807, several distinct tables: those of the Princes and Princesses of the Imperial family, who often gave grand dinners; that of the Grand Marshal of the Palace, with twenty-five places; that of the Empress's Maid of Honor, with the same number; and, finally, a last table for all

those who had received no special invitation. The
Princesses paid the cost of installing themselves
there out of their own purses, while under Napoleon
III., at Fontainebleau, or at Compiègne, all the ex-
penses were defrayed by the Emperor. Under the
first Empire only those holding high official position
were invited to the Imperial residences; under the
second, many were invited who were famous only
for their elegance. Under Napoleon I., where everything was formal, scarcely anything but tragedy was
played at the court; under Napoleon III., lighter
plays were often given. The hunts were very simple
under the second Emperor and very magnificent
under the first. In 1807 Napoleon had ordered that
women who went to the coursing should wear a
special costume; that of the Empress and of all the
ladies of her household was of amaranthine velvet,
embroidered with gold, and a cap with white feathers;
that of the Princesses, blue for the Queen of Holland,
pink for the Princess Murat, lilac for the Princess
Borghese, all adorned with silver embroidery. The
Emperor and all his guests wore the same hunting
dress for coursing: a green coat with gold buttons
and lace, breeches of white cassimere, Hessian boots
without tops; for shooting, a green coat, with no
other ornament than white buttons, on which were
carved hunting emblems. Under the first Empire,
etiquette was most rigid; under the second, it hardly
existed. At every moment of day and evening,
Napoleon I. wore a twofold air as commander-in-

chief and sovereign; Napoleon III. was like a man of the world receiving his friends in his own castle.

From September 21 to November 15, 1807, the great general had commanded that there should be amusement in the Palace of Fontainebleau. Pleasure was ordered, but it does not come at call. The Emperor, accustomed to have his every wish obeyed, was surprised to see that not every face was radiant. "Strange," he said, "I have gathered a good many people here at Fontainebleau; I want them to amuse themselves, I have arranged their pleasures, yet every one seems tired and sad." The Italian songs, even when sung by the best singers, in costume and with all the scenery, produced but a feeble impression. The tragedies seemed to induce slumber. The little balls, or, more exactly, the little hops in the apartment of the Maid of Honor, Madame de la Rochefoucauld, were very dull. Sometimes little games were played there; they gave a flash of gaiety, but as soon as the Emperor appeared, every one assumed a serious, composed air. Might one not say once more what La-Bruyère said when speaking of the court of Louis XIV.: "Who would believe that this eagerness for shows, that meals, hunts, ballets, tilting-matches, crowned so many anxieties, pains, and diverse interests, so many fears and hopes, so many lively passions, and serious affairs?" A palace is not built for ease. All its formalities hang heavy on every guest; the whole of every day is spent in playing a part.

Amid all these empty pleasures and hollow joys

there was no lack of sorrow. It was there that the wretched Queen Hortense, spitting blood, mourning the past and dreading the future, said to Napoleon: "My reputation is tainted, my health ruined, I expect no more happiness in life; banish me from your court; if you wish, lock me up in a convent, I desire neither throne nor fortune. Give peace to my mother, glory to Eugene, who deserves it, but let me live a calm and solitary life." She had been happier as an unknown schoolgirl at Madame Campan's, just as her mother, the Empress of the French and the Queen of Italy, must have often sighed for the island of Martinique, where she would have preferred the splash of the waves to the courtiers' murmur of obsequious flattery. Napoleon himself, at the height of human glory, had lost the peace of heart which he enjoyed in his boyhood, and never found again.

The Empress Josephine naturally held the highest place in this brilliant court of Fontainebleau, and was the object of untiring homage; few, however, suspected the anxieties that tormented her, so calm and happy did she appear, with a kind word and a gracious smile for every one.

M. de Metternich, the Austrian Ambassador who was then at Fontainebleau, took pains to ascertain the causes of her secret sorrow, and sent the details to his government. He wrote to von Stadion: "In many of my previous reports I have had the honor of speaking to Your Excellency about the long current rumors regarding the approaching divorce of the Emperor. After circulating vaguely in the last two months, they have become the subject of general and public discussion. It is true of these rumors, as of all not stamped out at their birth, that they rest on some foundation of truth, or they would be promptly silenced, if they were not directly tolerated." Then the clear-sighted ambassador reported in the same despatch what he had learned, thanks to his relations with persons to whom the Empress had made revelations: "Since his return from the army, the Emperor's bearing towards his wife has been cold and embarrassed. He no longer lives in the same apartment with her, and many of his daily habits have undergone a change. Rumors of the Empress's divorce began at that moment to assume a more serious form; when they reached her ears she simply waited for some direct information, without letting the Emperor see the slightest anxiety."

Josephine was sorely stricken, and her sufferings were all the more intense because she had to hide them from every one, especially from her husband, and they made a marked contrast, by the irony of fate, with the pleasures and amusements that surrounded her. She was too clear-sighted and intelligent to proceed to question the Emperor. She feared light and dreaded the truth. She hesitated before the abyss that awaited her, and shuddered before the Emperor's glance. She suffered on the throne, as if it were an instrument of torture. It was then that Fouché took some steps which doubled her anguish.

The incident is thus recounted by Prince Metternich in the despatch already cited: " One day the Minister of Police visited her at Fontainebleau, and after a short preamble, told her that the public good, and, above all, the strengthening of the existing dynasty requiring that the Emperor should have children, she ought to ask the Senate to join with her in demanding of the Emperor a sacrifice most painful to his heart. The Empress, who was prepared for the question, asked Fouché, with great coolness, if he took this step by the Emperor's orders. 'No,' he replied; 'I speak to Your Majesty as a minister charged with a general supervision, as a private citizen, as a subject devoted to his country's glory.' 'In that case I have nothing to say to you,' interrupted the Empress; 'I regard my union with the Emperor as written in the book of Fate. I shall never discuss the matter with any one but him, and never will do anything but what he orders.'" Josephine, when she mentioned this conversation to her confidant, M. de Lavalette, who had married a Mademoiselle de Beauharnais, said to him in great perplexity: "Is it not clear that Fouché was sent by the Emperor and that my fate is settled? Alas! To leave the throne is nothing to me. Who knows better than I do how many tears I have shed there? But to lose at the same time the man to whom I have given my best love, that sacrifice is beyond my strength."

But to return to Prince Metternich's despatch: " Many days passed without incident, when suddenly the Emperor began to share again the Empress's apartment and took a favorable moment to ask why she had been so sad for some days. The Empress then told him of her interview with Fouché. The Emperor confirmed his statement that he had never given him any such orders. He added that she ought to know him well enough to be sure that he had no need of any go-between to manage matters with her, and made her promise to report to him anything further she might hear about the matter." Josephine was not at all comforted. Napoleon's explanation was very embarrassed, and who could think that so crafty and ambitious a man as Fouché could assume the responsibility of such a negotiation if he supposed that thereby he exposed himself to his master's wrath?

The Minister of Police did not confine himself to mere spoken words. A few days after his interview with the Empress, he wrote to her a long letter on large paper, in which he set forth all the arguments he had already brought forward, to urge upon her the spontaneous sacrifice which would be the more meritorious, the more painful it was. Josephine, who received this letter in the evening, summoned M. de Rémusat at midnight to show it to him. "What shall I do," she asked, "to ward off this storm?" "Madame," replied the First Chamberlain, "my advice is to go this very moment to the Emperor, if he has not gone to bed, or else the very first thing to-morrow morning. Remember, you must seem to have consulted no one. Make him read this letter; watch him as closely as you can; but, whatever happens, show that you hate these roundabout methods, and tell him again that you will never listen to anything but a direct order from him."

The Empress did as he said. Napoleon, to use a common expression, was " cornered." He pretended to be much surprised, and very angry; promised "to comb Fouché's head," and even added that if she desired he would take away his portfolio; and to calm her he went so far as to write to the Minister of Police this letter, dated Fontainebleau, November 5, 1807 : —

" MONSIEUR FOUCHÉ: In the last fortnight I have heard of your foolish actions; it is time for you to put an end to them, and to stop interfering, directly or indirectly, in a matter which in no way concerns you; that is my wish."

Fouché was not at all disturbed by his master's reproach. He was at heart convinced that he had not displeased him; he kept his portfolio, and was sure that the divorce, though postponed, was irrevocably decided on by the Emperor. Josephine had no more illusions. It was in vain that Napoleon spoke to her kindly, and tried to console her with kisses and even tears, — for Napoleon used to cry sometimes, — after Fouché had made his overtures she had no more peace of mind.

The end of the stay at Fontainebleau was very gloomy. All became tired of this life of empty show, of the perpetual constraint, of the pleasures which by dint of repetition became dull and monotonous. Every one longed for home, to escape from this master's glances; for his presence inspired an admiration tempered with dread. The women had spent vast sums in their dress. The men had indulged in ambitious plans almost always futile. The German princelings had suffered in their lordly pride and German patriotism by having to bow their heads before the formidable man whose humble vassals they were, and these men, vain of their coat-of-arms, had not seen without a secret spite the crushing superiority of a poor Corsican gentleman. This great conqueror himself was not happy in all his splendor. Although he was no longer in love with his wife, it was not without sadness that he had seen her uneasiness and grief. Anxiety about the condition of Spain, which was so fatal to him, cast a cloud on his brow. When hunting in the forest, he was often seen to lose himself in thought and to let his horse wander as he pleased. At the theatrical performances it was noticed that, absorbed and distracted, he appeared to think less of the play than of his vast plans.

Not long since I visited the palace and the forest of Fontainebleau, in one of those cold but bright autumn days when the half bare trees have a strange appearance, when some leaves are as red as blood, others as yellow as gold, and nature wears all the countless hues which defy the artist's brush. The

forest is wonderfully beautiful with its marvellous
combination of trees and rocks. All the kings of
France since Louis VII. have inhabited this palace.
The holy head of Louis IX. appears there with
his aureola on his head. In the gallery of Francis
I., with its nymphs and fauns, amid garlands, fruits,
and emblems, one recalls that King and Charles V.
who entered the palace by the gilded door, and
who took part in the great festival in the forest,
when nymphs, fauns, and gods seemed to issue from
the trunks of oaks to the sound of tambourines, and
a band of maidens flung flowers before the feet of
the Spanish court. One recalls, too, Catharine de'
Medici with her squadron of young and brilliant
amazons — Catharine de' Medici who in this palace
brought forth her two sons, Francis II. and Henry
III. At the end of the oval court is a dome of rich
and picturesque construction, called the baptistery of
Louis XIII. because that king was baptized there.
Then there are the apartments of the queen
mothers: Catharine de' Medici, Maria de' Medici,
Anne of Austria, and those of Pius VII., a captive
at Fontainebleau. In the bedroom of the queen
mothers an altar was raised where the Vicar of Christ
said mass. The hangings of embroidered satin in
this room were a wedding-gift from the city of Lyons
to Marie Antoinette. The room is a model of luxury
and elegance, and is called the Chamber of the Five
Maries because it has been inhabited by five sovereigns bearing that name, Maria de' Medici, Maria

Theresa, Marie Antoinette, Marie Louise, and Marie Amélie. It was also the Empress Eugénie's chamber.

This marvellously picturesque palace of Fontaine-bleau is full of interesting reminiscences, but of all the figures it recalls, no figure is more impressive than that of Napoleon. There is much gorgeous furniture in the palace of various sorts, in the style of the renaissance, of Louis XIV., Louis XV., and Louis XVI.; but no piece attracts more attention than the plain mahogany table on which Napoleon signed his abdication. Then how impressive is the bedroom where he spent terrible nights, unable to sleep, and at last seeking in suicide a cure for his despair! Consider the contrast between 1807 and 1814! Meanwhile there had been changes of face, many apostasies. "Ah! Caulaincourt, mankind, mankind!" exclaimed the deserted Emperor. Every one left him, promising him a speedy return, but no one thought of it. Fontainebleau became a desert. If the sound of wheels was heard, it was never of carriages arriving, but only of carriages going away. It was at Fontainebleau that Napoleon's pride triumphed, and there that his pride suffered its cruelest humiliations. What anguish he endured, this man of destiny, in that room where he wrote: "To finish my career by signing a treaty in which I have not been able to stipulate a single general interest, nor even one moral interest, such as the preservation of our colonies, or the maintenance of the Legion of Honor! To sign a treaty by which money is given to me!" What anguish tore his mind and body when, having taken too small a dose of poison, he said between his spasms : " How hard it is to die, and it is so easy on the battle-field ! Why didn't I die at Arcis-sur-Aube !" Did he then recall the splendor of his return from Jena, from Friedland, from Tilsitt? Did he remember the crowd of courtiers who resembled priests whose God he was? The only courtiers left were those to whom he had given neither money nor honors, the old soldiers of his guard, with their gray mustaches, who could not restrain their sobs and tears when, in the Court of the White Horse, he bade them farewell, saying, " I should like to embrace you in my arms, but let me embrace this flag which represents you."

XXVI.

THE END OF THE YEAR 1807.

WHILE the court was still at Fontainebleau, the Empress received a piece of news, which had been kept back from her for some days, and which added materially to her sorrows. Her widowed mother, Madame Tascher de la Pagerie, whom she had not seen since September, 1790, had died June 2, 1807, at the age of seventy, in her home at Martinique. Josephine, who was much attached to her mother, had done her best to persuade her to come to France, where she would have been sure of the warmest welcome. But that venerable lady had perhaps chosen more wisely in preferring her modest and quiet home to all the splendor and excitement of an Imperial palace. From afar she thought of her daughter at the summit of human happiness; near her, she would often have seen her sad and downcast. By not approaching the throne which, at a distance, appears like a magic seat, but, to use the Emperor's expression, is in fact only an armchair covered with velvet, Napoleon's mother-in-law was spared the sight of much misery, and she died, as she had lived, in peace.

′ The Emperor left for Italy November 16, 1807, and this departure was for Josephine, already so afflicted, another source of anxiety and sadness. She would gladly have gone with him, and have seen once more Eugene and her granddaughter, who was named after her; but Napoleon had decided otherwise. He was no longer unable to live without his wife, and he no longer thought with La Fontaine that absence was the greatest of evils. He alleged as reason, the inclemency of the winter, said that he should be back early in December — in fact, he did not return to the Tuileries till January 1 — and to the Empress's great despair set off without her, leaving her the prey of the liveliest anxiety, the cruelest fears.

In Italy Napoleon received the same ardent flattery as in France. He reached Milan November 22, before Prince Eugene had had time to ride out to meet him. After ovations, reviews, religious ceremonies at the Cathedral, grand performances at the Scala, he went to Venice. Here he was received with all the luxury that used to be displayed at the majestic marriage of the doge and the Adriatic. When he reached Fusina, he entered a gondola rowed by men in satin coats embroidered with gold. He entered the grand canal beneath an arch of triumph between a double line of boats adorned with festoons and garlands. At the Venice theatre he saw a grand performance representing Olympus, and then was played, amid applause, the popular air, *Napoleone il grande*. He had with

him in Venice his brother Joseph, King of Naples;
his sister, Elisa Bacciochi, Princess of Lucca; his
step-son, Prince Eugene, Viceroy of Italy; the King
and Queen of Bavaria, the father-in-law and mother-
in-law of this Prince; Murat, Grand Duke of Berg,
and Berthier, Prince of Neufchâtel. He left Venice
December 8, dining at Treviso. The 11th he was at
Udine, and the 14th at Mantua.

It was in this city that he had a secret interview
with his brother Lucien, with whom he wished to be
reconciled, but on one absolute condition, *sine qua
non*. It will be remembered that Lucien, against the
First Consul's wishes, had married Alexandrine de
Bleschamps, widow of M. Jouberthon; who, after
being a broker in Paris, had died in Saint Domingo,
whither he had followed the French expedition. Napoleon, who was anxious to marry Lucien with Queen
Marie Louise, daughter of Charles IV. of Spain, and
widow of Louis I., King of Etruria, wished to annul
this marriage. But this brilliant offer had been per-
emptorily declined by the man who preferred a woman's love to a crown. In the spring of 1804 Lucien
had voluntarily left France to seek in Rome an
asylum from his brother's incessant reproaches and
demands. His mother, Madame Letitia, who thoroughly approved of him, had followed him to Rome,
and the Emperor had met with some difficulty in
persuading her to return to Paris, which she only did
after the coronation.

M. de Méneval went by night to fetch Lucien from

the inn where he was staying, and led him mysteriously to the palace which the Emperor occupied. Lucien, instead of falling in his brother's arms, greeted him coldly, with dignified reserve.

Stanislas de Girardin, in his interesting "Journal," has recounted the interview of the two brothers, as he heard it from Lucien himself. They said very much what follows: —

"Well, sir, do you still hold to Madame Jouberthon and her son?"

"Madame Jouberthon is my wife, and her son is my son."

"No, no, since it is a marriage which I do not recognize, and consequently null."

"I contracted it lawfully, as citizen and as Christian."

"The civil act was illegal, and it is known that you gave a priest twenty-five louis-d'or to persuade him to marry you."

"Doubtless Your Majesty, when he invited me here, did not do so for the purpose of paining me; if that is his intention, I withdraw."

"I have conquered Europe, and certainly I should not flinch before you. You owe your peaceful life in Rome to my kindness; but you are acquiring there a consideration which displeases me, and in time you will annoy me; I will order you to go away, and I will make you leave Europe."

"And if I should not obey?"

"I will have you arrested."

" And then ? "

" I shall have you sent to Bicêtre and then if — "

" I should defy you to commit a crime ! "

" Don't speak to me in that way ; don't imagine you can impose on me. I repeat, I have not conquered Europe to flinch before you. Leave the room."

Lucien did not leave, and Napoleon, after a few violent words, became a little calmer. Lucien then renewed the stormy discussion, trying to pacify his brother.

" I had no intention of displeasing Your Majesty by saying what should show the high opinion I have of the greatness of his soul."

" Never mind that; cast your eyes on the map of the world then. Join us, Lucien, and take your share; it will be a fine one, I promise you. The throne of Portugal is empty; I have declared that the King shall cease to reign. I will give it to you; take command of the army destined to make an easy conquest of it, and I will make you a French Prince and my lieutenant. The daughters of your first wife shall be my nieces; I will establish them in life. I will marry the eldest to the Prince of the Asturias; the King of Spain asks it of me as a favor; I can prove it by this letter."

" My eldest daughter, Sire, is not yet thirteen; she is not old enough to be married."

" I thought she was older."

" In a year or two, I will gladly let you dispose of her."

" Then there are no difficulties about the children of your first wife. You have daughters by your second wife. I will adopt them; you have a boy too; I shall not recognize him; his mother will have an important duchy, and he can be her heir. As for you, go to Lisbon, leave your wife and your son in Rome; I will look after them. Your ties are broken. I will find a way."

" That can only be by divorce."

" And why not? That is a frank and positive way which perfectly suits me. I want to be reconciled with you, and you know the price attached to the Portuguese crown."

" I see that to get it I should have to consent to make my wife a concubine, my son a bastard. Your Majesty knows me ill if he has been able to believe that the offer of a crown could tempt me to a dishonorable action."

" He who is not for me, is against me; if you don't enter into my system, you are my enemy; and thereby I have the right of persecuting you and I shall persecute you."

" I do not want to be your enemy, Sire; I cannot become one by preserving my honor and my virtue, by refusing to give up my reputation for a throne; and that this disagreement may be unknown, let Your Majesty give me some conspicuous proof of his kindness; give me the broad ribbon of the Legion of Honor, I beg of you ! "

" No; by taking my colors you would ruin your

reputation; it is a great thing to be opposed to me, and it is a fine part to play; you can continue it for two years without inconvenience, but then you will have to leave Europe."

"Much sooner, and I shall prepare to leave for America. Only the entreaties of my mother and Josephine have kept me here so long."

"I don't ask that of you; my propositions are not too unreasonable to be thought over; ponder them, with your wife, and let me know your answer within eighteen days."

At the end of the interview the two brothers parted with emotion. Lucien flung himself into his brother's arms, saying that doubtless he was embracing him for the last time, and left for Rome with his head high. He was obliged to yield only on one point, by sending to Paris his oldest daughter, Charlotte Marie, the issue of his first marriage with Christine Boyer. (She was born at Saint Maximini in February, 1795, and in 1815 married Prince Marius Gabrielli.) But the young girl had all her father's independent spirit. In Paris she was entrusted to the care of her grandmother, Madame Letitia, and she spoke so severely about the Imperial family in her letters, which were opened, that she was sent back to her father in Rome almost as soon as she had arrived in France. As for the idea of an annulment of the marriage or a divorce, Lucien absolutely rejected it. He preferred his wife to all the wealth, all the honors, all the kingdoms of the world. Jerome had yielded. Lucien did not yield.

Napoleon left Mantua after his interview with his brother, and returned to Milan, where, December 17, he witnessed some naval sports in the arena of the circus, which was turned into a lake. There too, December 20, in the grand hall of the palace, he adopted Prince Eugene as his son and declared him his heir to the crown of Italy. At the same time he issued these two decrees: "Wishing to give especial proof of our satisfaction with our good city of Venice, we have conferred, and by these letters-patent here present do confer, upon our dearly loved son, Prince Eugene Napoleon, our heir presumptive to the crown of Italy, the title of Prince of Venice." "Wishing to give especial proof of our satisfaction with our good city of Bologna, we have conferred, and by these letters-patent here present do confer, the title of Princess of Bologna upon our dearly loved granddaughter, the Princess Josephine." Napoleon left Milan, December 24, to return to Paris by way of Turin.

The letters which the Emperor wrote to his wife during this trip were very empty and unimportant, wholly unlike those he had written in 1793. Only a few need be quoted. "Milan, November, 25, 1807. I have been here, my dear, two days. I am glad I did not bring you. You would have suffered terribly crossing Mount Cenis where a storm detained me twenty-four hours. I found Eugene very well; I am much pleased with him. The Princess is ill; I went to see her at Monza; she has had a miscarriage, but is improving. Good by, my dear." "Venice, No-

vember 30, 1807. I have your letter of the 22d. I
have been for two days in Venice. The weather is
very bad, which has not prevented my going through
the lagoons to see the different forts. I am glad to
see that you are amusing yourself in Paris. The
King of Bavaria and his family and the Princess
Elisa are also here. After December 2, which I
shall spend here, I shall be on my way back, and glad
to see you. Good by, my dear." " Udine, December
11, 1807. I have your letter of the 3d, and I see you
are much pleased with the Jardin des Plantes. I am
at the furthest limit of my journey ; it is possible
that I shall be soon in Paris where I shall be glad to
see you again. The weather has not been very cold
here, but very wet. I have taken advantage of the
last fine weather of the season, for I suppose that at
Christmas the winter will be here. Good by, my
dear. Ever Yours."

During the Emperor's absence the triumphal return
of the Guard brought a slight diversion to the Em-
press's anxiety and distress of mind. Though unhappy
as a wife, she was at least happy as a Frenchwoman.
She, alas! had a presentiment of divorce, but not of
the invasion and dismemberment of France. At noon,
November 25, the twelve thousand old soldiers of the
Guard, bronzed, covered with glorious wounds, some
already gray, made their solemn entry into Paris.
An arch of triumph, broader and higher than the
Porte Saint Martin, had been built at the gate of
La Villette. The Prefect of the Seine and the muni-
cipal authorities there awaited the veterans.

The prefect welcomed the brave soldiers: "Heroes of Jena, of Eylau, of Friedland," he said, "conquerors of peace, immortal thanks are due you, for the country you have conquered! Your own country will ever remember your triumphs; your names will be handed down to the remotest posterity on bronze and marble, and the story of your exploits, firing the courage of our latest descendants, will be recalled, and you, by the example you have set, will still protect this vast Empire which you have so gloriously defended with your valor. . . . Hail! war-like eagles, symbols of the power of our magnanimous Emperor; carry over all the earth, with his great name, the glory of the French name, and may the crowns with which the city of Paris has been allowed to decorate you be everywhere a proof at once august and formidable of the union of monarch, people, and army!"

Marshal Bessières, who was in command, replied: "The most perfect harmony will always exist between the populace of this great city and the soldiers of the Imperial guard, and if their eagles should march again, recalling their oath to defend them to the death, they would remember that the wreaths adorning them redouble the obligation." After these two speeches the standard bearer left the ranks and bent down the flags on which the magistrates placed golden crowns bearing this inscription: "The city of Paris to the Grand Army." Then the troops marched past in the following order: the fusiliers, the riflemen, and grenadiers, the light cavalry, the Mamelukes, dragoons, the horse grenadiers, and the picked body of gens des armes. While they passed beneath the arch of triumph, a large band and chorus performed a cantata, with words by Arnault and music by Méhul. Passing through the dense crowds that lined the way, the guard came to the Tuileries, passing beneath the arch of the Carrousel, where the eagles were set down. Then it entered the palace garden, leaving its arms there, and proceeded to the Champs Elysées, where a banquet for twelve thousand men was laid. The tables were arranged under tents on each side of the Champs Elysées, along their whole extent, from the Place de la Concorde to the gate de l'Etoile. The tent of the staff was in the middle, half-way up. Marshal Bessières proposed a toast to the city of Paris, and the Prefect of the Seine one to the Emperor and King, and another to the Grand Army.

The next day there were three performances in every theatre. The pit, the orchestra, and principal rows of boxes and galleries were reserved for the Imperial Guard. The opera gave *The Triumph of Trajan*. The Français gave *Gaston and Bayard*. "That historical play," said the *Moniteur*, "which presents so noble and true a picture of French honor, of warlike victories, of chivalric enthusiasm, — never did this tragedy have spectators better fitted to appreciate it." In the minor theatres various plays on the events of the day were given. The performance at the opera was magnificent; the *Moniteur* described it with its usual lyrical enthusiasm : " This picked band of braves, who, in their swift conquests, in their distant marches, have seen such diverse climates, visited so many shores, and in so few months have seen the springs and the mouths of so many rivers, know also the banks of the Tiber; hence in the scenery they at once recognized Rome; in the triumphal march, in the eager throng, in the vast populace, bursting through the ranks of the Roman soldiers, and flinging themselves beneath the hoofs of their horses, they saw the touching picture of the reception they had met the day before. Their emotion baffles description. The Imperial Guard gazing at Trajan's triumph was itself an admirable spectacle." The opera was but a series of ingenious allusions to Napoleon's glory. Trajan was represented as burning, with his own hand, papers containing the secret of a conspiracy, recalling Napoleon's throwing into the fire the letters by which he could have ruined M. Hatzfeld; and when the Roman Emperor appeared in his chariot, drawn by four white horses, it was not Trajan who was applauded, but Napoleon.

December 14, at the Military School, Marshal Bessières, to celebrate the victories of the Grand Army, and to thank the city of Paris for its reception of the Imperial Guard, gave a grand entertainment which the Empress honored with her presence. The Invalides was brilliantly illuminated and connected with the Military School by a long row of lights. In the middle of the Champ de Mars was a vast hemisphere, on which was a pedestal holding a colossal statue of the Emperor, surrounded by allegoric figures. The trophies set aside for each one of the Grand Army were marked with the corps number. The Imperial Guard was under arms, and formed an interesting part of the spectators, and of the spectacle as well. Bengal fires lit up the warlike scene. The heights across the Seine were also ablaze with lights. The Empress arrived at the Military School at about eight in the evening. The entertainment began with a ballet performed by dancers from the opera. Then there were fireworks. The Champ de Mars was one sea of flame, and the Imperial Guard fired blank cartridges for half an hour. Then there was a grand ball with a fine supper; after which the dances continued till morning.

This worldly and military entertainment, at which the Empress queen appeared in all her glory, may be regarded as the crowning point of her splendors. And here, at the end of 1807, we close this study. We have left to narrate in a final volume only the last seven years of Josephine's life. We have already recounted nearly the whole career of this attractive woman, of this justly famous sovereign. We have descibed her infancy in Martinique, in her modest, patriarchal home, where she was born, June 23, 1763. We have admired her as a young girl, loving flowers, music, and nature, beneath the clear sky of the Antilles, amid banana and orange trees, tropical flowers, and birds of paradise, where the fortune-telling negress said to her: " You will be a queen." We have seen her in France, marrying, December 13, 1779, the young and brilliant Viscount Alexandre de Beauharnais, by whom she had one son, the future Viceroy of Italy, and one daughter, the future Queen of Holland. We have seen her going through that period of illusions, so well called the Golden Age of the Revolution, receiving in her drawing-room in the rue de l'Université the flower of the liberal nobility and leaders of the Constituent Assembly, then suddenly passing from the Golden to the Iron Age, shuddering at the dangers to which war, and above all the Terror exposed her husband, the general in chief of the Army of the Rhine, the leader of the democracy, rewarded for his patriotism and his devotion to the Republic by the scaffold. She herself, during her husband's captivity, was imprisoned in the Carmes April, 1794; for one hundred and eight days of inexpressible anguish and torment, she occupied in this dungeon the Room of the Swords as it was called, because the walls still bore traces of the three swords which the men of September had leaned against them after the massacre of the one hundred and twenty priests who were in the prison. Beauharnais, the man of the old régime, who had embraced the new ideas with so much ardor, this grand lord who got himself treated like a *sans-culotte*, was guillotined four days before Robespierre, whose death would have saved him. His young widow left prison, reduced to extreme want, and took refuge with her father-in-law, at Fontainebleau; then she made her appearance in the motley society which first showed itself in the drawing-room of Madame Tallien, then at the Luxembourg under Barras. Rivalling Madame Tallien and Madame Récamier in popularity, she smiled through her tears, like Andromache in Homer. Her means becoming greater, thanks to the support of men in authority, she bought in the rue Chantereine, afterwards rue de la Victoire, a little house belonging to Talma, the tragedian. There she received with her customary courtesy the few survivors of French aristocracy who said behind well-closed doors: "Let us talk about the old court; let us take a turn at Versailles."

Bonaparte, commander of the Army of the Interior, after the 13th Vendémiaire, when he saved the expiring Convention, had just ordered the disarmament of the sections and the delivery of all arms found in private houses, when a boy of fourteen called upon him to ask to have back the sword of his father, who had commanded the armies of the Republic. This boy was Eugene de Beauharnais, afterwards Viceroy of Italy. Bonaparte, touched by this action, received him graciously. The next day Madame de Beauharnais called upon him to thank him. He was much struck by her charms and proposed to her; she accepted him and they were married March 9, 1796. The Viscountess of Beauharnais became Citizeness Bonaparte. No sooner married, than the young husband, who was only twenty-six, tore himself from her arms and started for the army of Italy. Then Napoleon's love for Josephine was much greater than hers for him. It was he who was jealous, he who wrote burning letters; he it was who was all enthusiasm, ardor, and ablaze with passion. It was only with reluctance that Josephine decided to leave Paris, where she was happy, but in Italy she found a real royalty. At Milan she took possession of the Serbelloni Palace, where she did the honors most admirably and received the homage of the proud aristocracy of Milan. She followed her husband to the war, for he could not bear to be separated from her, and one day when, beset with dangers, she was crying, he exclaimed: " Wurmser shall pay dearly for the tears he causes you." After Arcole, Madame Bonaparte resembled a sovereign. She singularly aided her husband to play the double part which was soon to carry him to the highest rank. When it was a question of repelling royalism, the young conqueror relied on men like Augereau; when it was necessary to attract men of the old régime, Josephine was the bond of union between him and the French or Italian aristocracy. On her return to Paris, June 2, 1798, she shared her husband's glories. The little house in the rue Chantereine became more famous than the grandest palaces.

Bonaparte left for Egypt, embarking at Toulon, May 19, 1798, after taking tender leave of Josephine. During her husband's absence, she bought the estate of Malmaison, an unknown spot which soon became famous. She skilfully defended Bonaparte's inter- .

ests with the Directory, and in her drawing-room met celebrities of every kind. But malicious persons soon sent to Egypt hostile rumors, and her impetuous husband, wild with jealous wrath, spoke of nothing but separation and divorce. He reached Paris unexpectedly, October 16, 1799, and not finding his wife there, started off to meet her on a different road from hers, wild with jealousy. His brothers, Josephine's enemies, deceived him, and at first he refused to see her again; but, softened by the supplications of Eugene and Hortense de Beauharnais, he pardoned his wife and opened his door to her; she defended herself, and he let himself be convinced, so that, instead of a divorce, there was a complete reconciliation. Josephine was of use to her husband in the preparations for the 18th Brumaire; she helped him to lull the vigilance of the Republicans and to rise to the highest rank.

Citizeness Bonaparte had become the wife of the First Consul. Like the ladies of the old régime, she was addressed as Madame until she should be called Empress, or Your Majesty. She was at the head of the Consular Court, rich in youth, glory, and hope. At the Tuileries she took possession of the apartments of Marie Antoinette. At Malmaison she enjoyed the pleasures of the country. The hero of Marengo looked upon her as his good angel, his good genius. Their happiness was interrupted by the infernal machine, but this gloomy incident was soon forgotten. Under Josephine's guidance Parisian society soon resumed its former brilliancy. Monarchical customs reappeared. The Concordat effected a reconciliation of the church with the government, and the wife of the First Consul, surrounded by a real court, heard a *Te Deum* in the rood-loft of Notre Dame. At heart she was a Royalist by her memories and her feelings, although she was made by fate an Empress. The crown, so far from tempting her, filled her with fear. She yearned to descend as her husband yearned to rise. The proclamation of the Consulate for life, the prelude of the Empire, filled her with gloom and apprehension. Neither the pomp of Saint Cloud, nor the triumphal trip in Belgium, robbed her of her wise and modest ideas. She much preferred Malmaison to any splendid palace, and looked back with regret at the time when she was simply Citizeness Bonaparte. Grandeur, so far from turning her head, only made her less ambitious. She gave her husband excellent advice, which, unfortunately, he did not follow. Had he listened to her, he would not have had the Duke of Enghien killed, he would have been modest in good fortune, and would have remained the first citizen of a great Republic.

Crowned at Notre Dame by the hands of Napoleon, Josephine played a sovereign's part with as much ease as if she had been born on the steps of the throne. The greatest names of the old régime figured in her house. She adorned magnificent festivities by her presence. In Italy, whither she accompa-

nied her husband, she received as Queen the same
homage she had received as Empress. - Yet, amid all
this splendor, she was not happy. The terrible wars
in which Napoleon engaged filled her with anxiety.
At Strassburg, during the Austerlitz campaign, at
Mayence during that of Jena and that of Poland,
she was a victim of the greatest distress of mind and
nervous terror. Then, too, her husband's infidelities
filled her with despair. Towards the end of 1807
the spectre of divorce arose before her. The loss of
a crown would be a trifling matter, but the sight of
another woman reigning as lawful wife over Napoleon's heart was a thought to which she could not
reconcile herself. From that moment she knew no
peace or happiness. She was like a convicted criminal awaiting sentence at any moment, and she had to
hide her terrible grief from every one. She always
imagined that in the homage paid her by force of
habit, there was something false and ironical. She
thought of herself only as disgraced, betrayed, repudiated. All that was left of her crown was its mark
on her brow. Few peasant women in their huts were
ever as thoroughly unhappy as was this sovereign in
her palace.

We have seen Josephine in her springtime, in her
summer; it remains for us to describe only the
autumn of this wonderful and melancholy career.
This last study will be profoundly sad. "In the season which despoils nature," said Madame Swetchine,
"there is no breeze, no puff of air so light that it

fails to detach the leaf from the tree that bore it. In the autumn of the heart there is no movement that does not carry away a happiness or a hope." The great afflictions of Josephine's later years were the divorce, the invasion, and the long agony. Driven from the Tuileries forever, she took refuge at Malmaison one rainy, cold, December night, recalling, doubtless, the starlit evenings when the conqueror of Italy sought calm and happiness in that favorite spot. And after draining the cup of bitterness, the deserted wife exclaimed: "It sometimes seems to me as if I were dead and there was nothing left of me except a sort of vague power of feeling that I no longer exist." She could truly say with Queen Margaret of Navarre: "I have borne more than my share of the weariness which is the common lot of man." A still harder trial awaited her. Napoleon was unhappy, and she was forbidden to comfort him! He was exiled, and she was forbidden to follow him! The Empire she had seen so magnificent she was to see conquered, invaded, dismembered. No one was to mourn the woes of her country more than she. She was to die of grief, and when, May 29, 1814, she had breathed her last after uttering in her death agony these three words which sum up the anguish of her soul: "Napoleon! Elba! Marie Louise!" Mademoiselle Avrillon, the First Lady of her Bedchamber, was to say, "I have seen the Empress Josephine's sleeplessness and her terrible dreams. I have known her to pass whole days buried in the gloomiest thought. I know what I have seen and heard, and I am sure that grief killed her!" Was there ever a life of greater vicissitudes? It was a career full of smiles and tears, presenting every contrast of light and shade, of joy and grief, reproducing all the splendor and all the misery that can be crowded into human existence! It was a career, as fascinating as it was strange, which could only have been seen in those pathetic and disturbed epochs, when one surprise follows another, and the actors are perhaps even more astonished than the spectators at the shifting scenes and the incidents of the drama, in which events always take an unexpected turn, when men and things suffer shocks unknown to previous generations, and when history reads like the wildest romance.

INDEX.